RETHINKING JUVENILE JUSTICE

RETHINKING
JUVENILE JUSTICE

ELIZABETH S. SCOTT • LAURENCE STEINBERG

Harvard University Press

Cambridge, Massachusetts

London, England

First Harvard University Press paperback edition, 2010

Library of Congress Cataloging-in-Publication Data
Scott, Elizabeth S., 1945–
Rethinking juvenile justice / Elizabeth S. Scott and Laurence
Steinberg.
p.   cm.
Includes bibliographical references and index.
ISBN 978-0-674-03086-2 (cloth: alk. paper)
ISBN 978-0-674-05746-3 (pbk.)
1. Juvenile justice, Administration of—United States.
I. Steinberg, Laurence D., 1952–   II. Title.
KF9779.S36   2008
345.73'08—dc22   2008005133

Contents

RETHINKING JUVENILE JUSTICE

CHAPTER 1

Introduction:
The Challenge of Lionel Tate

In 1999 a twelve-year-old Florida boy named Lionel Tate killed Tiffany Eunick, a six-year-old neighbor girl half his size. According to initial press reports, Lionel, an avowed fan of professional wrestling, had executed a knee drop on Tiffany's chest during a wrestling match with her. Lionel later changed his account and admitted that he jumped down from a staircase onto his younger playmate. In any event, he broke the girl's ribs, fractured her skull, and lacerated several internal organs; the consequent hemorrhaging caused her death.[1]

Two years later, Lionel was tried as an adult on charges of first-degree murder. The prosecution offered him a plea bargain of a relatively short sentence in a juvenile facility followed by probation. On the advice of his mother, Lionel turned down the plea offer and opted to go to trial. He was convicted and sentenced to life in prison without parole—reportedly the youngest person to receive such a sentence in modern American history. According to news stories, the prosecutor said that he had no choice but to seek this sentence, given Florida law and the extent of Tiffany's injuries, which some took as evidence that her death was not accidental.[2]

Public outcry was immediate and strong at the severity of the sentence for a crime committed by a twelve-year-old.[3] Advocates for the boy insisted that the killing was accidental and that Lionel

1

did not pose a threat to society. In addition, many questioned whether Lionel was competent to stand trial, raising concerns about the fairness of adult criminal adjudication for a (by then) fourteen-year-old. Grassroots groups appealed to Florida Governor Jeb Bush, the Pope, and the United Nations to intervene on Lionel's behalf. Although many speculated that the governor would intervene and commute Lionel's sentence, this did not happen, and at age fourteen Lionel entered prison to begin serving his life sentence.

Lionel appealed, challenging the verdict on several grounds, and in December 2003 an appellate court reversed his conviction on the ground that the trial court should have ordered an assessment of Lionel's competence to stand trial before proceeding.[4] This result pleased advocates who had opposed the verdict, but some were troubled. Tiffany's family and the prosecutor appeared on television talk shows, expressing disappointment at the court's decision. The following month, Lionel was released from prison under an agreement not unlike the one he had originally declined; he pled guilty to second-degree murder and received credit for the time he had already served—three years in prison. Under the new agreement, Lionel, by then seventeen, was sentenced to a year of house arrest and ten years' probation. He was released in January 2004.

Unfortunately, Lionel's contact with the justice system did not end with his victory in the appellate court. In September 2004, just nine months after his successful appeal, sheriffs' deputies discovered the boy, still under house arrest, outside his home with a knife in his possession, a clear violation of his parole. A judge extended his probation to fifteen years. Then, in May 2005, Lionel was arrested for holding up a pizza delivery-person at gunpoint. He was charged with armed robbery and violation of probation. In May 2006, Lionel was sentenced to thirty years in prison for having violated his probation; according to news reports, the judge told Lionel, "In plain English, Lionel Tate, you've run out of chances. You do not get any more."[5]

The Lionel Tate story is a good place to begin a discussion of contemporary juvenile justice policy. What one should make of the story, however, is not immediately clear. Lionel was an immature youth when he killed Tiffany, but one who caused the gravest of harms. Was he as culpable as a twenty-year-old killer would have been? Should he have received the same punishment as an adult, or was the sentence that the prosecutor proposed at the outset fairer and more appropriate for a twelve-year-old? And does Lionel's post-release behavior shed any light on the right answers to these questions? On the one hand, his subsequent behavior could be interpreted as evidence that Lionel was a dangerous criminal who *should* have been locked up for life, and that the benign view that he was an immature youth who killed Tiffany accidentally was simply wrong. On the other hand, Lionel's conduct at age seventeen does not resolve the question of whether a twelve-year-old deserves the same punishment as an adult. Moreover, the three years Lionel spent in prison may have affected him in adverse ways, molding a wayward adolescent into a criminal; Lionel might have been a different person at age seventeen had the disposition for his crime been different. Either way, the case suggests just how difficult it is to construct a juvenile justice policy that responds satisfactorily to the multiple challenges that society faces in dealing with youth crime. An optimal (or even adequate) juvenile crime policy must pursue and balance several goals. These include fair punishment of young offenders, which means recognizing their immaturity and yet also holding them accountable for their crimes. The goals also include fair hearings, as well as dispositions that will enhance rather than harm the future prospects of youths in the justice system and reduce rather than increase the likelihood that they continue their criminal activities. Last, but certainly not least, juvenile justice policy will fail unless it satisfies the community's need for retribution and assures adequate protection of public safety. Accommodating the tensions among these diverse policy goals is a daunting challenge.

Youth Crime Policy in the Late Twentieth Century: A Period of Transformation

Lionel Tate's case unfolded during a period in which American juvenile justice policy was undergoing dramatic changes. In less than a generation, a justice system that viewed most juvenile lawbreakers as youngsters whose crimes were the product of immaturity has been transformed into one that often holds young offenders to the same standard of criminal accountability it imposes on adults. Under the traditional legal regime, the transfer to criminal court of a minor charged with a crime was a rare occurrence. That is no longer the case. Through legal reforms in almost every state, youths barely in their teenage years can be tried and punished as adults for a broad range of crimes. Florida law is not unusual in providing that twelve-year-olds accused of murder can be tried and punished as adults. Although such cases are rare, a youth of Lionel's age who is charged with murder could be subject to trial in criminal court and sentenced to prison in most states.[6] Other reforms have broader impact. In some states, teenagers in mid-adolescence are categorically excluded from juvenile court—either in general or when charged with designated felonies. Moreover, sentences imposed by juvenile courts have become longer—closer to those received by adult criminals.

Politicians and the media tend to focus on juveniles like Lionel who are accused of murder. In general, public alarm about violent youth crime has been an important catalyst for legal reforms. But such reforms extend also to youths charged with less serious crimes. Of the more than 250,000 individuals under eighteen years of age who are tried as adults each year in the United States, only about half are accused of violent crimes—and a *very* small percentage are charged with murder.[7] In many states, youths charged with selling drugs or stealing property fall under the jurisdiction of criminal court. Until 2005, Illinois had a particularly strict law under which any person age fifteen or over who was apprehended for selling drugs near a school or public housing project was automatically transferred to criminal court, regardless of his or her prior record.[8] The eroding distinction between the justice system's treatment of juveniles and of adults represents a pervasive and far-reaching policy shift that has touched the lives of many young people. The shift marks a dramatic departure from nearly a century of American juvenile justice policy.

The policy changes are not limited to an expansion of criminal court jurisdiction over juveniles. During the past twenty-five years, the juvenile justice system itself has come to treat young offenders with increasing severity. Incarceration has replaced community probation as a standard disposition in many cases, and youths who are adjudicated in juvenile court can receive long sentences that are completed well into their adult years, often in prison. Juvenile convictions also increasingly have repercussions in adulthood, in the form of criminal records or enhanced sentencing. Moreover, the system's reach is now appreciably broader, such that more juveniles are being referred to the justice system for less serious crimes. In response to fears about school violence, for example, police are routinely called into schools to respond to student misconduct.[9] Under "zero-tolerance" policies, students who might have received a short school suspension a few years ago are sent to juvenile court today.[10] Many cities have enacted curfew ordinances as a crime control tool; youths out late at night are charged with violations, and chronic violators can receive real penalties.[11] In other words, the normative misbehavior of adolescence—such as fighting in school or staying out too late at night—are increasingly being handled in court rather than at the kitchen table or in the principal's office.

The Traditional Court under Fire:
The Collapse of the Rehabilitative Ideal

What explains the growing trend for young offenders to be processed and punished as adults? Why has the boundary between the juvenile and the adult justice systems, intact for almost a century, eroded in less than a generation? In part, it is important to recognize that the reforms of juvenile crime regulation were part of a larger trend toward more punitive justice policies. A backlash against the liberal policies of the 1960s (the era of the Warren court and of spare use of imprisonment) began in the 1970s. By the 1980s, prison rates were skyrocketing. As national crime rates rose in the late 1980s and early 1990s, politicians competed to demonstrate that they aimed to get tough on crime, whether the criminals were adults or juveniles.

Supporters of the juvenile system reforms suggest that they simply provided a straightforward response to the sharp increase in violent youth crime that began in the late 1980s—an increase that made it glaringly evident that the juvenile justice system was inadequate to the task of protecting the public from the threat of young "super-predators."[12] According to this view, modern juvenile offenders are very different from young troublemakers of one hundred or even fifty years ago. The juvenile court, established at the turn of the last century as a key part of the Progressive Era's social reforms, may have met the needs of a simpler time when kids got into schoolyard fistfights, but the system has failed to deal with today's savvy young criminals who use guns to commit serious crimes.[13] Even seemingly innocuous behaviors (schoolyard fistfights, for example) warrant serious attention because they are precursors to violence. On this view, the recent law reforms simply recognize that the juvenile court is an outmoded institution that cannot meet the needs of contemporary criminal justice.

There is some truth to this account. The crimes of contemporary juvenile offenders *are* different from those perpetrated by young delinquents in earlier times, in part because of the widespread availability of firearms beginning in the 1980s.[14] Although there is little evidence that young criminals today are more prone to violence than were their predecessors owing to the "moral poverty" of modern culture,[15] the injuries that modern youths inflict on their victims are more likely to be fatal. Predictions of a coming wave of superpredators and "fledgling psychopaths" have proved to be exaggerated, but there is no question that lethal violence committed by juveniles increased markedly during the 1980s and early 1990s.[16]

Critics of the traditional juvenile court pointed to the increase in violent crime as justification for less forgiving justice policies. Indeed, many argued that the lenient policies and practices of the juvenile court were the *cause* of the youth crime problem, because young criminals assumed that their punishment would not be severe.[17] Although youth advocates strongly challenged this proposition, the criticism was generally well received by a public already disillusioned with the juvenile court and the rehabilitative model on which it was based.

Some of the criticism of the traditional system was quite justified. By the late 1980s, two key premises of the rehabilitative model had been largely discredited. The first was that young offenders were blameless but misguided children who were simply in need of redirection with the guidance of the court. Although this sympathetic image of delinquent youths probably served a useful political purpose in the early twentieth century when social reformers were promoting their new court to legislatures and the public, it later appeared naive when applied to older youths committing violent crimes. The second premise, related to the first, was that the sole purpose of state intervention in delinquency cases was to promote the welfare of delinquent youths through rehabilitative interventions. Though ardently defended by the architects of the juvenile court, this premise also turned out to be deeply flawed. It rested implicitly on an optimistic prediction that rehabilitation would "cure" young offenders of their criminal propensities, a prediction that allowed the Progressive reformers to avoid confronting the public's interest in protection from youth crime. When it became clear that juvenile correctional programs were failing to reduce recidivism, the conflicting interests of the state and of youths involved in crime became apparent. The rise in juvenile crime was seen as evidence not only that the juvenile justice system was too soft on young criminals, but also that the system's well-intentioned rehabilitative interventions were completely ineffective.

Even before the dramatic reforms of juvenile crime policy in the 1990s, the juvenile court had already undergone substantial changes from the model envisioned by the Progressive reformers. In the 1960s, it was disillusioned youth advocates (not politicians concerned about public safety) who launched a far-reaching reform initiative. These critics argued that the problem with the juvenile justice regime was not the failure of the rehabilitation model, but the failure of the system to deliver the treatment it promised while at the same time denying juveniles the procedural rights provided to adult criminal defendants.[18] In 1967, the Supreme Court responded to this challenge in *In re Gault,* a landmark opinion that extended to juveniles in delinquency proceedings some of the same constitutional rights that defendants in criminal proceedings enjoy under the Due Process Clause of the Fourteenth Amendment—most important, the right to an attorney.[19]

In the view of many observers, *Gault* marked the beginning of the end of the traditional juvenile court. To be sure, at least two decades would pass before there were serious challenges to the idea that juvenile offenders should be subject to more lenient treatment in the juvenile system. *Gault* nonetheless dealt a severe blow to the already faltering rehabilitative model. Moreover, in the 1970s and 1980s no coherent contemporary rationale for maintaining a separate juvenile justice system emerged to replace the traditional framework.[20] Although youths continued to be processed in the juvenile system, it was not clear what its purposes should be or how it should differ from the adult system. In short, the American juvenile justice system was floundering and in search of a rationale for its existence. In this environment, when violent juvenile crime became a hot issue in the late 1980s, the public and lawmakers were ready for radical reform.

Youth Violence and Law Reform as Moral Panic

Advocates for tougher laws governing youth violence focused on three themes: first, that young offenders were not children but dangerous criminals; second, that violent juvenile crime was epidemic, partly due to the laxity of juvenile court dispositions; and third, that rehabilitation was a dismal failure, at least when it came to reforming serious juvenile offenders.[21] A growing chorus of angry critics argued that youth crime policy should focus primarily (or even exclusively) on the goal of protecting the public. These critics ridiculed the juvenile system for coddling youths, whom they depicted as hardened criminals who deserved "adult time for adult crime." Albert Regnery, head of the Office of Juvenile Justice and Delinquency Prevention during the second Reagan administration, offered a typical comment: "Although there may be a good reason to give a more lenient sentence to a first offender, there is no justification for punishing an offender less simply because he is sixteen."[22]

Youth advocates who challenged the punitive reforms did not deny that public safety was an important consideration in responding to juvenile crime. Many of these advocates, however, tended to invoke the paternalistic rhetoric of the traditional juvenile court and characterized delinquents as children who were victims of poverty and racism.[23] In the polarized debate that unfolded during the 1990s, participants on both sides seemed to assume that youths charged with crimes would either be treated as children in juvenile court or be tried and punished as adults. Given this choice, lawmakers responded by opting for public protection over leniency and by redefining many adolescent offenders as adults.[24]

Although supporters saw the punitive law reforms as a coherent policy response to a new generation of dangerous young criminals, closer inspection reveals that these policy changes, even when driven by legitimate concerns, have often been adopted in a climate of fear and, sometimes, near hysteria. Indeed, juvenile crime policy has been transformed by a process that has the hallmarks of what sociologists describe as a "moral panic," in which politicians, the media, and the public reinforce each other in an escalating pattern of alarmed response to a perceived social threat.[25] Other features of a moral panic are evident in the response to juvenile crime that has led to the reforms, such as intense public hostility toward young offenders, exaggerated perceptions about the magnitude of the threat, and the conviction that drastic measures are urgently needed. For example, rigid "zero-tolerance" policies were implemented on a widespread basis to protect American schoolchildren in response to the school shootings of the 1990s, although the probability of an American student being murdered while in school is lower than that of being struck by lightning.[26] Moral panics are often triggered by highly publicized events; in the context of juvenile justice reform, the events are usually horrendous crimes committed by young perpetrators. In California, for example, reports of drive-by shootings by gang members that killed innocent bystanders generated enthusiasm for a punitive referendum expanding criminal court jurisdiction over juveniles.[27]

Although moral panics subside in time as the perception of the threat recedes, the impact can be enduring when lawmakers rush to protect the public through legislation and policy change. Moreover, once the legislative reform process is initiated, it seems to take on a life of its own. In many states, reform initiatives triggered by fears of violent youth crime have led to wholesale changes in juvenile justice policy, resulting in criminal court jurisdiction over youths charged with a broad range of nonviolent crimes, as well as the violent offenses that were initially targeted.[28] What has been missing, for the most part, is the kind of thoughtful deliberation and consideration of consequences that one would expect to inform legal and institutional changes of such sweeping importance.

A Window of Opportunity

After more than a decade of steadily declining juvenile crime rates, the moral panic finally seems to have subsided, leaving many people feeling uneasy about the dramatic policy changes that occurred and uncertain about the soundness of the reforms. As we discuss in a later chapter, recent polls indicate that the public opposes adult prison for most juveniles and favors rehabilitative interventions even for serious first-time juvenile offenders so long as they are held accountable for their crimes.[29] Even some enthusiasts for getting tough on kids seem a bit embarrassed at the punitive way the law has dealt with some young offenders. For example, John DiIulio, who coined the term "super-predators" in the mid-1990s, recently expressed regret at this characterization of young offenders and acknowledged that his predictions about the growing threat had not come to pass.[30] Legal commentators increasingly have challenged the punitive reforms, pointing out that juvenile justice policy stands out as a glaring anomaly in the legal regulation of minors: In virtually every other area of legal regulation, adolescents (and especially younger teenagers) are *not* treated like adults.[31]

There is also evidence that lawmakers are having second thoughts about policies that treat youths like adults, particularly as they begin to internalize the budgetary impact of tough sanctions. Recent legislative and policy reforms in states as diverse as Illinois, New

Hampshire, Connecticut, and California indicate that the pendulum may be swinging back toward a more moderate approach. In 2005, for example, Illinois abolished the statute under which youths charged with selling drugs near a school were automatically tried as adults, partly in response to evidence that the statute was enforced almost exclusively against African American youths.[32] The recent Supreme Court decision in *Roper v. Simmons,* abolishing the juvenile death penalty, is further evidence of this trend.[33]

This period of relative calm provides an opportunity to step back and evaluate the recent punitive reforms and, if they are unsatisfactory (as we shall argue), to devise a model of juvenile justice that can better serve the needs of society in the twenty-first century. Doing so seems particularly important at this time; juvenile crime rates have begun to climb slightly in the past year or two, and, if we are to avoid a new wave of reforms based on moral panic, policy makers must have a framework on which to build policies that are both sensible and fair. We undertake this challenge.

At the outset, we emphasize that we think the question of how society should respond to juvenile crime is much harder than either zealous youth advocates or defenders of punitive policies acknowledge—and we admit that we have no easy solutions to offer. Although we argue that most adolescents should not be subject to the same procedures and punishment as adults, we recognize the legitimacy of the concerns about violent youth crime that drove the reforms. Social scientists continue to debate what caused the escalation of serious juvenile crime that led to the punitive reforms, but the fact remains that violent crime *did* increase during the 1980s and early 1990s, and the availability of inexpensive handguns made the crimes more lethal and the young offenders more dangerous. In the early 1990s, homicides by juveniles were at an all-time high, several times the number in 1970.[34]

Furthermore, in light of research indicating high recidivism rates among serious juvenile offenders, the argument that the juvenile justice system was doing a poor job of rehabilitating violent young criminals is hard to refute; in truth, the lack of confidence in the system and in the rehabilitative model of juvenile justice was warranted. The response of some youth advocates to public concerns about youth crime—minimizing the threat, charging racism, and clinging to an outmoded image of young offenders as children—has not been helpful. Protecting the public from violent youth crime must be a core concern of a viable juvenile justice policy. At the same time, we aim to persuade the reader that a justice regime that focuses narrowly on public safety and that fails to attend to the differences between juveniles and adults ultimately will be unsatisfactory.

The Psychology of Adolescence and the Regulation of Crime

Adolescents are different from adults—and juvenile offenders are different from adult criminals—in ways that are important to the regulation of youth crime. In the chapters that follow, we propose an evidence-based developmental model of juvenile justice. Our model is grounded in wide-ranging scientific knowledge about psychological maturation in adolescence, patterns of involvement in crime during this developmental stage, and the impact of various dispositions on youth development and the transition to adulthood. A vast body of recent research that was not available a generation ago offers insights about both adolescence and youth crime from which we can draw important lessons for the design of juvenile justice policy. The research demonstrates convincingly that this developmental stage is distinctive in ways that are relevant both to the involvement of adolescents in crime and to effective legal responses. Developmental knowledge provides the material needed to construct a satisfactory framework for regulating juvenile crime in the twenty-first century.

First, available scientific knowledge confirms what parents of adolescents surely know—that although teenagers are not childlike, they are less competent decision makers than are adults. Although adolescents' capacities for reasoning and understanding (what might be called "pure" cognitive abilities) approach adult levels by about age sixteen, the evidence suggests they may be less capable than are adults of *using* these capacities in making real-world choices.[35] More important perhaps is that emotional and psychosocial development lags behind cognitive maturation. For example, teenagers are considerably more susceptible to peer influence than are adults, more likely to focus on immediate rather than long-term consequences, and more impulsive and subject to mood fluctuations. They are also more likely to take risks and probably less skilled in balancing risks and rewards. Finally, personal identity is fluid and unformed in adolescence.[36] This is a period when individuals separate from their parents, experiment (often in risky endeavors), and struggle to figure out who they are.

In combination, these developmental factors undermine adolescent decision making and contribute to immature judgment—as this term is used in common parlance.[37] Again, as most parents of teenagers can attest, immature judgment can lead adolescents to make "bad" decisions—that is, choices that threaten the welfare of the teenager or others—to a greater extent than do adults. Although not every teenager displays poor judgment, the effects of immature judgment on decision making are *normative*, as psychologists use this term: that is, typical of adolescents as a group and developmental in nature. Moreover, recent research has elucidated the biological underpinnings of many of these psychological attributes. Studies of brain development show that during adolescence, significant maturation occurs in brain systems and regions involved in long-term planning, impulse control, regulation of emotion, and evaluation of risk and reward.[38] Thus, the immature judgment of teenagers to some extent may be a function of hard wiring.

The psychological immaturity of adolescents affects their decision making in contexts that are relevant to justice policy. First, immature judgment likely plays a role in decisions by teenagers to engage in criminal activity, and the developmental influences sketched above (and described more fully in Chapter 2) combine to distinguish the criminal choices of adolescents from those of adults. The differences between teenagers and adults are more subtle than those that distinguish young children and severely impaired persons from ordinary criminals, but they are substantial and, we will argue, justify the conclusion that the punishment imposed on young offenders should be less severe than that which adult criminals receive. Further, due to their immaturity, adolescents may be less capable than adult defendants of participating effectively in criminal proceedings. This is important because of constitutional restrictions on adjudicating defendants who fail to meet basic standards of trial competence.[39]

Developmental psychologists view adolescence as a critical stage in an individual's development, not only because it is a period in which decision-making capacities mature, but also because during adolescence individuals begin to learn many essential skills required for optimal functioning in adulthood.[40] The basic capacities needed to fulfill the conventional adult roles of spouse (or intimate partner), employee, and citizen are acquired through the ordinary experiences of adolescence. Severe disruption of this process may impede, or completely sidetrack, the transition to productive adulthood. The successful completion of these developmental tasks involves reciprocal interactions between the adolescent and his or her social environment, an important consideration for the structuring of correctional programs.

Scientific knowledge about patterns of criminal behavior in adolescence and early adulthood also plays an important role in our developmental model. Ironically, many of the developmental factors that make the criminal conduct of adolescents less culpable than that of adults also contribute to the tendency of many teenagers (especially males) to get involved in criminal activity. This tendency is so pervasive that psychologist Terrie Moffitt, one of the world's leading experts on the development of antisocial behavior, has described delinquent behavior as "a normal part of teenage life."[41] It is not surprising, then, that seventeen-year-olds commit more crimes than any other age group; after that age, the crime rate declines dramatically. Predictably, as normative adolescents move into adulthood, they mature in all areas of psychological development, and, of particular importance for our purposes, most of them also desist from criminal activity. A much smaller group of more intractable youths, who are described as "life-course-persistent" offenders by Moffitt,[42] continue to engage in criminal activity beyond early adulthood. Policy makers are well advised to pay attention to these diverse patterns and to consider the impact of sanctions on a young offender's transition to adulthood.

The Developmental Model: Adolescence as an Intermediate Legal Category

Our developmental model of juvenile justice treats (most) adolescent offenders as a separate legal category, neither children whose crimes are excused nor adults who are fully responsible for their crimes. This approach, we argue, is the key to a fair and effective juvenile justice system, although it is not typical in the legal regulation of minors generally. On most issues, childhood and adulthood are binary legal categories; young citizens are treated as children until they cross the legal threshold and become adults. The boundary between childhood and adulthood is age eighteen, the age of majority, for most purposes, although occasionally it is set at a different age.[43] In this classification scheme, adults are presumed to be competent, autonomous persons who are responsible for their choices, while minors, whether they are toddlers or teenagers, are presumed to be incompetent, dependent, and not responsible. There is no middle ground where most issues are concerned.[44]

For the most part, as we explain in Chapter 3, this binary approach works quite well, although it often distorts the developmental reality of adolescence. It has not worked well, however, in juvenile justice policy. As we have noted, the rehabilitative model of juvenile justice collapsed, in part, due to its naive characterization of delinquent youths as innocent children who were not responsible for their crimes. The contemporary model errs in the other direction, depicting youths who are legal minors for all other purpose as adults when it comes to criminal adjudication and punishment.

The contemporary approach is deficient on both theoretical and practical grounds. First, it offends the core principles of proportionality and due process that are deeply embedded in our criminal justice system—and are essential to its fairness. Proportionality holds that criminal punishment should be based not only on the harm of the offense but also on the actor's blameworthiness. A justice system that is ready to hold adolescent offenders fully responsible for their crimes violates proportionality because young lawbreakers are less blameworthy than are their adult counterparts due to developmental immaturity. Beyond this, criminal adjudication of younger teenagers threatens the justice system's commitment to procedural fairness, because cognitive and psychosocial immaturity can undermine the ability of youths to function as criminal defendants. Second, although advocates argue that tough policies will protect the public and promote social welfare, in reality, adult punishment of delinquent youths, for the most part, is likely to be ineffective in achieving these practical goals. Punitive reformers have never confronted hard questions about the impact of adult punishment on adolescents, in terms of both their future criminal conduct and their development into adult members of society.

The research evidence suggests that their approach is shortsighted at best.

The developmental model is superior to both of the alternative frameworks that have shaped juvenile justice policy for more than a century. First, the research on adolescence has important implications for creating a justice system that is compatible with the theoretical commitments of the criminal law to fair punishment and fair process. Second, under the developmental model, scientific knowledge guides the formulation of policies that maximize social welfare at the least cost.

The Developmental Model and Principles of Criminal Law Fairness

Consider proportionality, a bedrock principle of the criminal law. Proportionality seems a rather abstract concern, but it is crucial to the legitimacy of state-sponsored punishment and an important dimension of a fair and stable juvenile justice system. Indeed, some of the ridicule directed at the traditional juvenile court and the uneasy response to recent punitive reforms may reflect public concerns about accountability and fairness. Scientific research and theory support the conclusion that adolescents, even sixteen-year-olds and seventeen-year-olds, make decisions to get involved in criminal activity that are less culpable than those of adults, largely because their choices are driven by developmental factors that contribute to immature judgment. But adolescents are also not children whose crimes should be excused. Thus, *mitigation* should apply to their criminal conduct. The distinction between mitigation and excuse is an important one that is often lost in the public debate, where the alternative options are often cast as either adult punishment or "a slap on the wrist," suggesting that if teenagers are not held fully responsible for their crimes, they bear no criminal responsibility at all. The developmental model holds that adolescents are responsible for their criminal conduct and should be sanctioned for their misdeeds but deserve less punishment than do typical adult offenders.

The principle of proportionality is at the heart of the substantive criminal law, but procedural fairness is also an important element of a satisfactory system for regulating youth crime. The U.S. Constitution requires that defendants in criminal proceedings be competent to stand trial, but substantial research indicates that the capacity of younger adolescents to function adequately in the trial context is highly uncertain.[45] This evidence has important implications both for the adjudication of youths in criminal court and for formulating a competence standard in juvenile delinquency proceedings. It should be underscored—because it often seems to be the source of confusion—that the issues of culpability and competence are quite distinct; the former involves the quality of the actor's decision to engage in criminal conduct, while the latter pertains to the actor's capacity for trial participation. Juvenile justice policy that is grounded in developmental knowledge attends to the impact of immaturity in both contexts.

The Developmental Model and Social Welfare

The theoretical mandates of proportionality and due process are important constraints on the design of juvenile justice regulation, but they are unlikely to carry the day in the political arena. Ultimately, the most compelling arguments for our proposed developmental framework are consequentialist. From society's perspective, crime policies are evaluated largely on the basis of their effectiveness at reducing crime at the least cost. At the heart of our model is the claim that social welfare will be enhanced and the cost of juvenile crime minimized if society adheres to the lessons of scientific research in responding to youth crime.

Supporters of the recent reforms claim, of course, that punitive policies promote public safety and therefore serve society's interests.

Their calculus is distorted, however, exaggerating the threat (and thus the social costs) of youth crime and the societal benefits of adult punishment, while miscalculating or discounting an array of potential costs of punitive policies, including recidivism costs and economic costs that have strained budgets in many states. Unnecessary costs have been generated because legislative enthusiasm for cracking down on youth crime has swept into the adult system many nonviolent offenders who represent little threat to public safety.[46] To be sure, at one level, tough sanctions can reduce juvenile crime. Youths who are locked up for long periods are not on the street committing crimes. But there is little evidence that long incarceration is effective at deterring crime or at reducing recidivism—indeed, most evidence indicates that adult imprisonment increases juvenile re-offending.[47]

The developmental research provides essential lessons for the construction of justice policies that promote social welfare. The first lesson is that most adolescent offenders are not headed for careers in crime—unless correctional interventions push them in that direction. Legal sanctions can have a profound impact on the trajectory of young offenders' lives and affect the likelihood that they will become productive (or at least not criminal) adults. Because adolescence is a critical developmental stage during which teenagers acquire essential competencies and skills, correctional dispositions have the potential either to disrupt or to enhance social and educational development, and thus either undermine or promote prospects for gainful employment, successful family formation, engaged citizenship—and criminal involvement. Twenty years ago, most social scientists were pessimistic about the effectiveness of delinquency programs in reducing recidivism.[48] That view has changed dramatically. A growing body of research indicates that interventions that invest in the social development of young offenders diminish the risk of re-offending, thus benefiting society, potential future victims, and youths themselves.[49]

Our consequentialist analysis explicitly recognizes that the promotion of social welfare is an essential criterion for evaluating juvenile justice policy. A key lesson we can take from the disillusionment with the traditional juvenile court is that youth crime policy will fail if it is not perceived as achieving this goal. Harms caused by young offenders must be minimized; occasionally tough measures (including adult imprisonment) may be required to achieve public protection against youths who persist in committing serious violent crimes. But most young criminals do not pose the kind of risk that justifies long incarceration in either the adult or the juvenile system. Policies that invest in their future lives will benefit young offenders and, ultimately, the rest of society. This conclusion is not based on paternalism, but rather on the conventional policy goal of maximizing public welfare at the least cost. In short, like the punitive reformers, we are utilitarian; we simply argue for a more comprehensive and accurate utility calculus.

A road map of the book may help guide readers through our proposed model. Chapter 2 elaborates on the scientific evidence about adolescence that forms the building blocks of the developmental model. First, we focus on cognitive, emotional, social, and neurobiological maturation, as well as identity formation, key aspects of development that influence the decision-making capacities of adolescents in ways that distinguish them from adults. We then explore patterns of antisocial conduct in adolescence and explain how psychological factors contribute to criminal conduct during this developmental stage and to desistance from criminal activity in late adolescence or early adulthood. This pattern reinforces the point that most young offenders are normative adolescents, teenagers whose involvement in crime is largely the product of developmental influences and begins and ends during adolescence; only a small percentage of teenagers are likely to become career criminals.

Although the criminal conduct of these two categories of young offenders in adolescence may be similar, the underlying causes and prognoses are different. Finally, this chapter examines recent evidence that mid- to late adolescence is a critical period for the development of the skills and competencies necessary for success in work, family, and citizenship roles and the importance of social environment in the accomplishment of these developmental tasks.

In Chapter 3 we describe the key features of legal regulation of minors generally, as a backdrop for understanding and evaluating justice policy in the chapters that follow. Many aspects of contemporary regulation can be traced to the ambitious Progressive agenda to improve the lives of children at the turn of the past century. From these early reforms came the concept of the state as parent and protector of children and the assumption that the overriding purpose of regulation is to promote children's welfare and to facilitate their development to healthy adulthood, ideas that continue to shape legal regulation. This chapter describes the standard binary approach to legal regulation under which adolescents, for most legal purposes, are subject to the same restrictions and protections as are younger children, although occasionally they are classified as adults. In this classification scheme, the intermediate stage of adolescence is virtually invisible. The chapter analyzes how the boundary between childhood and adulthood is determined, first by examining the age of majority and then by exploring contexts in which the line is shifted either downward (for example, under statutes authorizing minors' consent to particular medical treatments) or upward (for example, through laws authorizing child support through college). Our analysis suggests that departures from the presumptive boundary occur when youth welfare and social welfare converge on a different age as superior to the presumptive age of majority.

Chapter 4 examines crime regulation as a type of legal regulation of minors. This perspective makes clear that the traditional juvenile justice regime fit comfortably within the general paternalistic framework, treating young offenders as children whose welfare was of paramount concern in the legal response to their crimes. The chapter explains why the standard paternalistic approach failed in the context of crime regulation and examines the forces that led to a dramatic policy transformation in the last decades of the twentieth century. After briefly describing the various legal strategies through which the jurisdictional boundary between the juvenile system and the criminal system has shifted, we focus on one jurisdiction, California, that adopted tough juvenile justice reforms by referendum in 2000. Analysis of the campaign that led to the adoption of Proposition 21 provides an informative case study of the politics of juvenile justice reform under conditions that have the hallmarks of a moral panic—in this case, focusing on juvenile gang activity. This account suggests that an appeal to racial bias played a role in the campaign and that, generally, the process by which the reforms were undertaken was deeply flawed.

In Chapters 5 and 6, we locate juvenile justice policy within the broader framework of the criminal law and examine how two key elements of a fair justice system apply to the prosecution and punishment of juveniles. Chapter 5 undertakes a standard proportionality analysis that identifies three conventional sources of mitigation in criminal law—diminished capacity, external coercion, and the lack of bad character—as important to assessing the culpability of normative adolescent offenders. We also explain why mitigation based on immaturity generally should operate as a categorical constraint on punishment of teenagers rather than as a basis of individualized assessment of culpability. Implementation of this principle will reinforce the jurisdictional boundaries of the juvenile court and affect transfer and legislative waiver policies, as well as juvenile dispositions. We address the vexing question of whether "immature" adult offenders should qualify for mitigation—and explain important psychological differences between these actors and adolescents that disqualify the former group. The chapter concludes with an examination of the juvenile death penalty, recently struck down by the Supreme Court in *Roper v. Simmons*. Adopting elements of our mitigation framework, the Court concluded that juveniles are not culpable enough to deserve the ultimate punishment of death, and that the prohibition should be categorical.[50]

In Chapter 6, we turn to procedural fairness, examining the application to juveniles of the constitutional mandate that criminal defendants must be competent to stand trial. The due process requirement of adjudicative competence evolved as a protection for mentally impaired defendants, but it applies with equal force to youths who may be incapable of competent participation in a criminal proceeding due to developmental immaturity. The chapter examines how younger teenagers' immature decision-making capacities and limited experience may affect their abilities to assist their attorneys and otherwise to function as criminal defendants. We describe compelling research evidence, including findings of a major study conducted by the authors with colleagues, that a substantial percentage of younger teenagers are at risk for incompetence using standard measures applied to adults.[51] These findings have important practice and policy implications for the criminal adjudication of youths; they present policy makers with important policy choices, one of which is whether to shift the jurisdictional boundary of criminal prosecution to exclude younger teenagers. The research evidence also has implications for delinquency proceedings. We argue that to avoid the exclusion of many younger teenagers from adjudication in *any* court, dual standards of competence should be applied in criminal and juvenile court, an approach that is constitutionally acceptable so long as the dispositional stakes faced by youths in juvenile court are lower than those faced by adults.

In Chapter 7, we undertake a social welfare analysis of youth crime policy, shifting the focus from fairness to young offenders to the prevention of crime at the least cost to society. One aim of this chapter is to probe the claim that tough policies are justified on the ground that they promote social welfare. We do this by the evaluating available evidence on the costs and benefits of alternative approaches—an analysis undertaken against the backdrop of scientific knowledge about adolescence and the pattern of youth offending. First, we examine economic costs, which have increased dramatically since 1990, a period in which juvenile crime has steadily declined. This increase in costs is due primarily to a substantially greater use of incarceration in both the adult and the juvenile systems for both violent and nonviolent young offenders. The chapter then examines whether severe sanctions themselves have reduced juvenile crime and concludes that the policy reforms in recent years may have had a modest effect through general deterrence and incapacitation, but have also resulted in the incarceration of many youths who do not present a great risk of re-offending. Moreover, the empirical evidence does not support that harsh sanctions reduce recidivism—indeed, youths sent to prison appear more likely to recidivate than do comparable youths in the juvenile system.

An examination of prisons and of juvenile facilities as social environments against the backdrop of developmental knowledge provides some insight into why this might be so. The developmental model clarifies that delinquency interventions should aim to avoid what may be irremediable disruption of developmental trajectories of adjudicated youths, and to facilitate, to the extent possible, preparation for conventional adult life. The chapter concludes with a description of programs in the juvenile system that incorporate developmental knowledge with considerable success. Several promising programs, some of which have been replicated and studied extensively, have been found to reduce recidivism substantially in young offenders at considerably less cost than incarceration.

Chapter 8 extracts lessons for juvenile justice policy from the fairness and social welfare analyses presented in earlier chapters. Although we offer no detailed blueprint for an ideal regime, our model provides guidelines for a justice system that is fair to young offenders and at the same time minimizes the social cost of youth crime. First, our analysis indicates the importance of retaining a separate juvenile justice system with a clear boundary separating it from the adult system. Most youths should be retained in this system and subject to sentences that are proportionate in duration in correctional settings promoting healthy development through investments in the human capital of young offenders. We argue that the dispositional jurisdiction of the juvenile court should be extended into early adulthood, so that youths who commit serious crimes can be held accountable while remaining in the juvenile system. In a regime grounded in the developmental framework, only older youths are eligible for transfer to criminal court, under rules that are designed to separate normative offenders from career criminals and to limit judicial and prosecutorial discretion. Thus, only serious violent felonies are transferable offenses, and waiver to the criminal court is limited to juveniles with a record of serious violent crimes. These youths have the least claim to mitigation and pose the most severe threat to public safety. Finally, even in the adult system, fairness and social welfare dictate that juveniles should not be subject to toxic environments or receive the most severe sentences, such as life without parole.

Chapter 8 then deals with the "hard cases," the small group of youths whose crimes do not appear to result from developmental influences and who are at substantial risk of becoming career criminals. For some, a pattern of antisocial behavior may begin in early childhood; they may come into the justice system in late childhood or early adolescence and by mid-adolescence have a long criminal record. Containing the substantial costs that these youths inflict on society is an essential condition of a viable juvenile justice policy. We examine the sources of persistent antisocial behavior and explore appropriate responses for the justice system. Older youths in this category are likely to be well represented among juveniles transferred to the adult system. More challenging from a policy perspective is how to deal with pre-teenage or young adolescent offenders, youths who are at high risk for recidivism but also have the most compelling claims for mitigation due to immaturity. Intensive and comprehensive interventions offer the best hope for changing the developmental course of these very young offenders, but, on proportionality grounds, the disposition should be a mix of correctional programs and social, educational, and psychological interventions available to children not in the justice system. The costly investment in developing effective programs will be justified if it can be linked to enhanced public protection.

In Chapter 9, we return to an issue raised earlier—the politics of juvenile justice—and ask whether a stable justice regime grounded in our developmental model can be established and sustained. We are cautiously optimistic about the possibilities of reform in this direction. Recent evidence from several sources indicates that enthusiasm for punitive policies is waning and that the pendulum may be swinging back toward moderation. Several state legislatures have revised their juvenile justice laws, backing off from the punitive reforms enacted just a few years earlier. Moreover, policy makers appear to be focusing to a greater extent on the monetary costs of criminalizing juvenile justice—and perhaps on human costs as well. Research evidence also indicates that public attitudes toward young offenders are considerably less punitive and have more nuances than conventional wisdom would suggest.[52] This evidence can reassure lawmakers that responding cautiously to public pressure in the wake of high-profile crimes may not carry the political risk some seem to fear. Deliberation and the passage of time can result in more rational policy formation. On our view, the time is ripe for a new period of juvenile justice reform. Translating the developmental framework into legal policy is the key to creating a stable regime that is fair to juvenile offenders and promotes social welfare.

CHAPTER 2

The Science of Adolescent Development and Teenagers' Involvement in Crime

The study of adolescence has "a long past, but only a short history."[1] Philosophers and educators have recognized for centuries that there is a distinctive stage of life between childhood and adulthood—more than two thousand years ago, Aristotle described a seven-year period of life from about age fourteen until twenty-one that followed childhood and preceded adulthood. But scientists did not turn their attention to adolescence as a unique developmental period until the turn of the twentieth century. Most scholars of adolescence mark the beginning of its systematic study with the publication of G. Stanley Hall's book, *Adolescence: Its Psychology and Its Relations to Physiology, Anthropology, Sociology, Sex, Crime, Religion, and Education*, but Hall's writings were based more on speculation than science.[2] Psychoanalytic thinkers, like Anna Freud and Erik Erikson, published treatises on adolescence in the middle of the twentieth century, but like Hall's, their writings were not grounded in empirical inquiry.[3] The systematic scientific study of psychological development during adolescence did not really begin until the early 1970s, and it did not genuinely come of age until at least ten years later. Indeed, the first meeting of the Society for Research on Adolescence—today, the major professional organization of scientists interested in adolescent development—took place in 1986. Only 150 persons attended.

Despite its short history, the scientific study of adolescence has generated a remarkably comprehensive literature on many key features of human development during the second decade of life. Scientists now have a thorough understanding of physical, emotional, cognitive, and social development in adolescence, and a burgeoning and complementary literature on adolescent brain maturation has emerged that has fascinated both scholars and laypersons.[4] Although not all of the conjectures offered by Aristotle, Hall, Freud, and Erikson have been borne out by empirical research, the long-standing popular belief that adolescence is characterized by a unique set of features that warrant its consideration as a distinct period of development is indisputably supported by the research of the past three decades. In this chapter, we focus on the scientific study of adolescence as a distinctive developmental period that bridges childhood and adulthood.

The argument that we advance is that scientific knowledge about cognitive, psychosocial, and neurobiological development in adolescence supports the conclusion that juveniles are different from adults in fundamental ways that bear on decisions about their appropriate treatment within the justice system—and that this scientific knowledge should be the foundation of the legal regulation of juvenile crime. In the chapters that follow, we argue that these differences should inform discussions about adolescents' criminal blameworthiness, their competence to stand trial, and the types of sanctions and interventions they should receive when they are convicted of a criminal offense.

The assertion that adolescents are "different" from adults will strike many as self-evident, especially those who are (or have been) parents of teenagers. To be useful in policy discussions about how the legal system should deal with adolescents involved in crime, however, the evidence must go beyond common sense or anecdotal observation. In particular, in constructing our developmental model, we focus on differences between adolescents and adults that have the following three characteristics. First, the differences must be related to their criminal conduct and society's response to it. Teenagers and adults might differ in countless ways, and while some of these differences may be relevant to justice policy, others are not. Thus, for our purposes, differences between teenagers and adults in their susceptibility to coercion are important, but not differences in their taste in music.

Second, these differences are of interest only if they are integrally linked to adolescent development. A trait or tendency that distinguishes adolescents from adults is linked to adolescent development if adolescents' capacities in regard to the trait are deficient or immature, either intrinsically or in practice—that is, in specific social contexts. For example, adolescents tend to consider the future consequences of their choices and conduct less than do adults.[5] One explanation for this tendency is that adolescents are simply inherently less capable than adults of thinking ahead or anticipating consequences; if true, this would be evidence of developmental immaturity that is relevant to their criminal choices. However, even if, in the abstract, adolescents could plan and contemplate future consequences as well as adults, they may be less capable of doing so when they make real-world choices (such as the choice "on the street" of whether to join their friends in holding up a convenience store).[6] If individuals in this developmental stage systematically demonstrate this deficiency in practice *and* predictably improve with maturity, then this tendency can be described as developmental and is relevant to the evaluation of their criminal choices.

Finally, the relevant features of adolescence that distinguish teenagers from adults must be characteristic of juveniles in general.[7] Put differently, the psychological attributes that are of interest to us are traits and tendencies that reasonably can be said to characterize the "typical" adolescent and are part of what psychologists call "normative" patterns of development. The conclusion that adolescents, as a class, are inherently different from adults does not mean necessarily that *all* adolescents are different from *all* adults—but it does mean that the *typical* individual who is categorized as an adolescent differs from the typical individual who is categorized as an adult.

Developmental research supports our contention that adolescents do, in fact, differ from adults in ways that are relevant to justice policy, that the distinguishing features of adolescence are linked to this period of development, and that these features are sufficiently characteristic of adolescents as a group to warrant their consideration as a separate and distinct class. Before examining these factors in detail, however, we turn to a more general discussion of adolescence as a developmental period.

Adolescence as a Developmental Stage

Adolescence generally is not considered a distinct legal category, but it is regarded as a separate life stage by psychologists who specialize in cognitive, emotional, and social development. Whether the changes that are characteristic of development into, during, and out of adolescence should be thought of as continuous or categorical in nature has been the subject of unresolved debate among scientists who study adolescence, but few scholars today view adolescents as either mature children or immature adults. Contemporary psychologists universally view adolescence as a period of development distinct from either childhood or adulthood with unique and characteristic features.[8] For example, adolescents, who are typically struggling to establish independence from their parents—a central psychological task during this stage—are quite different from children, who look to their parents to make decisions for them and for whom autonomy has not yet become a goal. At the same time, adolescents also differ from young adults, whose independence from parental control has already been achieved.[9]

As a developmental stage, adolescence is a complex mixture of the transitional and the formative. The period is *transitional* because it is marked by rapid and dramatic change within the individual in the realms of biology, cognition, emotion, and interpersonal relationships, and by equally important transformations in major social contexts—family, peer group, and school. Even the word "adolescence" has origins that connote its transitional nature: it derives from the Latin verb *adolescere,* to grow into adulthood. At the same time, adolescence is a *formative* stage in the sense that events and experiences that take place during this period place individuals on particular pathways into adulthood that may set the course of their future lives.[10] For example, adolescence is the period during which educational and vocational trajectories are typically launched and preparation for adult roles begins in earnest; young people whose educational paths are impeded or disrupted during this time often do not fully recover. Further, most of the serious psychological problems that afflict adults, such as depression or substance abuse, appear first in adolescence.[11] The fact that adolescence is a formative period does not minimize the importance of childhood experience in shaping what happens during adolescence or ignore the possibility of life-changing experiences during adulthood. But what happens during adolescence undoubtedly shapes individuals' views of the world, their mental health, and their likelihood of success as adults.

Nonindustrialized societies recognize the importance of adolescence as a period of preparation for adult roles through rites of passage that often mark both the beginning and end of this preparatory period. Although such formal ceremonies are of less significance today, modern adolescents also prepare for the occupational, familial, and citizenship roles they will occupy as adults. True, the transition from adolescence to adulthood has been delayed in some segments of society by the lengthening of formal education, postponement of marriage, and prolongation of individuals' financial dependence on their family of origin, but this has only reinforced the significance of adolescence as a period of preparation for adulthood.[12] Adolescents make decisions about whether to enter the workforce full time or pursue post-secondary education, decide on possible career paths, and establish serious intimate relationships with potential marital partners. The choices they make and the experiences they have in the domains of school, work, and romance potentially have long-lasting implications.[13]

Drawing Developmental Boundaries

When lawmakers focus on the legal regulation of young people (including the regulation of their criminal activity), the distinction between adolescence and adulthood is of primary interest. However, in virtually all major theories of psychological development, adolescence is distinguished not only from adulthood, but from childhood as well. Indeed, the research on psychological development during the second decade of life has focused more extensively on the transition into adolescence than on the transition to adulthood.[14] Only in recent years has scientific interest focused intensely on the psychological transition between adolescence and adulthood, largely in response to new research showing continued brain maturation through the end of the adolescent period.[15] Until this research began to appear in scientific journals and the popular press, the line between adolescence and adulthood was seen primarily as a legal or sociological boundary, rather than a psychological one.

In contrast, the psychological distinctions between childhood and adolescence have long been well understood. A substantial psychological literature documents changes in intellectual, emotional, behavioral, and interpersonal functioning during the transition from childhood into adolescence. These include changes in reasoning abilities, personality characteristics, problem behavior, psychological distress, family and peer relationships, and various aspects of psychosocial maturity (such as self-reliance and resistance to peer pressure). These studies, which include much longitudinal research, have tracked development through puberty, the transition from elementary to secondary school, and the emergence of increasingly sophisticated reasoning abilities.[16]

The research shows that several important developmental shifts distinguish childhood and adolescence. First, a gradual increase in logical reasoning abilities takes place between ages eleven and sixteen, as indexed by improvements in abstract and hypothetical thinking (the consideration of alternative outcomes that do not exist in the present reality).[17] Interestingly, although gains in hypothetical thinking level off in mid-adolescence, the consideration of the future consequences of choices continues to improve through late adolescence.[18] Second, emotional arousal and affective lability increase in early adolescence, coincident with the onset of puberty.[19] This change has been linked to increases in emotional intensity, in the pursuit of pleasurable experiences (such as the sensations achieved through the use of drugs), and in sensation-seeking.[20] Third, a significant social shift occurs; parents become less salient than in childhood while peers become more so. Orientation to the peer group increases markedly between the ages of ten and fourteen. [21] Fourth, the desire for emotional and behavioral independence increases in adolescence, impelling some adolescents to challenge the authority of parents and other adults.[22]

More recently, developmental scientists have turned their attention to the biological and psychological transition out of adolescence, providing support for the uniqueness of adolescence as a stage of life that is also distinct from adulthood with respect to several aspects of brain and psychosocial development. The transition from adolescence to adulthood is characterized by psychosocial maturation and the maturation of the brain's executive functions, which together result in improved judgment in decision-making; the transition is also marked by the attainment of a settled identity.[23] Most of the remainder of this chapter focuses on these distinctions between adolescence and adulthood—which form the basis for policy arguments for differential treatment of adolescent and adult offenders in the chapters that follow.

Psychological Development and Decision-Making in Adolescence

Two related features of normative psychological development influence adolescent decision-making and conduct in ways that distinguish teenagers from adults and are relevant to youthful criminal choices. First, several features of cognitive and psychosocial development undermine competent decision-making in adolescence. These features contribute to immature judgment, leading adolescents to make decisions that are harmful to the interests of others or themselves. Cognitive and psychosocial immaturity also may undermine the capacity of youths to participate competently in criminal proceedings. Second, adolescents are in the process of separating from their parents and forming their adult personal identities, a process that involves exploration and (for many teenagers) experimentation in risky activities. To the extent that youthful criminal activity represents this kind of experimentation, it is quite different from that of adults, whose criminal choices can be attributed to *individual* preferences and values.

Over the past twenty years, a substantial body of scientific research has greatly enhanced our understanding of influences on decision-making that are constitutive of the developmental stage of adolescence and that change as normative adolescents move into adulthood. Until the past decade or so, this research was largely based on standard tools of psychological investigation, such as interviews and instruments eliciting verbal or written responses. Recently, however, brain research has begun to contribute to our understanding of adolescence and to clarify the biological underpinnings of psychological development. Both kinds of research are important to understanding developmental influences on adolescent decision-making.

Cognitive Development in Adolescence—Understanding and Reasoning

The most familiar capacities involved in decision-making are *understanding* (i.e., the ability to comprehend information relevant to the decision) and *reasoning* (i.e., the ability to use this information logically to make a choice). These capacities increase through childhood into adolescence. Between late childhood and mid-adolescence (roughly between the ages of eleven and sixteen), individuals' general knowledge base expands and they show marked improvements in reasoning (especially deductive reasoning) and in both the efficiency and capacity of information processing. Research over a period of twenty-five years has demonstrated conclusively that, as a result of gains in these areas, individuals become more capable of abstract, multidimensional, planned, and hypothetical thinking as they develop from late childhood into mid-adolescence. By mid-adolescence, teenagers' capacities for understanding and logical reasoning in making decisions roughly approximate those of adults, at least in the abstract.[24]

This conclusion—that adolescents and adults demonstrate comparable capacities for understanding and reasoning—must be viewed with caution, however. The findings are based on laboratory studies in which individuals are presented with hypothetical decision-making dilemmas that may not accurately test decision-making capacities in the real world. There is reason to believe, for example, that adolescents may be less able to deploy their cognitive capacities as effectively as adults in making decisions in their everyday lives, in part because they simply have less experience (and thus less information) to draw on. In laboratory studies, subjects are typically provided with the information necessary to make the decisions presented; in the real world, individuals must draw on their own resources.[25] Moreover, research indicates that information processing becomes more efficient as individuals mature; thus, adolescents may be less capable than adults of *quickly* processing information accurately.[26] In life, and particularly on the street, the capacity to marshal information quickly may be essential to optimal decision-making.

Psychosocial Development—Immaturity of Judgment in Adolescence

Other developmental factors may also influence adolescent decision-making. New perspectives on adolescent "cognition-in-context" emphasize that adolescent thinking in everyday settings is a function of social and emotional, as well as cognitive, processes and that a full account of youthful decision-making capacities must examine the interaction of all of these influences. This is another way in which laboratory-based studies of intellectual functioning may give an incomplete picture of adolescents' performance. Even when adolescent cognitive capacities approximate those of adults, youthful decision-making may still differ from that of adults due to psychosocial immaturity.[27] Moreover, research indicates that psychosocial maturation proceeds more slowly than cognitive development, and that age differences in decision-making may reflect social and emotional differences between adolescents and adults that continue well beyond mid-adolescence.[28]

The psychosocial factors most relevant to age differences in criminal conduct include susceptibility to peer influence and orientation toward peers, the evaluation of risk and reward, future orientation (the extent to which one considers short- versus long-term consequences when making decisions), and the capacity for self-management and self-regulation. Available research indicates that adolescents and adults differ significantly with respect to each of these attributes. While cognitive capacities shape the process of decision-making, psychosocial maturity can affect the actual outcomes of individuals' deliberations, because these developmental factors interact with cognitive factors to shape values and preferences in real-world situations.[29]

PEER INFLUENCE. Substantial research evidence supports the conventional wisdom that teenagers are more oriented toward peers and responsive to peer influence than are adults. Susceptibility to peer influence increases between childhood and early adolescence as individuals begin to separate from their parents. Peer influence appears to operate through two processes, social comparison and social conformity.[30] Through social comparison, adolescents use others' behavior as a measure of their own behavior. Social conformity, which is especially heightened in mid-adolescence, leads adolescents to adapt their behavior and attitudes to that of their peers, especially in day-to-day matters, as opposed to long-term plans or fundamental values. Social scientists have studied age differences in response to peer pressure by presenting individuals with hypothetical dilemmas involving some sort of peer influence and asking them what they would do in the situation. Several studies using this method show that susceptibility to peer influence in situations involving pressure to engage in antisocial behavior increases between childhood and mid-adolescence, peaks around age fourteen or fifteen, and declines slowly during the late adolescent years.[31] Increased susceptibility to peer pressure in early and mid-adolescence may reflect changes in individuals' capacity for self-direction (as parents' influence declines) as well as changes in the intensity of pressure that adolescents exert on each other. The net result is that adolescents are more likely than either children or adults to change their decisions and alter their behavior in the face of pressure from age-mates.

Peer influence affects adolescent judgment both directly and indirectly. In some contexts, adolescents might make choices in response to direct peer pressure, as when they are coerced to take risks that they might otherwise avoid. More indirectly, adolescents' desire for peer approval, and consequent fear of rejection, affect their choices even without direct coercion. The increased salience of peers in adolescence likely makes approval-seeking especially important in group situations. Thus, it is not surprising, perhaps, that adolescents are far more likely than adults to commit crimes in groups.[32]

Peers also may provide models for behavior that adolescents believe will assist them to accomplish their own ends. For example, there is some evidence that during early and mid-adolescence, teenagers who engage in certain types of antisocial behavior, such as fighting or drinking, may enjoy higher status among their peers as a consequence.[33] Accordingly, some adolescents may engage in antisocial conduct to impress their friends or to conform to peer expectations.

FUTURE ORIENTATION. Future orientation, the capacity and inclination to project events into the future, may also influence judgment because it affects the extent to which individuals consider the long-term consequences of their actions in making choices. Between mid-adolescence and young adulthood, individuals become more future-oriented, with increases in the consideration of future consequences continuing over this extended period.[34] In addition, adolescents tend to discount the future more than adults do, and to weigh more heavily short-term consequences of decisions—both risks and benefits—in making choices. This may account for the greater inclination to take risks among teenagers than adults.[35] Thus, compared to adults, adolescents are less likely to think about the longer-term consequences of their actions and, when future consequences are considered, they are likely to assign relatively less weight to them than to more immediate ramifications.

There are several plausible explanations for this age gap in future orientation. In part, adolescents' weaker future orientation may reflect their more limited life experience. To a young person, a short-term consequence may have far greater salience than one five years in the future. The latter may seem very remote simply because five years represents a substantial portion of her life.[36] Behind this common-sense explanation, however, is scientific evidence linking the differences between adolescents and adults in future orientation to age differences in brain structure and function. One recent study linked future orientation to performance on a neuropsychological test known to assess functioning of the brain's frontal lobe, suggesting that increasing future orientation may be related to improvements in functioning in brain regions that continue to mature between adolescence and adulthood.[37]

RISK EVALUATION. Research evidence also suggests that adolescents differ from adults in their evaluation of risk, although not necessarily in their ability to perceive risks. By mid-adolescence, teenagers perform similarly to adults on measures of risk perception—responding similarly to paper-and-pencil questionnaires asking them to rate various activities (e.g., "How dangerous is it to have unprotected sex?").[38] This seems somewhat puzzling, given that adolescents and young adults take more health and safety risks than do older adults by engaging more frequently in behaviors such as unprotected sex, drunk driving, and criminal conduct. If adolescents and adults are equally likely to perceive a dangerous activity as risky, why are adolescents more likely to engage in the activity?

One explanation of the puzzle is that laboratory studies of risk perception may fail to capture differences between adults and adolescents that affect risk assessment in the real world. This intuition was corroborated in a recent study by one of the authors, in which participants were directed to play a video game in which they could take risks while driving a car.[39] The study found that adolescents and adults engaged in comparable levels of risk-taking when acting alone, but when asked to play the game in the presence of friends, risk-taking increased among adolescents (aged thirteen to sixteen) and young adults (aged eighteen to twenty-two), but did not change among adults (whose average age was in the thirties). Most laboratory-based comparisons of adolescent and adults test individuals in isolation and thus do not detect these differences—but, in the real world, risk preference and peer influence may interact in a dynamic way that contributes to adolescents' risky choices.

A story about the son of one of the authors illustrates this point aptly. When he was fourteen, Ben and several of his friends secretly left the house where they were spending the night at 2 A.M. to visit the nearby home of the girlfriend of one of the boys. When they arrived at the girl's home, they threw pebbles at her window to wake her. Unfortunately for the boys, the pebble-throwing set off a burglar alarm, which sounded a siren and sent a dispatch to the local police station. Upon hearing the siren, the boys ran—right into a patrol car that was racing toward the house. Instead of explaining their situation to the police, Ben and his friends panicked and scattered. One of the boys was apprehended by the police and taken home. The others returned to the house where they were spending the night. The next morning, Ben's father received a phone call from the girl's parents, explaining what had happened. After picking Ben up and lecturing him about the dangers of running, in the dark, from armed police who thought they had interrupted a burglary, his father asked him, rhetorically, "What were you thinking?" "That's the problem, Dad," Ben said. "I wasn't."

It seems probable that the presence of peers, together with the sense of urgency created by the arrival of the police, overwhelmed the decision-making capacities of an otherwise intelligent and law-abiding teenager. In a laboratory setting, Ben likely would have identified the risks of his situation as well as any adult. The lesson of the story is that risk assessment and decision-making on the street may present challenges to teenagers that are greater than those faced by adults.

A different, although compatible, account of why adolescents take more risks than do adults concerns how people of different ages evaluate the *benefits* of risky activity. Adolescents and adults may perceive risks similarly (both in the lab and in the real world) but evaluate rewards differently, especially when the benefits of the risky decision are weighed against the costs.[40] Psychologists refer to the outcome of weighing risks and rewards in making decisions as the "risk-reward ratio"; the higher the ratio, the less likely an individual is to engage in the behavior in question. Studies suggest that in calculating the risk-reward ratio, the key difference between adolescents and adults may be not in their assessment of the risks, but in the calculation of anticipated rewards. So, for example, in deciding whether to speed while driving a car, adolescents and adults may estimate the risks of this behavior (e.g., being ticketed, getting into an accident) similarly, but adolescents may weigh the potential rewards (e.g., the thrill of driving fast, peer approval, getting to one's destination sooner) more heavily than adults, leading to lower risk-ratio ratios for teenagers—and a higher likelihood of engaging in the (rewarding) activity. Thus, what distinguishes adolescents from adults in this regard is not the fact that teenagers are less knowledgeable about risks, but rather that they attach greater value to the rewards that risk-taking provides.[41]

Emerging evidence suggests that the special salience of rewards to adolescents may be driven, at least in part, by neurobiological changes that take place at puberty. In particular, the tendency of adolescents to seek more novelty and pay more attention to the potential rewards of a risky decision is likely due to dramatic changes in the brain's reward circuitry that take place at puberty.[42] Although most of the relevant brain research on this question comes from animal studies, there is some support for the notion that developments in the limbic system of the brain and in connections between the limbic system and the prefrontal cortex around puberty may account for at least part of this change in reward-seeking.[43] We will look more carefully at this brain research shortly.

Finally, age differences in risk-taking may be due to age differences in specific values and priorities that are linked to other psychosocial influences on decision-making.[44] For example, consider a teenager whose friends are encouraging him to join them in trying a new drug. If adolescents value enhanced status among their friends more than do adults, that reward may be given more weight by a teenager than by an adult in deciding how to respond. By the same token, adolescents may weigh more heavily than adults the cost of peer disapproval, and thus, that possibility may have a relatively greater impact on the decision-making of teenagers.

SELF MANAGEMENT.   In addition to age differences in susceptibility to peer influence, future orientation, and the calibration of risk and reward, adolescents and adults also differ with respect to their ability to control impulsive behavior and choices. Thus, the widely held stereotype that adolescents are more reckless than adults is supported by research on developmental changes in impulsivity and self-management over the course of adolescence. In general, studies show gradual but steady increases in the capacity for self-direction through adolescence, with gains continuing through the high-school years.[45] Impulsivity, as a general trait, declines between adolescence and adulthood, as does sensation-seeking (the tendency to place oneself in sensation-arousing situations).[46] Research also indicates that adolescents are subject to more rapid and extreme mood swings (both positive and negative) than are adults;[47] although the connection between moodiness and impulsivity is not clear, it is likely that extreme levels of emotional arousal (either anger or elation) are associated with difficulties in self-control. Although more research is needed, the available evidence indicates that adolescents may have more difficulty regulating their moods, impulses, and behaviors than do adults.

Adolescent Brain Development

Although most of the developmental research on cognitive and psychosocial functioning during adolescence involves psychological studies, recent work in the field of developmental neuroscience—the study of changes in the brain with age—is beginning to shed light on the underlying causes of immaturity of judgment in middle and late adolescence. The evidence that differences in the decision-making capacities of adolescents and adults are linked to predictable changes in brain structure and function has generated considerable interest. Both the public and policy-makers appear to view this research as relevant to legal regulation and particularly to justice policy. For this reason, we review the evidence in some detail.

Scientists have found clear evidence that the brain continues to mature through adolescence and into the early twenties, with large-scale structural change taking place during this period in the frontal lobes, most importantly within the prefrontal cortex, and in the connections between the prefrontal cortex and other brain regions.[48] The prefrontal cortex is central to what psychologists call "executive functions," advanced thinking processes that are employed in planning ahead and controlling impulses, and in weighing the costs and benefits of decisions before acting. Individuals employ executive functions when they think through the likely consequences of an action, compare the costs and benefits of alternative choices, pause before acting to envision the way a scenario is likely to unfold, or stop themselves from behaving impulsively.

Brain maturation typically occurs through several processes. Two of the most important are "synaptic pruning," the selective elimination of unused connections between brain cells (neurons), and myelination, the development of the white fatty substance (myelin) that forms a sort of insulation around the neural circuits in the brain. Both of these processes make information processing more efficient. Myelin functions similarly to plastic insulation on electrical wires, and myelination is associated with more efficient transmission of electrical impulses in the brain. Myelin production increases during adolescence and into adulthood.[49] In contrast, synaptic pruning improves brain functioning by *reducing* the number of synapses (the connections between neurons) and strengthening those that remain. Through pruning, unnecessary synapses produced during the early years are eliminated and information processing becomes more efficient. Synaptic pruning occurs in different regions of the brain at different times; it occurs in the prefrontal cortex mostly during adolescence.[50]

Research also indicates that the connections between the frontal regions of the cortex and other parts of the brain that are involved in processing social and emotional information undergo maturation through adolescence and into early adulthood. Recent studies show substantial changes during this period in brain regions and systems associated with impulse control, the calibration of risk and reward, and the regulation of emotions.[51] The studies show, for instance, that adults are not only better than adolescents at inhibiting a response that is difficult to restrain (e.g., looking away from, rather than toward, a flash of light in a dark room), but that adults employ many more regions of the brain in a coordinated effort to perform this task.[52] Adolescents, relying on a more limited number of brain regions, are vulnerable to being overwhelmed when the task becomes complicated.[53]

Scientists study brain development in several ways. *Functional* imaging, which allows actual observation of brain functioning while individuals engage in specific tasks, has only recently been used to study the adolescent brain. More common are studies that employ *structural* imaging, which allows comparison of the brain anatomy of people of different ages, without any reference to task performance. But most of what we know about actual decision-making differences between adolescents and adults comes from behavioral, rather than neurobiological, research. Research directly linking anatomical brain development with actual behavioral change is still very sparse, but the behavioral and structural research considered together indicate that performance on tasks thought to involve the frontal lobe improves at the same general time that significant structural changes take place in this region of the brain.

An illustration of behavioral research that sheds light on age differences in brain development is the study of performance on a task known as the Tower of London, which is known to activate the dorsolateral region of the prefrontal cortex.[54] In this test, the subject is presented with an arrangement of colored balls, stacked in a certain order, and several empty vertical rods onto which the balls can be moved. The subject is then presented with a picture of a different configuration of balls and asked to turn the original configuration into the new one by moving one ball at a time, using the fewest number of moves.

This task requires thinking ahead, because extra moves must be used to undo a mistake. In several studies, our research group found that individuals in early and mid-adolescence performed similarly to adults when the problem presented was an easy one (i.e., one that could be solved in two or three moves), but that they did not plan ahead as much as did late adolescents and young adults on the harder problems; unlike the older subjects, the younger participants spent no more time before making their first move on the complex problems than they did on the simple ones.[55] These findings are consistent with casual observations of teenagers in the real world, which also suggest that they are less likely than adults to think ahead before acting.

Researchers have also found improvement during adolescence in performance on tasks known to activate the ventromedial region of the prefrontal cortex, which regulates activities associated with the balancing of risk and reward. This has been shown in studies employing the Iowa Gambling Task, in which subjects are given four decks of cards, face down, and are instructed to turn over cards, one at a time, from any deck.[56] Each card has information about how much money the subject has won or lost by selecting that card. Two of the decks are "good," in that drawing from them will lead to gains over time, and two of the decks are "bad"; drawing from them will produce net losses. Because a few cards in the "bad" decks offer very high rewards, though, a person who is especially sensitive to rewards will be drawn to the "bad" decks, even if he or she keeps losing money as a result. At the beginning of the task, people tend to draw randomly from all four decks, but as the task progresses, normal adults pick more frequently from the good decks.[57] Studies, including our own, find that children and younger adolescents do poorly on this task. Performance improves with age, with the most dramatic improvement taking place during mid-adolescence.[58] This likely reflects a decrease in susceptibility to choosing based on the prospect of an immediate, attractive reward.

Our research group has also examined age differences using a task called Delay Discounting, a task that measures how much individuals discount the value of a reward in order to receive it sooner. Performance on this task is known to activate parts of the brain that are especially sensitive to reward.[59] The participant is asked to choose between a larger reward (say, $1,000) at some specified point in the future (say, in one year) or a smaller amount of money sooner (say, $500 in one week).[60] In our research, we found a direct correlation between the age of the participant and the amount of money he would accept sooner rather than waiting longer for the larger reward. Adolescents were more likely than adults to settle for less money if they could get it sooner—a correlation that existed regardless of the amounts of money offered or the length of the shorter and longer time periods.[61] This is consistent with the view that adolescents are more sensitive to rewards than are adults and also are more inclined to value immediate consequences and to discount the future.

One of the lessons that emerged from both brain and behavioral research on executive functioning is that changes in the relevant regions and abilities are gradual, occurring over a long period of time that continues into early adulthood. This relatively late and steady maturation of the brain regions implicated in executive functioning stands in contrast to the timing of changes in emotional arousal and the processing of social information, activities that are controlled mainly by the brain's limbic system. Relatively early in adolescence, individuals experience increases in the intensity of negative and positive emotions, in sensitivity to social stimuli, and in the importance of status in a peer group.[62] Scientists know less about the anatomical maturation of the limbic system than about frontal lobe development, but it appears that these emotional and social changes are most dramatic around the onset of puberty, when there is a proliferation of receptors for dopamine, a neurotransmitter important for the experience of pleasure, and oxytocin, a neural hormone important for social bonding.[63] We are now beginning to understand the neurobiological underpinnings of the increase in risk-taking, especially in group situations, that takes place during the first half of the adolescent decade.

The upshot of this work is that changes in the limbic system at puberty may promote reckless, sensation-seeking conduct (especially in peer groups) in early and mid-adolescence, while the regions of the prefrontal cortex that control the executive functions of planning, emotion regulation, impulse control, and evaluation of risk and reward continue to mature over the course of adolescence and into young adulthood. This gap in time, between the increase in sensation seeking around puberty and the later development of "regulatory competence," may combine to make adolescence a time of inherently immature judgment. One scientist has likened the situation to "starting the engines without a skilled driver."[64] Because adolescents' executive functions are not mature, their capacities for planning, for anticipating future consequences, and for impulse control are deficient—as compared with those of adults— at a time when their inclination to engage in risk-taking behavior in the company of peers is greater than it will be in a few years. This seems like a prescription for bad choices based on immature judgment.

What role do these developmental influences play in youthful choices to engage in criminal activity? Consider for a moment an individual who is inclined to act impulsively and who, in making choices, discounts or ignores risks and future consequences, while assigning substantial value to peer approval, immediate rewards, and the excitement of risk-taking. It takes little imagination to see how a group of individuals with these adolescent traits, hanging out on a street corner, might decide to hold up the nearby convenience store.

Our inquiry into scientific knowledge about adolescents' cognitive and psychosocial development points to the conclusion that ordinary teenagers differ from adults in their decision-making capacities, that their "deficiencies" are developmental in nature, and that the psychological deficits that contribute to immature judgment are grounded in underlying neurobiological immaturity. These developmental deficits likely are important in driving much youthful involvement in criminal activity and, as we will explain in Chapter 5, affect teenagers' criminal choices in ways that are mitigating under criminal law. Youthful immaturity may also undermine the capacities of some youths to assist their attorneys and otherwise function as criminal defendants, issues that we take up in Chapter 6. Clearly, developmental knowledge confirms the commonly held intuition that although teenagers are cognitively and psychologically quite different from children, they are less capable decision-makers than are adults, and their choices may reflect immature judgment.

Deficiencies in self-control and future orientation have been highlighted in other influential theories of criminal behavior—most notably, Michael Gottfredson and Travis Hirschi's "General Theory of Crime."[65] These authors argue that poor self-control (which they define as "the tendency to consider or ignore the long-term consequences of one's acts.") is the root cause of all criminal activity.[66] They fail to distinguish, however, between poor self-control that is part of normative adolescent development and deficits in adults that are more enduring and characterological. As we discuss in Chapter 5, antisocial acts that can be reliably attributed to bad character—as would be the case for an individual who continues to act like a teenager well into adulthood—appropriately are seen in a very different light than those of normative teenagers.

Personal Identity Formation and Experimentation in Risky Activities

The features of psychosocial maturation that we have described play a key role in an important developmental function of adolescence, the emergence of personal identity. As developmental psychologists explain, two interrelated processes contribute to identity formation: individuation—the process of separating from one's parents—and identity development—the process of creating a coherent and integrated sense of self. Although both processes are ongoing throughout this period, individuation is more salient in early and mid-adolescence (when teenagers struggle for independence from parental control), while identity development is more important in late adolescence and early adulthood.[67]

A predictable developmental sequence can be described. Until age ten or eleven, most children strive to please their parents and other adults by complying with their wishes and "parroting" adult beliefs and values. But during early adolescence, as part of normal emotional development, youths individuate from parents, a process that sometimes involves engaging in risky behavior that reflects both challenges to parental control and a shift in orientation from parents to peers. By mid-adolescence, individuals have distanced themselves from their parents and oriented themselves toward their peers, but genuine autonomy has not yet been established; teenagers at this stage can be slavish conformists to peer values and norms. By late adolescence, however, the process of individuation is normally accomplished, autonomy from both parental and peer influence is largely achieved, and the individual is well on the way toward the establishment of personal identity.[68]

Adolescence has often been described as a period of "identity crisis"—an ongoing struggle to achieve self-definition.[69] Under developmental theory, identity formation is a lengthy process that involves considerable exploration and experimentation with different behaviors and identity "elements." These elements include both superficial characteristics, such as style of dress, appearance, or manner of speaking, as well as deeper dimensions, such as personality traits, attitudes, values, and beliefs. As individuals experiment, they gauge the reactions of others—peers and adults—as well as their own satisfaction and, through a process of trial and error, over time select and integrate the identity elements of a realized self.

The experimentation that is a part of normal identity formation often involves risky, illegal, or dangerous activities—alcohol and drug use, unsafe sex, delinquent conduct, and the like. This is not surprising, perhaps, given adolescent preferences for immediate rewards and their sensation-seeking tendencies—perhaps combined with rebellion against parental values in pursuit of individuation. For most teenagers, this period of experimentation is fleeting; it ceases with maturity as identity becomes settled. Only a relatively small proportion of adolescents who experiment in risky or illegal activities develop entrenched patterns of problem behavior that persist into adulthood.[70] Thus, predicting the development of more permanent and enduring traits on the basis of risky behavior patterns in adolescence is an uncertain business.

While individuation, exploration, and experimentation are ongoing from early adolescence, coherent integration of the various retained elements of identity into a developed "self" does not occur until late adolescence or early adulthood. Empirical research indicates that the final stages of this process often occur during the college years. (Very few studies have examined identity development among non-college youth, so it is impossible to say whether this timetable holds true across all socioeconomic strata of the adolescent population.) Elements of adult personhood include social and political attitudes, moral values, occupational commitments, religious beliefs, and personal habits and lifestyle choices. Until at least late adolescence, the values, attitudes, beliefs, and plans expressed by adolescents are likely to be tentative and exploratory expressions, rather than enduring representations of personhood.

The Age-Crime Curve and Psychological Development

Our account of identity formation and of general psychological development in adolescence and early adulthood informs our understanding of patterns of criminal conduct among teenagers. The relationship between chronological age and patterns of criminal offending—called the "age-crime curve" by criminologists and sociologists—shows that criminal behavior follows a predictable course during adolescence and early adulthood.[71] Criminal behavior is rare in childhood and preadolescence. Its incidence increases sharply through age sixteen, a pattern that represents what vast amounts of other research demonstrates—that participation in criminal activity of some kind during adolescence is very common, especially among males. From age seventeen onward, the age-crime curve declines sharply. This steep drop-off in criminal activity reflects the reality that *most* adolescents desist in late adolescence or early adulthood. Only a small group of young offenders—about 5 percent by many estimates—will persist in criminal activity in adulthood. The upshot is that the vast majority of teenage offenders are individuals whose offenses are linked to adolescence and who are not destined to become adult criminals.

Criminologists and sociologists offer accounts of desistence from criminal activity in late adolescence or early adulthood that focus on societal role expectations. According to Robert Sampson and John Laub, as individuals assume normal adult roles (employee, spouse, parent) the time demands and daily routines of a conventional lifestyle make engaging in criminal behavior both less rewarding and more costly.[72] Gainful employment diminishes the relative monetary benefits of engaging in income-producing crime. Moreover, at home and in the workplace, social pressures to abide by the law begin to carry more weight than does pressure from antisocial friends to engage in criminal activity.

Our explanation for adolescents' involvement in and desistance from criminal activity is compatible with this account, but it focuses on psychological development rather than social role transitions—although the two are clearly related. In our view, a large portion of youthful criminal activity represents the experimentation in risky behavior that is a part of the developmental process of individuation and identity formation—combined with the psychosocial immaturity that contributes to poor judgment and deficient decision-making generally. Most teenagers desist from criminal behavior during the period when risky experimentation generally diminishes as individuals develop a stable sense of identity, a stake in their future, and mature judgment. The assumption of adult roles that Sampson and Laub associate with desistence from crime may facilitate this process; at the same time, it seems likely that psychological maturation makes it possible for individuals effectively to assume those roles.

The distinction between youthful criminal behavior that is attributable to transitory developmental influences of adolescence and conduct that is attributable to relatively more permanent elements of personality is captured in psychologist Terrie Moffitt's influential work on the developmental trajectories of antisocial behavior.[73] In Moffitt's view, adolescent offenders fall into one of two broad categories: "adolescence-limited offenders," whose antisocial behavior begins and ends during this developmental stage, and a much smaller group of "life-course-persistent offenders," whose antisocial behavior begins in childhood and continues through adolescence and into adulthood. Adolescence-limited offenders have little notable history of antisocial conduct in childhood, and, predictably, in late adolescence or early adulthood, they "mature out" of their inclination to get involved in criminal activity.

According to Moffitt, the criminal activity of both groups during adolescence may be similar, but the underlying causes of their behavior are very different. Life-course-persistent offenders show longstanding patterns of antisocial behavior that appear to be rooted, at least in part, in relatively stable psychological attributes that are present early in development and that are attributable to psychopathology, deficient socialization or neurobiological anomalies. Adolescence-limited offending, in contrast, is driven by forces that are inherent features of adolescence as a developmental period, including susceptibility to peer pressure (and peer orientation), sensation-seeking, experimentation with risk, a tendency to discount the future, and impulsivity. All of these developmentally driven forces abate as individuals mature into adulthood.

The typical delinquent youth does not grow up to be an adult criminal, in part because the developmentally linked values and preferences driving his criminal choices as a teenager change in predictable ways as he matures. As our description of identity formation suggests, adolescents are not yet the persons they will become—persons whose choices reflect their *individual* values and preferences, developed through the process of identity formation. As the typical adolescent offender matures, he becomes an adult with personally defined commitments and values and a stake in his own future plans. He is no longer inclined to involve himself in crime because his adult values (components of his personal identity) no longer lead him in that direction and because his choices are guided by more mature psychosocial judgment.

Understanding patterns of criminal conduct in adolescence and into early adulthood is important for several reasons. First, the fact that many adolescents who engage in criminal activity predictably will desist as they attain maturity is evidence that the criminal choices of these typical young offenders are quite different from those of adults. Crime rates begin to climb in early adolescence and then decline steeply in late adolescence *because* much adolescent crime reflects developmental influences that are characteristic of this period of life, and most youths will outgrow their criminal tendencies as they mature. This pattern is important for another reason. Because most teenage lawbreakers are not on a trajectory to pursue a life of crime, a key consideration in responding to their criminal conduct is the impact of dispositions on their prospects for productive adulthood.

The Social Conditions of Successful Adolescent Development

Thus far we have focused on *what* it is that changes during adolescence that contributes to the attainment of psychological maturity. We turn now to the *process* through which psychological and social development takes place and the conditions and circumstances that facilitate positive change. Although aspects of brain maturation described above drive this development, the pathway from adolescence to successful adulthood is not determined by biology alone and does not take place in a vacuum. Social context influences the course of psychological development in many ways, and certain conditions are important in facilitating the attainment of skills and capacities that allow individuals to assume successfully the conventional adult roles of spouse (or partner), employee, and citizen. Understanding the elements of social context that contribute to healthy development is important for several reasons. It offers some insight into why some youths get involved in crime and others do not, and, just as important, why some desist as they mature—and others become career criminals. Related to this latter point, as we discuss in Chapter 7, this knowledge has significant implications for creating correctional environments that enhance rather than undermine the likelihood that young offenders will become productive adults.

An extensive and remarkably consistent scientific literature describes the contextual conditions that are associated with the development of psychosocial maturity in adolescence and young adulthood.[74] Three conditions appear to be crucial. The first is the presence of at least one adult—typically, but not necessarily, a parent—who is involved in the adolescent's life and invested in the young person's success. This person also interacts with the adolescent in a way that is characterized by the expression of warmth, the establishment and enforcement of age-appropriate guidelines and expectations, and the acceptance and encouragement of the teenager's attempts at individuation.[75] This combination of warmth, firmness, and the encouragement of individuation is known as authoritative parenting. Almost all of the relevant work on this topic comes from studies of adolescents and their parents, although a few studies have looked at adolescents' relationships with other important adults, such as teachers or coaches. The basic pattern of findings is the same. Countless studies, conducted across samples of families around the world that vary in their socioeconomic background, household composition, and ethnicity show unequivocally that adolescents who have been raised by authoritative parents are less impulsive, more self-reliant, less vulnerable to peer pressure, and more successful in school than are their age-mates who were raised in other ways.[76] Not surprisingly, adolescents with authoritative parents are also less likely to commit antisocial or criminal acts, less likely to have drug or alcohol problems, and less likely to develop significant mental health problems.

Second, healthy psychosocial development during adolescence is facilitated by membership in a peer group that models and values pro-social behavior and academic success and by having a supportive, satisfying relationship with at least one close friend.[77] Most of what we have written about the peer group in this chapter—indeed, most of what has been written about adolescent peer groups by researchers on adolescence—has emphasized the potentially negative influence of exposure to antisocial peers. But the same susceptibility to peer influence that leads some adolescents to crime leads others to emulate friends who are pro-social in their orientation. Behaving in ways believed to enhance one's status with peers is a hallmark of adolescence, but the nature of the behavior produced through this motivation varies, because peer groups vary in what they value. Antisocial peer pressure is problematic; pro-social peer pressure, which also exists, is not.

A third contributor to successful psychosocial development in adolescence is participation in activities that permit the adolescent to develop and practice autonomous decision-making and critical thinking.[78] Research on this dimension of social context has mainly examined the impact of these sorts of influences in school, extracurricular activities, and work. Regardless of the setting, allowing adolescents to think for themselves, helping them learn to think critically, and giving them chances to make decisions that genuinely matter, as opposed to involving them in "make-work" (so long as bad decisions do not have severely harmful consequences) promote the development of self-reliance, self-efficacy, moral thinking, and more sophisticated reasoning abilities.

Scientists who study adolescent development agree that these three aspects of the social environment provide the conditions for the successful accomplishment of important developmental tasks of middle and late adolescence. During this period (and into early adulthood), individuals normally make substantial progress in acquiring and coordinating skills in several areas that are essential to making the transition to the conventional roles that are part of self-sufficient adulthood. First, they acquire basic educational and vocational skills that enable them to function in the workplace as productive members of society. They also acquire the social skills necessary to establish stable intimate relationships and to cooperate in groups. Finally, they begin to learn to behave responsibly without external supervision and to set meaningful personal goals for themselves. This process of development toward psychosocial maturity is one of reciprocal interaction between the individual and healthy social contexts that provide opportunity structures that facilitate normative development. The aspects of social environment that we have described contribute in important ways to the successful completion of these developmental tasks.

The social environment, of course, can also undermine the process of healthy development.[79] Parents can be neglectful, absent, or abusive, and if no adult steps in as a substitute to provide authoritative parenting, the likelihood that youths will accomplish the essential developmental tasks of adolescence is reduced. Moreover, peers, as we have discussed, can encourage or even coerce antisocial behavior. For youths who succumb to peer pressure, desistance from involvement in criminal activity may be difficult if the social context does not change. Finally, for some youths, school does not provide the setting for developing autonomy and critical thinking. If extracurricular activities or positive work environments do not fill this gap, psychosocial development toward mature adulthood may be inhibited.

Understanding the reciprocal interaction between youths and their social context is important for at least two reasons. It allows us to see why some adolescents get involved in criminal activity and others do not, and it helps inform the design of prevention programs designed to diminish the likelihood that young people will become involved in crime. To be sure, many youths who grow up in adequate or even supportive social environments get in trouble—due to the influence of the psychological developmental factors we described earlier. But youths in social contexts that do not promote healthy development are at far greater risk for offending. In some high-risk neighborhoods, many teenagers experience extraordinary pressure from peers to get involved in criminal activity, and they lack authoritative parents and opportunities to participate in school, extracurricular, or employment activities that might exert positive influences that offset the influence of peers. In such social contexts, only extraordinary youths will proceed along a path of healthy psychological development.

Beyond this, understanding the importance of social context to the maturation process is critically important in structuring juvenile correctional programs that will promote desistance and facilitate the transition of young offenders to productive adulthood. As we discuss in Chapter 7, recent research indicates that juvenile justice programs that pay attention to the importance of social context and to the goal of accomplishing essential developmental tasks have been far more effective at reducing recidivism than sanctions that ignore the differences between adolescents and adults. The social contexts of youths in the adult and juvenile systems are shaped by such factors as the attitudes and roles of parents and other adult supervisors, the identity and behavior of other offenders, and the availability (or not) of good educational skill-building and rehabilitative services. In combination, these factors may affect the inclination of young offenders to persist in criminal activities and facilitate or impede their development into adults who can function adequately in society.

This chapter has offered a scientific account of adolescence as a developmental stage, focusing on dimensions that are relevant to the involvement of teenagers in criminal activity and to the response of the justice system to their crimes. The research clarifies that substantial psychological maturation takes place in middle and late adolescence and even into early adulthood. It also supports the conclusion that the cognitive and psychosocial immaturity of teenagers can contribute to ill-advised choices that reflect immature judgment. The differences between youths and adults in these domains, combined with differences in identity formation and in underlying brain development, point to the conclusion that the criminal choices of typical adolescent offenders also are different in important ways from those of adult criminals. Not only do adolescent choices reflect deficiencies in decision-making, but the developmental meaning of choices as risky experimentation that is part of normal identity formation distinguishes typical young offenders from their adult counterparts. Finally, social context plays a critically important role in adolescent development; environmental influences in the family, peer, school, and community settings can promote or inhibit progress toward mature adulthood. In the chapters that follow, we will explore the implications of this scientific account of adolescence for youth crime policy. Our hope, ultimately, is to persuade the reader that optimal juvenile justice policy—policy that serves the interests of society as well as those of young offenders—will be grounded in this scientific account.

CHAPTER 3

Regulating Children in American Law:
The State as Parent and Protector

[A] child lacks . . . maturity, experience, and capacity for judgment in making life's difficult decisions. . . . Most children, even
in adolescence, simply are not able to make sound judgments . . .
concerning their need for medical care

— Parham v. J.R., 442 U.S. 584 (1979)

[The state's requirement of parental notification of abortion] is
[a] . . . state-imposed obstacle to the exercise of the minor
woman's free choice.

— H.L. v. Matheson, 450 U.S. 398 (1981), J. Marshall, dissenting

The developmental model of juvenile justice that we propose in
this book treats adolescents involved in crime as a separate legal
category, distinct from children and adults. Our approach is compatible with that of developmental psychologists, who view adolescence as a discrete stage that bridges childhood and adulthood.
This, however, is *not* the conventional approach toward adolescents in American law—including the law regulating youth crime.
Lawmakers tend to think of childhood and adulthood as binary
categories; the transitional stage of adolescence for the most part is
simply ignored in this classification scheme. For most purposes,
lawmakers lump teenagers and toddlers together as legal children

(or "minors") and subject them to the same paternalistic treatment. When an individual crosses the line to legal adulthood, she is assumed to be an autonomous person who is responsible for her conduct and choices and who no longer needs special protections. For most purposes, that line is drawn today at age eighteen, the modern *age of majority*. However, for some purposes, as we will see, adolescents attain adult legal status either before or after this age. As a general matter, the goals of promoting children's welfare and facilitating their development to healthy adulthood shape legal policies—and determine where the boundary between childhood and adulthood is drawn in different contexts.

In this chapter we explore the law's general approach to the regulation of children and adolescents as a useful backdrop for understanding and evaluating justice policies in the chapters to come. In responding to juvenile crime, lawmakers have tended to adopt the standard binary categories. The traditional regime fit comfortably within the larger framework of paternalistic legal regulation of minors as children, while contemporary justice policy classifies many adolescents as legal adults long before they reach age eighteen. Formally this move is not unique; however, in its purposes and consequences, it represents a dramatic departure from the law's conventional approach and a rejection of values and attitudes toward young people that are deeply embedded in our law and culture.

Images of Childhood and Adolescence in American Law

Modern legal regulation of children has its roots in the Progressive Era social and legal reforms of the late nineteenth and early twentieth centuries.[1] Until that time, the government took little interest in the health and welfare of its youngest citizens, who grew up subject to the virtually absolute authority and responsibility of their parents. It is no great exaggeration to describe parental rights until the late nineteenth century as akin to property rights; children "belonged" to their parents in concrete ways that would be foreign to us today.[2] For example, public schools became common during the nineteenth century, but, until compulsory education laws were enacted in the Progressive Era, parents decided whether their children attended school and for how long.

The Progressives were ambitious social reformers who aimed to educate children and improve their lives; they conceptualized the state as a benign super-parent with the authority and duty to protect children and promote their development into productive adults. To be sure, some historians have questioned the motives of these enthusiastic reformers, arguing that their ultimate goal was to inculcate American values by diluting the influence of immigrant parents over their children.[3] Whatever their "real" goals, the far-reaching legal and institutional reforms of this period redefined the relationship between the government and children (and their parents) in ways that most observers would agree served children's interests. Public education was an important mission of these reformers; important initiatives included the enactment of compulsory school attendance laws and restrictions on child labor.[4] These laws operated in tandem to keep children out of sweatshops and factories where many were employed and to ensure that they would stay in school, regardless of the desires of their parents, who may have wanted children to work so that their families could benefit from their meager earnings. Reformers of the Progressive Era also created the child welfare system and established the juvenile court, a court with the mission of promoting the welfare of delinquent youths as well as that of children whose parents failed to provide adequate care.[5]

A deep paternalism and solicitude toward young persons drove the Progressive agenda and shaped its rhetoric. At the turn of the twentieth century, psychologists began to study adolescence as a developmental stage and to recognize that during this period, individuals were emerging from childhood but were not fully formed adults.[6] This new scientific knowledge influenced the agenda of the Progressives, who focused not on the differences between adolescents and younger children but on their differences from adults. In an era in which mid-adolescents often were obliged to assume adult roles and responsibilities, the reformers ambitiously sought to expand the boundary of childhood and to promote the idea that older youths as well as younger children should enjoy the protection of the state. To achieve their reform goals, the Progressives worked to reshape the public image of adolescents, depicting vulnerable youths working in sweatshops, suffering at the hands of neglectful and ignorant parents, and gullibly falling prey to the influence of evil adults.[7] In short, the paternalistic rhetoric of the Progressives did not distinguish adolescents from younger children in describing the vulnerability, dependency, and innocence of youth.

The general regulatory approach to children that we have today is firmly grounded in the foundation laid by the Progressives a century ago. Although the idealistic rhetoric of the early reformers has moderated considerably, legal minors, both children and adolescents, are still viewed as "children," a unique class of citizens who require special government protections. Over the years, lawmakers have constructed a complex picture of the attributes of childhood that are important to their special legal status. Children are assumed to be dependent on others for survival in the early years and, as they get older, for the care and resources that will enable them to mature into productive adulthood. This dependency means that others must provide for children's basic needs, such as food, shelter, and health care, and supervise their socialization and education if they are to become productive members of society. Children also are assumed to be unable to make sound decisions. Due to their immature cognitive development, they cannot reason or process information sufficiently to make rational choices. Children's decision-making also can reflect immature judgment, which may lead them to make choices that are harmful to their interests or those of others. These deficits justify restricting children's autonomy, mostly for their own good. Finally, children are assumed to be malleable and, thus, vulnerable to harm from those around them—ill-meaning adults as well as their peers. This trait, coupled with dependency, justifies special state protection of children from those who might harm them.

This account of childhood has led quite naturally to the conclusions that children need paternalistic care and oversight and that the core political values held by adult citizens (personal autonomy, responsibility, and political liberty) simply do not apply to them. At the heart of legal regulation of children today is the Progressive premise that the government has both the authority and the duty to care for this class of dependent persons. Some of that authority and responsibility is delegated to parents, of course, who have the primary job of raising their children. But the Progressive distrust of parents as competent caretakers continues; parental authority is subject to state supervision and oversight. Today, the belief that society, through the government, has an important stake in the healthy development of children into productive adulthood and a commitment to their welfare is pervasively embedded in legal policy.

Assumptions about children's incompetence, dependence, and vulnerability are expressed in several ways in modern legal regulation. First, children's legal rights and privileges are far more restricted than are those of adults. Because they are presumed to lack the capacities for reasoning, understanding, and mature judgment (as well as the life experience that presumably would contribute to better decision-making), children cannot vote, make most medical decisions, enlist for military service, drink alcohol, or drive motor vehicles. Their First Amendment right of free speech is more restricted than is that of adults, in part because it is assumed that children may be vulnerable to harmful effects of some forms of speech. Thus, for example, the Supreme Court upheld a New York statute restricting minors' access to soft pornography (*Playboy* magazine, for example) that would be protected speech for adults.[8] Juvenile curfew laws in many cities prohibit youths from being out on the street late at night, limiting the freedom of minors to move about in society through restrictions that clearly would be unconstitutional for adults.[9] Lawmakers sometimes justify restrictions of children's rights on social welfare grounds, arguing, for example, that voting restrictions are justified because society is better off if uninformed youths cannot choose our political leaders. But the legal rights of minors also are limited to protect their welfare. Thus, for example, curfew laws promote public safety, but they are also justified on the grounds that they protect children from getting in trouble through the exercise of their immature judgment and from the harmful influences of others who roam the streets at night.

Second, children are not held to adult legal standards of accountability for their choices and behavior because of their cognitive and psychosocial immaturity and vulnerability to undue influence. For example, under the infancy doctrine in contract law, minors are free to disaffirm most contracts; thus overreaching adults who might be inclined to enter contracts with minors have no legal recourse should the youth default on her side of the bargain. Most cases applying this doctrine involve youths who contract with adults to buy used cars or trucks or electronic equipment, purchases that courts assume children might be tempted to make without considering the obligations that they are undertaking. As one court put it, a minor is assumed to be "immature in both mind and experience and . . . therefore, he should be protected from his own bad judgments, as well as from adults who would take advantage of him."[10] In the same category was the traditional legal response to criminal conduct by juveniles. The founders of the Juvenile Court advocated against imposing criminal responsibility on juveniles for their offenses because they were presumed to lack the capacities for reasoning, judgment, and moral understanding on which attributions of blameworthiness must rest. In protecting minors from the costs of their ill-considered choices, lawmakers have recognized that imposing full responsibility would undermine children's welfare—and sometimes harm their future prospects.

The third category of policies directed at children includes legal protections and entitlements that respond to children's dependency and invest in their development into healthy, productive adulthood. The law requires parents and the government to provide children with care, financial support, and education—services that children are unable to provide for themselves and are needed for survival and healthy development. The child support duty of divorced parents and the public welfare support through such programs as Temporary Assistance to Needy Families (TANF), Head Start, and Medicaid provide a safety net that ensures that children's basic needs are met.[11] In all states, children are entitled to a public school education, so that they can develop the capacities needed for productive adult lives. Moreover, because children are vulnerable and unable to protect themselves, the state enforces parents' duty to provide adequate care through elaborate civil and criminal child abuse regulation.[12] Through child abuse reporting statutes and other means, the government monitors parental care and provides substitute parents through foster care when biological or adoptive parents fail egregiously to fulfill their responsibilities.[13]

Taken together, this complex regulatory scheme confirms that lawmakers view children as a very special class of citizens, a group whose unique traits and circumstances warrant different legal rules and policies from those that apply to adults. In general, these policies of restricted rights and privileges, special protections, and limited responsibilities are grounded in a consistent account of what it means to be a child, an account of human capacities in the early years of life that conforms quite well to the one offered by the developmental sciences. Embedded in legal regulation is an overriding commitment to promoting children's welfare and facilitating their development into productive adulthood, coupled with the assumption that this goal also promotes society's interest.

Where does adolescence fit in this policy picture? With rare exceptions, as we have noted, this transitional stage is invisible under the law since adolescents usually are incorporated into the binary legal categories of childhood and adulthood. The Progressives, in advocating paternalistic policies, grouped adolescents with younger children, in part for strategic purposes. To a large extent, this framework continues to define legal regulation. For most purposes—voting, enlistment in the military, domicile (legal residence), consent to most medical treatments, contracting, executing a lease or will, and entitlement to parental support—adolescents are legal children until they reach they reach their eighteenth birthday and attain adult status. On particular issues, teens attain adult status before or after this age. For example, minors can leave school at age sixteen in most states and are no longer subject to child labor restrictions; curfew restrictions under some ordinances apply only to youths under age seventeen. In contrast, young persons cannot purchase or drink alcohol until age twenty-one, and in some states, college students are entitled to financial support from noncustodial parents until they graduate—well after they attain adult status for most purposes. However, the law seldom recognizes adolescence as an intermediate category, distinct from childhood and adulthood.

When extending adult legal rights or responsibilities to minors is the subject of policy debate, adolescents are usually described either as children or as mature adults, depending on the desired classification. Abortion jurisprudence provides good illustrations of the elusiveness of adolescence in legal rhetoric. In *Bellotti v. Baird*, Supreme Court Justice Lewis Powell pointed to the vulnerability of children and their lack of experience, perspective, and judgment in justifying restrictions on adolescent abortion rights that would be unconstitutional if applied to adult women.[14] In contrast, advocates or judges who favor conferring adult abortion rights on pregnant teenagers present quite a different picture of adolescents. Justice Marshall, for example, challenged a Utah parental notification restriction as a state-created "obstacle to the exercise of the minor woman's free choice."[15] As we will see in Chapter 4, the rhetoric of juvenile justice policy over the course of the twentieth century also provides many examples of this same tension, with child advocates describing young offenders as children and supporters of tough laws describing them in the same terms applied to adult criminals.

The upshot is that lawmakers tend to ignore the developmental realities of adolescence and to depict teenagers either as immature children (and thus dependant, vulnerable, and incompetent) or as mature adults (and thus self-sufficient, responsible, and competent), depending on the policy (or political) agenda at hand. This does not mean that such binary classification is bad policy as a general matter, or that it usually harms the interests of adolescents. To the contrary, as we will explain shortly, this approach has worked quite well in most legal contexts. This may explain why juvenile justice policy adopted binary classification, where it has not been successful.

Before we turn to the question of how the boundary between childhood and adolescence is drawn, a final comment is warranted on the general approach to regulating children under American law. The state's authority to regulate children has two sources and is driven by two large purposes. First, the state's *parens patriae* authority is invoked when the government acts on the basis of society's moral obligation to care for its weak and dependent members; here, the focus is on the interest and welfare of individual children affected by the regulation. The role of the state as *parens patriae* goes back hundreds of years in English history to a time when the king was the protector of his people, but it became institutionalized by the Progressives as the basis of the state's relationship to children.[16]

A second source of government power to regulate minors is its *police power* authority to promote social welfare, both by ensuring that children receive adequate care and by investing in their human capital so that they will become productive adults and engaged citizens.[17] In this instance, the interest served is that of society, which ultimately benefits if children grow up to be healthy, educated adults. The societal purposes of regulation may not be emphasized; the paternalistic rhetoric that characterizes policy discussions often suggests that the sole justification for a particular policy is that it benefits the affected children. But this may present an incomplete picture; society's interest is usually a part of the calculus. Most of the time, as it turns out, legal regulations that protect children and promote their interests are compatible with social welfare. A public school education benefits the individual children whose life prospects are enhanced by the skills they attain, and it benefits society by creating self-sufficient citizens who are able to participate in democratic governance. Occasionally, however, tensions may appear to exist between the interests of individual children and those of society. As we will see, this is the case with juvenile justice policy.

The Boundary of Legal Childhood

Children cross the line into legal adulthood at different ages in different regulatory contexts. The default is the age-of-majority, the age at which presumptive adult status is attained—currently age eighteen in the United States. However, a complex system of age grading defines childhood as a category with multiple boundaries. Ten-year-olds charged with murder can be tried as adults in many states, and high-school students who are not yet age eighteen can obtain contraceptives and drive motor vehicles. Twenty-year-olds, however, cannot purchase alcohol, run for Congress, or, in many states, consent to sterilization.[18] What explains the variation?

To some extent, age grading suggests that lawmakers pay some attention to developmental maturity, conferring adult status when young citizens can meet maturity requirements for particular tasks. No one would challenge that the maturity required to fulfill the role of president (currently limited to citizens age thirty-five or older) is greater than that needed to drive a car or vote. However, even a cursory perusal of the regulatory scheme reveals that, although crude assumptions about maturity are usually important, other considerations are in play as well. In fact, examination of specific policies suggests that the lines between childhood and adulthood are drawn on the basis of diverse policy concerns. Concern about youth welfare, parental authority, societal benefit, and pure administrative convenience are all part of the mix. On most issues, these interests converge and point to a particular age as appropriate.

The Age of Majority

The age of majority is the natural place to begin a discussion of legal age boundaries. According to conventional wisdom, the common law age of legal adulthood was set at twenty-one years in the Middle Ages because it was judged to be the age at which a young man was capable of carrying a full suit of armor.[19] Currently set at age eighteen, this milestone signals the end of parents' legal authority and responsibility (including their financial support obligation), as well as the withdrawal of the state from its protective parental role (which means that, in many states, youths in foster care are discharged at age eighteen and assumed to be self-sufficient).[20] On reaching the age of majority, individuals acquire most legal capacities to function as citizens and adult members of society. These include the capacities to purchase real estate, lease an apartment, execute a binding contract, make a will, consent to medical treatment, register for the draft, serve on a jury, and, most important perhaps, to vote in state and federal elections.

The designation of a categorical legal age of majority reflects a crude judgment about maturity and competence. Society assumes that individuals of the specified age are mature enough to function in society as adults, to care for themselves, and to make self-interested decisions. Evidence from developmental psychology supports the position that by age eighteen, and certainly by age twenty-one, most individuals attain adult competence in many domains of intellectual and physical development. Although, as we have suggested, the process of psychological maturation continues into the adult years (and many eighteen-year-olds do not seem capable of functioning as autonomous adults), differences in decision-making capacity between late-adolescents and adults are more subtle than those that distinguish younger teenagers from adults.

It is true that the use of a crude, bright-line rule ignores individual variation in maturity among teenagers and fails to recognize that the range of adult rights and responsibilities that are conferred on the eighteenth birthday have varying maturity demands. Some children's rights advocates have argued for more tailored rules that would recognize that many younger adolescents have adult capacities in some domains.[21] In our view, however, the law's method generally works quite well despite some inevitable distortion of the developmental abilities of young people. For most purposes, no great harm results from postponing adult status until the designated age. Most adolescents have no pressing need to execute contracts or leases, for example, and, if they do, parental involvement is probably desirable in most cases. Moreover, entitlement to parental support and other protections of childhood are beneficial to young people. A rule that employs a bright-line age of majority is a clear signal of adult status; everyone who deals with the young person can quickly determine whether he has legal capacity based on his age. A more tailored approach under which adult status was decided on a case-by-case basis or fixed according to particular task demands could generate confusion and error—and would certainly be more costly to administer.

The upshot is that a categorical approach that treats individuals below a designated age as legal minors works well—as long as that age corresponds roughly to some threshold of developmental readiness to assume the privileges and obligations of adulthood. Indeed, because a bright-line age of majority offers so many advantages, variations that depart from the presumptive age should attract our attention.

The Twenty-Sixth Amendment and the Politics of Boundary-Setting

How is the presumptive boundary of childhood determined? The age of majority is based on a rough assessment of the maturity level needed to function as an adult in society—but, within a range, developmental considerations do not dictate any particular age. Indeed, a generation ago, the boundary was shifted downward. In 1972, at the height of the Vietnam War, the Twenty-Sixth Amendment to the U.S. Constitution was ratified, lowering the minimum age for voting in federal and state elections from twenty-one to eighteen. The right to vote has long been the defining marker of legal adulthood to which the age of majority is linked. Not surprisingly, therefore, Congress and state legislatures responded to the passage of the Twenty-Sixth Amendment by systematically revising statutes to change the age of majority from age twenty-one to eighteen for most purposes.[22] What this meant, in practical terms, was that a group of young people—those who were eighteen, nineteen, or twenty years old—who previously had been classified as children under the law suddenly became legal adults.

What forces drove the movement in the late 1960s to amend the Constitution to extend voting rights to eighteen-year-old citizens? Clearly, the political context was important. Many legal minors between the ages of eighteen and twenty-one were drafted into military service and sent to fight in Vietnam. At the same time, college students across the country demonstrated their interest in political participation through their involvement in anti-war and civil rights activities. The Senate Report that recommended the enactment of the Amendment pointed to these political facts. It also emphasized that the young adults who would be enfranchised under the Amendment were "mentally and emotionally capable of full participation in our democratic form of government."[23]

Several points about this constitutional initiative and the legislative response are interesting. First, supporters of the Amendment recognized that developmental maturity is a precondition to adult legal status, defending the Amendment on the ground that the common law age-of-majority distorted developmental reality in defining young adults as legal children. At the same time, the passage of the Twenty-Sixth Amendment suggests the extent to which the legally defined age of childhood and adulthood are political and social constructs; clearly contextual factors were at least as important to the legal change as were developmental facts.

Another important argument of advocates for passage of the Amendment was that fairness required some parity between rights and responsibilities. Many supporters believed that eighteen-year-olds should have the right to vote because they were subject to military service, the most onerous duty of citizenship. The image of young persons dying for their country in Vietnam who were not "mature" enough to vote in elections was compelling: It goes a long way toward explaining the timing of this constitutional reform.

A final observation about this constitutional reform is noteworthy. Proponents of the reform viewed the Amendment as beneficial to young citizens insofar as it recognized that they were full participants in the political process, and also good for the country in that it was hoped that the reform would transform college student protestors from troublemakers who were outside the system into citizens with a stake in the democratic process. As we have suggested, this convergence of youth welfare and social welfare is usually present when lawmakers shift the boundary of childhood.

Departures from the Presumptive Boundary of Childhood

We turn now to the somewhat unusual instances in which lawmakers confer adult status on young people before or after the legal age of majority. Perhaps the most familiar examples of legal policies shifting the threshold of adulthood are those regulating driving privileges and restrictions on the right to purchase and drink alcohol—policies that can be readily understood as promoting both youth welfare and social welfare. In most states, under restrictions imposed by federal highway funding legislation, teenagers can get a driver's license at age sixteen or seventeen, while young adults cannot purchase alcohol until age twenty-one.[24] The gap between the minimum legal age for driving and drinking offers young persons independence and mobility, which they (and often their parents) greatly value, while protecting young drivers (and the rest of us) from harms that they might cause due to immature, youthful judgment if they had ready access to alcohol.[25]

A closer look at regulations that restrict or expand the boundary of legal childhood provides insight into the forces that drive these departures from the age of majority. Laws that extend noncustodial parents' support obligation through college provide a good example of a regulation that expands legal childhood beyond age eighteen. On the other hand, minors' consent statutes treat teenagers who are legal children for most purposes as adults for the purpose of consenting to particular medical treatments. These laws are justified as measures that not only benefit the affected young people but also promote society's interest in the health and education of its members. Or put another way, in these contexts, maintaining the conventional age of majority as the threshold to adult status would cause harm to young people and create social costs—both of which can be reduced by shifting the age boundary.

THE CASE OF CHILD SUPPORT.   First, consider parental support. When state legislatures lowered the age of majority after the passage of the Twenty-Sixth Amendment, some courts interpreted this legal reform to mean that noncustodial parents' obligation to provide financial support to their minor children must end at age eighteen (because, by definition, the recipients were no longer minors).[26] The debate about these legal changes highlighted the reality that in a world in which college attendance has become the norm as preparation for a successful life, many eighteen-year-olds continue to be financially dependent on their parents although they may be ready to function as adults in other ways. If child support is only available to "minors," then children of divorced parents may expect no financial assistance from their noncustodial parent for college expenses; indeed, often support would end during the youth's senior year in high school, depending on the date of her eighteenth birthday. Under these conditions, many children would obtain a college education only with great difficulty, if at all. In intact families, parents who have the financial means usually contribute to their children's college education, recognizing that, in this domain, the extension of childhood status is important to their children's welfare. Noncustodial parents may be less likely to identify their own interests with that of children with whom they no longer reside, and less likely to provide college support voluntarily. Some courts and legislatures have authorized the continuation of child support to finance college expenses, effectively imposing a legal obligation on these parents to act toward their children as they presumably would have acted had the family stayed together.[27] A college education is a straightforward investment in the human capital of students, who benefit in enhanced career opportunities and general life prospects. At the same time, well-educated adults are more likely to be economically productive and engaged citizens than are those who lack education. Thus, in this domain, extending the boundary of childhood is beneficial both to the affected young persons and to society.

THE COMPLEX CASE OF MEDICAL TREATMENT DECISIONS. Whereas college support obligations extend childhood into early adulthood, other laws truncate legal childhood, conferring adult status on adolescents. For example, teenagers can attain adult status before the age of eighteen for the purpose of making certain medical decisions. These instances are exceptions to the general rule under which medical treatment of children under age eighteen requires parental consent.[28] In part, the general requirement is justified on the ground that medical treatment requires informed consent, which minors categorically are presumed incompetent to provide.[29] Although developmental evidence indicates that older adolescents are cognitively mature enough to make medical decisions, giving parents legal authority in this realm usually makes good sense. For most treatments, parents can be counted on to have their children's interests at heart in making treatment decisions. Giving authority to parents reduces uncertainty and cost for medical service providers, who would otherwise need to assess the competence of their young patients, and it encourages parents to take responsibility for their children's health care—and, of course, to pay their medical bills!

There are, however, several exceptions to the requirement of parental consent. Historically the most well established exception is the mature minor doctrine, under which physicians are authorized to treat older minors in situations in which obtaining parental consent may be difficult.[30] By insulating health care providers from legal liability, this doctrine encourages them to provide treatment to minors who are likely competent when the preferred decision-maker is unavailable. Minors' decisions about abortion are also subject to an exception from the straightforward requirement that parental consent is required for medical treatment. On this issue, courts, including the Supreme Court, and legislatures have struggled to accommodate the constitutionally protected reproductive rights of pregnant teenagers and the rights (also of constitutional stature) of parents.[31] The courts have recognized that parents may have a conflict of interest with their child in this situation, because their responses may be influenced by their religious or moral views about their daughter's sexual activity and pregnancy—or about abortion. Partly in response to this concern, and partly in deference to the reproductive choices of pregnant teens, the Supreme Court has endorsed the use of a judicial bypass hearing to determine whether the minor is mature enough to make her own decision, or, if she is not mature enough, whether allowing abortion without involving her parents is in her best interest.[32] The legal framework that has emerged represents a complex (some would say Byzantine) effort to find an acceptable resolution to a highly contested dispute about the boundary of childhood—a dispute that, in our view, is more about abortion itself than about the regulation of children and adolescents.

The minors' consent statute, another exception to the requirement of parental consent, raises issues that are more straightforward than abortion and more directly related to our interest. Legislatures in many states have enacted these statutes under which minors are deemed adults for the purpose of consenting to particular kinds of treatment—typically treatment for birth control, sexually transmitted diseases, substance abuse, mental health problems and pregnancy.[33] Minors' consent statutes usually do not prescribe a minimum age at which a minor is deemed an adult, but, given the nature of the specified medical conditions, only adolescents are likely to seek the designated treatments. The treatments all involve situations in which the traditional assumption that parents can be counted on to respond to their child's medical needs with her interest at heart simply might not hold. For example, some parents may become outraged to learn of their child's sexual activity or drug use and respond in a way that is harmful rather than helpful to her welfare. Moreover, even if many parents *would* act in the interest of their children's health, adolescents may be deterred from seeking treatment in these situations because they fear their parents' reaction or because they do not want to disclose private information.[34] Removing the obstacle of parental consent encourages teenagers to seek treatment that may be critically important to their health.

Minors' consent statutes represent a legislative judgment that adolescents should be deemed legal adults for the narrow purpose of consenting to the designated treatments, because harm may result from the standard classification of teenagers as children. In one sense, these statutes are curious in that they accord *adult* status to adolescents mostly out of a paternalistic concern for youthful vulnerability. The argument favoring this exception is not that teenagers are especially mature in making these particular treatment decisions, but that their welfare may be promoted if they can obtain these treatments on their own without involving their parents. In addition, society has an obvious public health interest in promoting treatment for sexually transmitted diseases, substance abuse, and mental illness and in reducing the incidence of teenage pregnancy. Thus, both youth welfare and social welfare support a downward shift in the boundary of childhood in this context.

Binary Categories and Age Grading: A Largely Successful Approach

The law's general approach to regulating young citizens results in a relatively well-functioning regime. Children are subject to an array of legal policies that restrict their freedom, protect them from harm, and invest in their human capital—all aimed, at least in part, at promoting their welfare and enhancing their prospects for productive lives. The bright-line age of majority marks the transition from legal childhood to adulthood efficiently for most purposes, even though at best it is a crude approximation of developmental maturity. When that line is shifted through legal regulation that lowers or raises the threshold of legal adulthood, some important policy objective is being served—usually a mix of paternalistic goals and public welfare. This point is underscored in each of the examples described—driving privileges, alcohol restrictions, minors' consent laws and child support rules—and even the passage of the Twenty-Sixth Amendment. On the whole, legal policy facilitates the transition to adulthood by calibrated steps that reflect society's concern for the individual well-being of its most vulnerable citizens and, moreover, its collective interest in their healthy development into productive adults. In part, the general legal account of childhood is a success story because the two objectives that dictate where the legal boundaries are drawn—youth welfare and social welfare—are usually aligned in pointing to a particular classification as child or adult.

The legal framework seems to work well in another way. Although some observers have criticized the law's simplistic classification system, there is little evidence that adolescents are harmed by a regime of binary categories in most contexts or would benefit from the creation of an intermediate legal category tailored to their developmental needs and capacities. Occasionally, to be sure, exceptions to binary classification are introduced, and lawmakers recognize that adolescents are different from younger children as well as from adults. For example, when parents in a divorce proceeding battle for custody of their children, the preferences of teenagers are given more weight than those of younger children.[35] Also, some states have enacted laws under which young drivers are accorded the adult privilege of operating motor vehicles, subject to special restrictions (no night driving, no driving with peers) as they gain experience and learn responsibility.[36] In this setting, youth welfare and social welfare are served by the creation of an intermediate category. However, in most areas, the costs of a tailored approach would likely outweigh the benefits, and binary categories function efficiently to serve the interests of youths and of the larger society.

In the next chapter we turn to juvenile justice policy, which, over the past century, has largely adopted the conventional approach of classifying adolescents involved in crime as either children or adults. As we will see, the binary classification approach has not been successful in this legal context, because of unique features that distinguish the regulation of criminal activity from other matters affecting minors that come within the state's concern.

CHAPTER 4

Why Crime Is Different

Why is it not just and proper to treat these juvenile offenders, as
we deal with the neglected children, as a wise and merciful father
handles his own child whose errors are not discovered by the authorities?

   —Judge Julian Mack, "The Juvenile Court"

Juvenile offenders are "criminals who happen to be young, not
children who happen to be criminal."

   —Albert Regnery, "Getting away with Murder: Why the Juvenile
   Justice System Needs an Overhaul"

Ben Lindsey, founder and judge of the Denver Juvenile Court in the
early twentieth century, believed that there were "no bad kids"—
only bad conditions that led to bad conduct. The purpose of his
court, as he explained in a magazine article in 1927, was to save the
youths who came before him, not to punish them.[1] He reported that
the young miscreants with whom he dealt were surprised by his
kindly manner and concern for their welfare. They were often fearful when they were brought to court (often by a police officer who
did not share Judge Lindsey's benign views), but they soon learned
to trust the judge. Realizing that he would not hurt them, most
spoke forthrightly about their misdeeds, sometimes persuading their
delinquent friends to come forward as well. In his biography, Judge

Lindsey recounted the story of Tony, the leader of a Catholic juvenile gang who shot a boy from a rival Protestant gang in the leg. Judge Lindsey won Tony's trust and, with the judge's guidance, Tony persuaded his fellow gang members to stop desecrating the Protestant church, an important step in the process of improving relations between the two gangs.[2]

Judge Lindsey embodied the ideals of the Progressive Era and, like the other social reformers who worked to establish the juvenile court at the turn of the twentieth century, he viewed youths involved in crime first and foremost as children. Judge Lindsey often emphasized that his court was *not* a criminal court and that the lawbreakers who came before him were not criminals.[3] His only goal was to provide aid and rehabilitation, which he accomplished with the help of probation officers, social workers, physicians, and psychiatrists. Judge Lindsey's court exemplified the rehabilitative model that dominated juvenile justice policy for much of the twentieth century, a model under which delinquents were dealt with as children whose welfare was of primary concern when the state intervened in response to their criminal conduct. Thus, traditional justice policy, to a large extent, simply adopted the conventional values and goals that generally have characterized the legal regulation of minors and applied them to the regulation of criminal behavior.

Unfortunately, as we will see, in this context, the standard paternalistic approach was not successful. It failed not only by sacrificing public safety, which received insufficient attention, but also, more surprisingly, by not promoting the welfare of youths in the system. The account of the rise and fall of the traditional juvenile court points to the conclusion that, in the regulation of crime, classifying youths as children is a fundamental error—despite the good intentions of Judge Lindsey and others who advocated enthusiastically for the rehabilitative model.

Under recent juvenile justice reforms, the legal boundary has shifted, and youths (or many of them) have been transformed into adults. This change is not so unusual in itself. As we saw in Chapter 3, lawmakers occasionally assign adult status to adolescents for particular purposes. What *is* unusual is that two goals that pervade legal regulation—the promotion of youth welfare and investment in their human capital—have been suspended under modern justice policy, with its single-minded focus on punishment and short-term public safety.

Why has American law, in a relatively short period, transformed young offenders from children into adults? We explore this question and conclude that the obvious answer—that a scourge of violent youth crime beginning in the late 1980s exposed the inadequacies of a justice system that seemed to ignore accountability and public safety—provides only a partial explanation. A puzzle remains: the punitive reform movement continued full force well beyond the mid-1990s, during an extended period of *declining* juvenile crime. Close inspection of one state, California, that adopted tough reform measures in 2000, sheds light on the politics of youth crime reform. This account does not answer the key question of whether the practice of reclassifying young offenders as adult offenders is fair or good for society—we leave that for later chapters. But it does suggest that the process by which these dramatic reforms have been undertaken is seriously flawed—a "moral panic" in which politicians, the public, and the media respond on the basis of exaggerated perceptions of threat.

The Traditional Court: Young Offenders as Children

The establishment of the juvenile court was at the heart of the Progressive agenda—a court with a mission of promoting the welfare of youths involved in crime, as well as that of children whose parents failed to provide proper care. At the dawn of the juvenile court movement, only young children were insulated from criminal responsibility; most youths were tried and punished as adults.[4] Pursuing the general goal of expanding the boundary of childhood to include adolescents, the reformers envisioned a court and correctional system in which older as well as younger youths would receive rehabilitation rather than punishment. Miriam Van Waters, a prominent advocate in the 1920s, described the underlying theory of the juvenile court, a theory that, in the minds of the reformers, applied with as much force to delinquent youths as to neglected children:

> [T]he child of proper age to be under [the] jurisdiction of the juvenile court is encircled by the arm of the state, which, as a sheltering, wise parent, assumes guardianship and has power to shield the child from the rigors of the common law and from neglect or depravity of adults.[5]

The challenge of reshaping the image of young criminals and of persuading politicians and the public that delinquent youths were deserving of sympathy and paternalistic attention was a daunting one—a harder sell, we might imagine, than urging the merits of child labor laws. Advocates like Van Waters and Lindsey deployed romantic rhetoric to promote their vision of the protective role of the state toward youths involved in crime. Youths were described as innocents without adequate parental supervision who (understandably) fell prey to the evil influences of the street. On Judge Lindsey's view, immoral or overworked and inattentive parents caused their children to become delinquent by failing to provide moral guidance and support.[6] Central to the philosophy of the new juvenile court, and to the political strategy of Progressive reformers, was the claim that delinquent youths and children who were neglected by their parents were not very different from each other, and the state's role in both delinquency and neglect cases was to intervene "in the spirit of a wise parent toward an erring child."[7] The political objective was to promote an image of young offenders as children whose parents had failed them rather than as criminals who threatened the community.

In service of this objective, advocates underscored the similarity between young delinquents and neglected children. In 1909, Judge Julian Mack of the Boston juvenile court issued a famous challenge in an article published in the *Harvard Law Review* (quoted at the beginning of the chapter): "Why is it not just and proper to treat these juvenile offenders, as we deal with the neglected children, as a wise and merciful father handles his own child whose errors are not discovered by the authorities?"[8] Other juvenile court evangelists, such as Judge Lindsey, emphasized the innocence and vulnerability of young lawbreakers. As his description of Tony's redemption suggests, Judge Lindsey offered heartwarming stories of wayward youths who came before his court and were set on the right path through his guidance and that of other court personnel. These romanticized accounts of young delinquents included tales of older youths as well as young boys and girls, and of serious crimes as well as minor misdeeds. All of the young miscreants were described sympathetically as innocent children gone astray who needed only the firm (but kind) treatment that the court could provide.[9]

In general, the Progressives viewed the legal regulation of delinquent youths to be simply an integrated component of a broader framework of legal policies directed at children. Because the states' primary purpose was to rehabilitate delinquents, the reformers were emphatic that concepts such as criminal responsibility and punishment had no place in the lexicon of juvenile justice. As Judge Lindsey declared, "Our criminal laws are as inapplicable to children as they would be to idiots."[10]

Judge Lindsey's account rings with sincerity, but in general, one should not exaggerate the benign paternalism of the Progressives or accept at face value their characterization of delinquent youths as wayward children whose welfare was the sole aim of government intervention. To some extent, as we have suggested, the paternalistic rhetoric was invoked strategically in service of the political agenda of selling the new court and justice system to a skeptical public. Also, some scholars have argued that the Progressives' intentions were mixed: along with their concern for child welfare, many reformers had a social control agenda, aiming to Americanize immigrant youths and generally to minimize the influence of poor, urban (often foreign) parents.[11] Finally, it is important to remember that the Progressives had faith in the effectiveness of rehabilitation. As the Progressive reforms unfolded, the profession of social work was established and psychiatry and psychology were emerging as scientific disciplines, creating optimism about the potential to understand human behavior and to treat pathological conditions.[12] The reformers believed that this knowledge and expertise would provide the basis for treatment that would lead delinquents to abandon their criminal ways; thus, youth crime would decline under the new regime. This belief made it unnecessary to sort out the interest of society from that of young law violators—in focusing on the latter, the Progressives assumed that society would also benefit.

For much of the twentieth century, the rehabilitative model shaped the operation of the juvenile court. The goal of treatment influenced the process by which delinquency was adjudicated, the type of dispositions imposed (at least in theory), and the roles of the various participants. Judge Lindsey was typical of the architects of the new court in insisting that the proceeding was *not* a criminal trial—or an adversarial hearing at all. Thus, the accused youth had no need of a defense attorney or of procedural protections that adult defendants enjoyed. The qualifications of the juvenile court judges reflected the informality of the proceedings, as many lacked legal training.[13] The announced purpose of the delinquency hearing was to discern the sources of the child's criminal conduct and to determine the correctional disposition that would set him on the right path; in pursuit of this goal, the judge, probation officers, and social workers were all to work together on the youth's behalf. Many larger juvenile courts in cities such as Boston and Chicago had affiliated court clinics, so that mental health professionals could also participate in the diagnosis and prescription of treatment for delinquent youths.[14]

Delinquency dispositions were open-ended and indeterminate—which made sense, given their purported rehabilitative purpose. Like treatment for an illness, rehabilitation, in theory at least, should end when the youth was "cured." Under the rehabilitative model, the duration bore no necessary relation to the seriousness of the offense; thus, the principle of penal proportionality, like criminal responsibility, had no place in delinquency proceedings. Although in practice, the seriousness of the crime usually played a role in the type and duration of dispositions, juvenile court judges were relatively free to order dispositions based on their judgment about the youth's "needs," without regard to the seriousness of his criminal conduct.[15]

The Collapse of the Rehabilitative Model

At one level, the Progressive Era reformers were successful in their efforts. By 1925 every state had established a separate juvenile justice system that assumed jurisdiction over the adjudication and disposition of most youths charged with crimes.[16] This represented a remarkable institutional transformation, when one considers that, before the juvenile court was established, adolescents age fourteen and older were all prosecuted and punished as adults. For more than seventy years after it was established at the turn of the twentieth century, the juvenile court operated with its informal procedures and proclaimed purpose of offering rehabilitation to children involved in crime.

The Liberal Challenge: *Gault* and Its Aftermath

Despite its initial success, the traditional juvenile court and the rehabilitative model on which it was built were largely a failure. By the 1960s the rehabilitative model began to crumble, and since that time, the juvenile court has been challenged from both the left and the right. The first successful assault did not originate with conservative politicians who spearheaded the punitive reforms of the 1990s. Rather, it was launched by youth advocates who claimed that adolescents charged with crimes were getting a bad deal in a system that was ostensibly designed to serve their needs.[17] These critics argued that the juvenile system failed to provide treatment, but that it maintained the myth that rehabilitation was its purpose as the justification for denying juveniles the procedural rights given to adult criminal defendants. In the words of Justice Fortas, juveniles had "the worst of both worlds."[18] They had no right to legal counsel, and delinquency proceedings lacked the careful fact-finding of an adversarial criminal trial; yet, dispositions, at least for some youths, meant confinement in correctional facilities that, from the incarcerated youth's perspective, may have been hard to distinguish from prison.

This push for reform ultimately led the Supreme Court, in the landmark 1967 opinion of *In re Gault,* to extend due process protections to youths in delinquency proceedings.[19] Gerald Gault, age fifteen, was arrested for making telephone calls to his next-door neighbor that the Supreme Court later described as being "of the irritatingly offensive, adolescent, sex variety."[20] Gerald was brought before a juvenile court judge, but he was not given notice of the charges against him and did not have an attorney to represent him. The neighbor never appeared in court as a witness; instead, the arresting officer testified, describing what the neighbor reported. The juvenile court judge committed Gerald to the Arizona State Industrial School for up to six years, for a crime that would have carried at most a sentence of two months in jail and a $50 fine if committed by an adult. These facts made *Gault* the perfect case to challenge the informality of the process by which guilt was determined in juvenile delinquency proceedings, an approach that was justified by the ostensibly rehabilitative purpose of the proceedings.

Gerald Gault appealed and ultimately prevailed in the United States Supreme Court. The Court, in an opinion by Justice Fortas, flatly rejected the state's justification for the informality of delinquency proceedings. Justice Fortas described the proceeding as a "kangaroo court," a description that might have led the Progressive architects of the court to shudder in their graves.[21] He noted that delinquents generally got little rehabilitation, and what they received was ineffective, as evidenced by the high recidivism rate in juvenile crime. The court concluded that youths facing adjudication in delinquency proceedings, like adult criminal defendants, faced a loss of liberty and thus were entitled to certain due process protections as mandated by the Fourteenth Amendment of the U.S. Constitution. Juveniles, like adults, had a right to notice of the charges, a right to confront witnesses against them, a privilege against self-incrimination, and, most importantly, a right to counsel.

Gault is a watershed case in the history of the juvenile court. The procedural changes ordered by the Court transformed delinquency proceedings into more formal adversarial hearings—not unlike criminal trials. Moreover, although *Gault* gave lip service to rehabilitation as a laudable if unrealized goal of juvenile dispositions, the rehabilitative model was in disrepute. By the 1970s it had pretty much collapsed, creating a conceptual vacuum. Whatever its flaws, the rehabilitative model had provided a coherent rationale for proceedings and dispositions that were very different from those of the criminal justice system. In the 1970s and 1980s most youths charged with crimes continued to be processed in the juvenile system, but its purposes and underlying "theory" were far less clear than in the days of the traditional court. What was needed was a new rationale for maintaining a separate justice system for juveniles.

During this period, a few law reform groups and legislatures responded to the decline of the rehabilitative model by undertaking to modernize the juvenile court.[22] For a brief time it seemed that a new model of juvenile justice might emerge—one that incorporated procedural regularity, accountability, and public protection, while retaining a commitment to leniency and to serving the needs of young offenders. Before these tentative initiatives could be firmly established, however, violent juvenile crime rates started to climb in the late 1980s, triggering a new wave of reforms under which young criminals increasingly were either classified as adults or punished severely within the juvenile system. Thus, the youth advocates who sought to change the traditional juvenile system ultimately lost control of the reform process. The justice system that has emerged is a far cry from the ideal that the reformers in the 1970s envisioned.

What Went Wrong with the Rehabilitative Model?

What went wrong? Why did the rehabilitative model of juvenile justice flounder when, in general, the Progressive reformers' ambitious framework defining the relationship between children and the state has endured in its basic outline and purposes and is embedded firmly in contemporary policy? In our view, the corrosive flaw at the heart of the rehabilitative model of juvenile justice can be found in its insistence that the purpose of the court's intervention in delinquency cases was indistinguishable from its goal in child welfare cases—solely to promote the welfare of the youngster before the court. This was always a shaky premise that ignored the fact that young offenders, unlike children whose parents provide inadequate care, intentionally cause social harm through their criminal conduct. When the harm is serious, and especially if the offender is an older youth, the claim that the state's overriding purpose is to promote that child's welfare rings hollow. In short the model failed to recognize and accommodate explicitly the inherent tension between the state's professed purpose of acting in the interest of young offenders and its interest in retribution and protecting society against those who engage in criminal conduct.

This tension might have been manageable had the "treatment" offered by the court and correctional system been more effective in "curing" young criminals. Public acceptance of the rehabilitative model likely was always predicated on its promise that young criminals would be rehabilitated—and thus that society would be protected. But recidivism rates were high among young offenders; according to a survey cited in *Gault,* 66 percent of youths referred to the juvenile court were recidivists.[23] When it became apparent that juvenile court interventions were failing to cure many young delinquents of their inclinations toward criminal activity, the conflicting interests that had been papered over with idealistic rhetoric became apparent.

Paradoxically, the rehabilitative model's insistent focus on promoting child welfare ultimately harmed the court's young clientele, as the advocates who brought *Gault* to the Supreme Court argued. Criminal defendants are given procedural rights because it is well understood that their interests are adverse to those of the state. In contrast, supporters of the juvenile court invoked its rehabilitative purpose to justify nonadversarial procedures, indeterminate sentences, and the lack of many procedural protections enjoyed by criminal defendants. Ultimately, it became clear that these hallmark features of the juvenile system harmed the interests of young offenders. Youngsters were defenseless against court officials who had virtually unbridled freedom to impose punishment on them, while claiming to act only in their interest. Gerry Gault's case provides a good example. Based on hearsay evidence and the judge's suspicion that the youth had been involved in an earlier incident (for which he had not been adjudicated), Gerry was sent off to a correctional facility for a minor crime.[24] To be sure, Gerald's punishment was unusually severe; in the 1960s probation was the typical sanction. But the point is not that most youths in juvenile court received harsher punishment than adults—they did not. The point is that the exaggerated emphasis on rehabilitation freed judges from constraints that limit judicial power in criminal proceedings and gave them exceedingly broad discretion. Most observers concur that the traditional model of juvenile justice not only failed to serve the larger societal interest in public protection, but also failed to fulfill its proclaimed purpose of promoting the welfare of the young charges of the system. The Supreme Court's mandate in *In re Gault* that courts adopt many of the procedures of criminal trials marked the beginning of the end of the traditional court.

Several lessons can be drawn from this brief historical account of the rise and fall of the traditional juvenile court. First, it should be noted that in the context of juvenile justice policy, the Progressive reformers followed faithfully the norms of legal regulation of children that guided their larger program of social reform. The focus on child welfare as the overriding purpose, the depiction and classification of adolescents as children, and the commitment to investment in their human capital as a legitimate and important function of government were important Progressive themes in the establishment of a separate justice system for children. They were also important in child welfare reforms and in the promotion of laws regulating school attendance and child labor. In the expressed aspirations of the early reformers can be heard the themes that continue to resonate powerfully in other legal contexts and to guide much of contemporary regulation of children—and, as we have suggested, quite successfully for the most part.

Ultimately, however, the conventional framework was *not* successfully adapted to juvenile justice policy, because this context is different in an important way from other areas of legal regulation.

As explained in Chapter 3, in most settings in which the government regulates children, the state's interest in promoting social welfare and its interest in promoting the welfare of children are transparently compatible with one another. Regulation of youth crime presents a more complex challenge. The public interests are several; they include the goals of reducing youth crime, protecting the public from young criminals, holding youths accountable, and producing noncriminal adults. Accommodating these interests to one another is difficult enough, but beyond this, society's interests sometimes may be hard to reconcile with the interests of the delinquent youths in retaining their liberty and preserving their prospects for productive adult lives. Critics of the traditional system, alarmed at youth violence, were quick to conclude that the paternalistic policies of the traditional court threatened public safety—and that the goal of promoting child welfare should be abandoned. In reality, as we have suggested and will argue more fully in later chapters, the public interest is more complex than promoting short-term public safety and can best be accommodated by including youth welfare in the calculus. Nonetheless, the rehabilitative model was inherently unstable because, at least in its rhetoric, it ignored the reality that society's interest in public safety was in tension with the interests of delinquent youths.[25]

Getting Tough on Kids

In the latter decades of the twentieth century, as violent youth crime rates rose, attacks on the juvenile court intensified. Critics railed at the depiction of young criminals as children, a characterization that was discordant with the media images of teenage street gangs spreading fear in city neighborhoods. By the 1990s young offenders became "super-predators" in the popular imagination, teenage criminals without moral inhibitions who were eager to kill and maim those who came in their paths.[26] Many observers (including much of the public, according to polls) thought the juvenile court's lenient treatment of young offenders contributed to the crime problem. On this view, the failure to hold young offenders accountable for their crimes encouraged them to engage in criminal activity.[27] A chorus of protest against the juvenile system intensified and continued for a decade or more. Without question, the lack of confidence in the juvenile court played an important role in fueling the punitive reforms of the past generation.

A reality check is in order at this point. By the 1980s when attacks on the leniency of juvenile court were gaining momentum and public confidence was waning, the court, in practice if not in rhetoric, had evolved beyond the rehabilitative model. After *Gault*, delinquency procedures became more formalized and, by the 1980s, accountability and public protection were emphasized increasingly in the disposition of young offenders.[28] Indeed, studies during this period suggested that severity of offense was the best predictor of the kind and duration of delinquency dispositions.[29] Moreover, even as enthusiasm for punitive reforms gained momentum in the 1990s, some states sought to accommodate the public's concern about safety and the interest of young offenders in rehabilitation, through laws based on a model of "Balanced and Restorative Justice."[30] These developments were local in their impact, however, and failed to halt the sweeping movement toward punitive laws.

A part of the problem may have been that some juvenile court's supporters continued to promote its benign mission and the romantic image of young offenders as beleaguered children.[31] The paternalistic rhetoric may have led many people to conclude that youths who committed crimes got nothing but slaps on the wrist. In any event, the country had internalized the Progressive maxim that in the juvenile court, young offenders were to be dealt with as children—and rejected the court on this basis.

Conservative reformers of the past few decades offer quite a different account of young law violators, describing them as criminals who should be held fully accountable for their offenses. Responding initially to higher rates of violent juvenile crime (particularly homicide), lawmakers in the 1980s and 1990s dramatically altered the regulation of juvenile crime, such that youths (at least those who commit serious crimes) increasingly have been subject to criminal court jurisdiction.[32] The primary goals of modern youth crime policy are protection of the public and punishment of the offender. In service of these goals, lawmakers have shifted the conventional boundary of childhood downward. The depiction of young offenders as hardened adult criminals by these modern reformers was a smart strategy, given their agenda. Punitive justice policies are more palatable if adolescent offenders are described as "super-predators" rather than as children, because childhood is associated with legal protection and leniency. Because the image of "child" and that of "criminal" are discordant, the intersection of childhood and criminality poses a difficult dilemma. The Progressive Era reformers resolved the dilemma by redefining the offense as something less than a crime. For modern proponents of punitive policies, the solution has been to redefine the offender as something other than a child. In an era in which the public perceives violent juvenile crime as a serious threat, the latter response is more appealing than the former.

The Range of Punitive Reforms

The modern reformers have pursued their goal of reclassifying young offenders as adults through several legislative strategies. First, the age of judicial transfer has been lowered in many states and revised in other ways to facilitate criminal prosecutions of juveniles.[33] In a transfer hearing, a juvenile court judge makes an individualized determination of whether the young defendant should be deemed a legal adult for purposes of criminal prosecution or adjudicated as a child in juvenile court.[34] Under the traditional system, judicial transfer functioned as a mechanism to exclude from the court's jurisdiction the occasional older youth charged with a serious violent crime (usually murder) who the judge determined was not amenable to treatment as a juvenile. In a sense, transfer functioned as a safety valve, providing recognition of the importance of public safety and acknowledgment that not every youth would benefit from rehabilitation. The inquiry focused on whether the youth was likely to respond to interventions offered by the juvenile system; thus, past treatment efforts, malleability, and general immaturity were important considerations.[35] Today, in a majority of states, ten-year-olds charged with murder can be transferred to criminal court, and a large minority of states have no statutory minimum age of transfer.[36] Almost all statutes that do set a minimum age designate age fourteen or younger.[37] Moreover, in contrast to the traditional approach, the transfer decision under many statutes need not incorporate consideration of maturity or lack of amenability to treatment; it is based, instead, on the seriousness of the offense and the criminal record. Judicial discretion also is constrained under some statutes by strong presumptions favoring transfer, reflecting legislative suspicion that juvenile court judges are too lenient. For example, California law includes a presumption favoring transfer of any minor who has committed two or more felonies while over the age of fourteen.[38]

This distrust of juvenile court judges is reflected in other recent legislative reforms that give criminal courts automatic jurisdiction over certain youths (without a judicial hearing). Under legislative waiver (or automatic transfer) statutes, young offenders charged with designated serious crimes are defined categorically as adults, and are excluded from juvenile court jurisdiction based on their age and the offense with which they are charged.[39] For example, under the California statute, a fourteen-year-old charged with murder, rape, or other sexual offenses against a child is automatically charged as an adult.[40] Legislative waiver statutes implicitly shift discretion from judges, who are deemed soft on crime, to prosecutors (who are not assumed to have this deficiency), as prosecutors are given authority to decide whether to charge the youth with a waivable offense or with some less serious crime over which the juvenile court has jurisdiction. In a few states, including New York, the general age of adult jurisdiction is age sixteen or seventeen—thus, all juveniles of the jurisdictional age are deemed adults for purposes of criminal prosecution—when they are legal minors for most other purposes.[41] Under "direct file" statutes, another modern reform, prosecutorial discretion is explicit; the district attorney can file charges against juveniles in either criminal or juvenile court for a range of serious offenses.[42] In some states, all felonies are subject to the prosecutor's direct-file discretion.[43]

The category of juveniles who can be subject to adult prosecution has been expanded in another way. Until recently, only the most violent crimes (usually murder, rape, armed robbery, aggravated assault, and kidnapping) could be the basis of criminal court prosecution of juveniles in most jurisdictions, but many statutes today include a long laundry list of transferable offenses or crimes subject to automatic waiver.[44] The California statute lists thirty transferable offenses.[45] Other statutes allow youths charged with *any* felony (or even any crime) to be tried and punished as adults.[46] The upshot is that although advocates for punitive reform repeatedly emphasize the threat to society of violent young criminals, criminal prosecution of adolescents is by no means limited to youths charged with serious violent crimes. In most states today, youths charged with drug and property offenses can be tried and punished as adults, and crime statistics indicate that a large percentage of youths sentenced to adult prisons have committed nonviolent offenses.[47]

Juvenile court sanctions also have become harsher, with longer sentences and far greater use of incarceration, and for longer periods, than was true a few decades ago.[48] Further, some states have extended juvenile court jurisdiction into adulthood or adopted blended sentencing statutes, under which juveniles who are convicted of designated felonies are subject to stiff sentences in juvenile court that are completed by transfer to prison when the offenders become adults. In some states, such as Texas, youths can be given forty-year sentences in juvenile court, for a broad range of felonies.[49] Most blended sentencing statutes include either a procedure when the offender reaches age eighteen for determining if the adult portion of the sentence will be carried out, or a provision suspending that portion for youths who have not violated institutional regulations or probation conditions. However, in many states, juveniles can be sentenced to life without parole.[50]

The upshot is that the mantra of punitive reformers, "adult time for adult crime," is a reality for many juveniles. Through a variety of legal initiatives, the boundary of childhood has shifted dramatically, and many offenders who are not yet in high school are tried and sentenced as adults.

The Punitive Reforms and the General Regulation of Minors

On first inspection it may appear that the recent reforms are consistent with regulations in other contexts under which the conventional legal boundary of childhood is adjusted on the basis of social welfare considerations. In the case of justice policies, the shift was triggered by skyrocketing violent juvenile crime—particularly homicide. The statistics made clear that the traditional regime, under which delinquents were dealt with as children, was ineffective in protecting the public. Described thus, the reforms bear some similarity to the minors' consent statutes, described in Chapter 3, that also aim to reduce the social cost of harmful behaviors by minors (for example, substance abuse and unprotected sex) by lowering the age of adult legal status. On this account, policy-makers have simply made the standard move of classifying adolescents as adults when it became clear that the costs to society of maintaining the conventional boundary of childhood were unacceptably high—and could be lowered through reclassification. Given that the system of binary categories has long defined the legal regulation of minors, the option of lowering the age threshold of adult legal status may have appeared to be the obvious policy choice.

Although there is a kernel of truth to this account, it does not acknowledge what a radical departure these policies represent from the law's conventional approach to juveniles. In other contexts, deviations from the presumptive age (in either direction) usually aim to advance societal interests, but they almost always are justified *also* on the paternalistic ground that they advance the welfare of young persons affected by the reclassification. Thus, minors' consent statutes (which also lower the age of adult status) have the dual purpose of reducing the public health costs associated with pregnancy, substance abuse, STDs, and so forth, but also of benefiting affected youths by encouraging them to get necessary treatment. In contrast, the rhetoric of the punitive reformers is striking: young offenders are portrayed by advocates for tough sanctions as predators, the enemies of society. This description signals strongly that promoting youth welfare is *not* the point of the reforms. Disinterest (or hostility) is also manifested in what appears to be a lack of concern about the impact of dispositions on the future lives of young offenders. Contemporary justice policy pays scant attention to investment in the human capital of young offenders, an overriding focus of regulation in other contexts and one that is presumed to benefit society as well as the youths themselves.

Contemporary justice policies are unique in another way. As we have suggested, the reforms have lowered the threshold of adult legal status so dramatically in this context that youths who are legal children for every other purpose are adults for the purpose of criminal punishment. Thus, fourteen-year-old Lionel Tate, described in Chapter 1, could be sentenced to life in prison under Florida law (for a crime committed at age twelve) at an age when he could not drop out of school, vote, consent to medical treatment, sign a lease, go out without his mother's permission, or (in many states) buy cigarettes or a *Playboy* magazine. Under a regime of age grading, youths may achieve adult legal status for different purposes at different times, but a disjunction of this magnitude is jarring.[51] As we saw in Chapter 3, Americans tend to favor some rough parity between rights and responsibilities; supporters of the Twenty-Sixth Amendment argued that young people who fought for their country in Vietnam deserved to have the right to vote. Substantial disparities, particularly when youths are subject to adult burdens but lack adult privileges, seem inequitable. The uneasy response to Lionel Tate's conviction may reflect discomfort about imposing the burden of adult punishment on one who so clearly was a child for all other purposes.

In essence, contemporary justice reforms are an anomaly within the general scheme of legal regulation of children. They are also inconsistent with policy values and objectives that are uncontroversial in other settings—and with widely shared social attitudes toward children and youth. We would expect such a departure to be justified by an important public interest and undertaken on the basis of careful deliberation. But close scrutiny of the law reform process is not reassuring in this regard. The standard justification for the recent reforms, that they were necessary to protect the public from the threat of young offenders, turns out not to be fully satisfactory. It is puzzling—especially in light of the generally benign attitudes toward youth—that these reforms proceeded apace for almost a decade after juvenile crime rates began to steadily decline. More troubling, perhaps, as we explain in the next section, is the political process through which legislatures have undertaken important changes in youth crime regulation, a process that belies the claim that these reforms are simply a rational response to a social threat.

Proposition 21 and the Politics of Reform

A complex political dynamic is often at work when juvenile crime policies capture public attention. It is a process that has many features of a moral panic, a phenomenon introduced in Chapter 1. To better understand this process, we focus on juvenile justice reform in one state, California, where 62 percent of adult voters in the year 2000 endorsed Proposition 21, a far-reaching initiative that dramatically altered the penal law regulating juveniles.[52] Some features of the California process are unusual; for example, few states have undertaken legislative reforms of crime policy through the mechanism of a voter referendum. However, the forces that led to the passage of Proposition 21 and the politics of the initiative were very similar to those that have driven legislatures across the country to substantially revise laws regulating youth crime in recent years. In California and elsewhere, the reforms were largely the product of a powerful interaction among three forces: intense media interest in violent juvenile crime, public outrage and fear in response to the perceived threat, and politicians seeking to capitalize on these fears to win elections or retain popularity. These are the ingredients of a moral panic.

The Story of Proposition 21

Proposition 21 was initiated by Republican Governor Pete Wilson after he failed twice to persuade the Democrat-dominated California Assembly to pass his administration's Gang Violence and Juvenile Crime Prevention Act of 1998. Governor Wilson took his bill to the California District Attorney's Association, and that organization agreed to sponsor it as an initiative on the 2000 ballot.

Many observers thought that Wilson's ambition to become the Republican presidential candidate in 2000 drove his enthusiasm for the get-tough reform measure. When Democrat Gray Davis was elected governor in 1998, he broke ranks with many in his party to vigorously advocate for the Proposition.[53]

How did Proposition 21 aim to change California law? The initiative proposed sweeping statutory revisions that expanded criminal court jurisdiction over juveniles and limited the authority of the juvenile court in several ways. First, automatic transfer for youths charged with murder or rape was lowered from age sixteen to fourteen under the initiative. Second, and of potentially broader impact, was a provision that expanded the list of about thirty "serious and violent felonies" and lowered from age sixteen to fourteen the application of a presumption at transfer hearings that youths charged with these crimes were not fit to be tried as juveniles. The list of "serious and violent felonies" already included various forms of assault, small-time drug sales, and car-jacking; Proposition 21 added robbery without a dangerous weapon and voluntary manslaughter. The initiative also expanded the authority of prosecutors to directly file charges in criminal court against fourteen year old youths facing a second felony charge, a charge for an offense involving a firearm, or a charge for an offense committed "in association with any criminal street gang." The last provision expanded the potential for criminal liability for youths on the fringes of gang activity, who were not actually gang members. Finally, the initiative removed the protection of confidentiality of juvenile records.[54]

Although many of the proposed legal changes did not specifically target gang members, Proposition 21 was promoted intensely to the public as a measure to combat criminal street gangs. This was a smart strategy; gang violence had been viewed as a major threat in California for a number of years, and public fears about juvenile crime were focused largely on gang activity. The rise of youth violence in the late 1980s was mostly attributed to street gangs and, in the early 1990s, gangs were largely responsible for a juvenile homicide rate in California that was at an all time high.[55] Most gangs were made up of non-white youths—African Americans, Latinos, and Asians—and they were organized along ethnic lines. Two African American street gangs in Los Angeles, the Crips and the Bloods, gained national notoriety in the 1980s, giving the city the dubious distinction of being known as "the gang capital of the nation."[56] Media fascination with gangs was intense throughout the 1990s; commentators routinely described the crisis facing California's cities and depicted gangs as alien forces who controlled the streets, making them unsafe for ordinary citizens. As one analyst put it, gangs represented "a breakdown of the moral order, an evil in which racial or ethnic ties have been perverted for criminal gain."[57]

Proposition 21 was not California's first legislative effort to punish and deter gang activity. Under the 1988 Street Terrorism Enforcement and Prevention Act, "active participation in a criminal gang" became a substantive offense separate from the underlying criminal activity.[58] Thus, a gang member charged with holding up a convenience store could also be convicted of a separate felony of "active participation," with both felonies counting under California's three-strikes law.[59] The 1988 statute included other sentence enhancement measures for gang-related activity as well. Given that California already had in place tough anti-gang regulation, why did politicians initiate Proposition 21 in the late 1990s, and why did the public respond with overwhelming support?

The California experience differed somewhat from that in many states in which punitive reforms were triggered by horrendous high-profile killings by juveniles that fueled public anger at laws that were perceived to be too lenient. In Arkansas, for example, pressure to lower the age of adult prosecution for murder was a direct response to the Jonesboro middle school killings, and to public outrage that William Mitchell and Andrew Golden, the thirteen-

and eleven-year-old perpetrators, could not be tried as adults.[60] In California, in contrast, no particular high-profile crime can be identified that aroused public outrage and served as a catalyst for Proposition 21. Instead, the situation in California involved a chronic, low-level public fear of gang violence—a fear periodically stirred up by reports of gang shootings in which innocent bystanders were killed. Advocates for Proposition 21 exploited this chronic anxiety over the threat of gangs.

Surprisingly, there was also no upsurge in gang activity in the period before the referendum. Indeed, the most puzzling aspect of the public enthusiasm for Proposition 21 is that by 2000, juvenile crime rates, including homicide rates, had fallen substantially for several years from their high point in the early 1990s and were lower than they had been in a generation.[61] Although there is disagreement about whether juvenile crime had declined 40 percent, as some analysts claimed, it is not disputed that there was significantly less violent crime by juveniles in 2000 than in the early and mid-1990s. Opponents of Proposition 21 emphasized these statistics, but the information fell on deaf ears. Public opinion polls indicated that California citizens in 2000 erroneously believed that youth crime was *on the rise,* and 60 percent also believed that juveniles were responsible for *most* violent crime.[62] The reality was that in 1998 only about 14 percent of arrests for violent crimes involved juveniles—a decrease from 30 percent in 1978. Thus, a majority of California voters had distorted perceptions of the threat of youth crime.

This perception was heightened by dire projections about a coming wave of teenage super-predators in the first decade of the new century, as the children born in the baby boom of the early 1990s reached adolescence. As we have indicated, some criminologists in the mid-1990s predicted "a bloodbath of teenage violence that is lurking in the future,"[63] to be perpetrated by youths who were growing up in "moral poverty." Proponents of Proposition 21 justified the need for tougher laws by emphasizing these predictions, while discounting the fact that teenage crime rates had dipped since the early 1990s. Moreover, some argued that the drop in youth crime was attributable to California's (already) tough laws, suggesting that crime would decline even more if the initiative were enacted.[64]

The argument that youth crime declined in response to punitive policies enacted in the late 1980s in California may have some merit; it is certainly plausible that some juveniles facing harsher punishment were deterred from crime. However, as we discuss in Chapter 7, the evidence of a connection between increased penalties and crime reduction is conflicting and inconclusive in states where the impact of policy changes has been studied; most research does not find that tough sanctions have a deterrent effect. Moreover, even if the reforms had a deterrent (or more likely, incapacitative) effect, this does not explain why public perceptions about the threat of youth crime were so distorted in the late 1990s—such that even tougher laws were deemed necessary.

To some extent there is a straightforward explanation for these distortions: public perceptions about the threat of crime naturally lag behind actual changes in the crime rate.[65] But beyond this, the public's fears were reinforced and amplified by media coverage of violent crime and gang activity in the 1990s. Studies indicate that media coverage of sensational crimes generally intensified during this period and that violence by street gangs was prominently featured in newspaper and television news stories, both in California and nationally. In the 1990s local news programs reported crime stories more frequently than any other topic. Network news programs also highlighted crime reports; stories reporting homicides increased by 473 percent on national news programs between 1990 and 1998, although the homicide rate declined by 33 percent during that period.[66] In California, much of this coverage focused on juvenile crime. A California study found that two-thirds of television stories featuring violent crime involved juveniles, even though, in reality, many more violent crimes were committed by adults than by adolescents. Further, more than half of the television stories focusing on children and youth involved violence—although only about 2 percent of California youths were crime victims or perpetrators.[67]

Race was also an element in the media coverage of crime. Studies indicated that members of minority groups were over-represented in the news as perpetrators of violent crime and under-represented as victims. The research also showed that many people assumed that young criminals were members of minority groups, even when race and ethnicity were not mentioned in news stories. In 2000 an overview analysis of 110 studies of media coverage of crime concluded that depiction of crime in the news exaggerated the violent crime rate, as well as the proportion of crime committed by juveniles and by persons of color.[68]

This background of sensational media coverage enabled politicians advocating the passage of Proposition 21 to draw on public fear of gang violence and to falsely portray juvenile crime as a growing threat. In this vein, Michael Bradbury, the Ventura County district attorney, wrote an op-ed column in the *L.A. Times* favoring Proposition 21 a few weeks before the referendum; "Gang violence is the most alarming of all crime trends . . . [C]urrent outmoded laws fail to address this growing problem."[69] Supporters of the initiative spent $1 million a week campaigning for passage; through an intense campaign of television commercials, appearances on talk shows, and newspaper op-ed columns, they drove home the message that juvenile gangs were a serious and growing threat and that tough laws were needed.

A Field Poll conducted shortly before the referendum suggests that the appeal to the fear of gang violence was important to the ultimate vote on Proposition 21. In the poll, two groups of likely voters were presented with descriptions of the pending initiative.

Those presented with a "short form" that stated that "Proposition 21 provides changes for juvenile felonies—increasing penalties, changing trial procedures, and required reporting" voted against the measure by 47 percent to 30 percent. Those who were presented with a "long form" that stated that Proposition 21 increases punishment for "gang-related felonies such as home-invasion robbery, carjacking, witness intimidations, and drive-by shootings, and creates a crime of gang-recruitment activities" favored passage by 55 percent.[70]

Opposition to Proposition 21 was also intense but ultimately ineffective. Most juvenile court judges, the California Association of Sheriffs, probation officers, child advocacy groups, religious leaders, and even the District Attorney of Los Angeles lined up against Proposition 21, portraying the initiative as a power grab by prosecutors that would sweep lots of teenagers who were not violent gang members into the adult system.[71] Opponents emphasized the declining juvenile crime rate as evidence that the get-tough measures mandated by Proposition 21 were unnecessary. They also predicted that the initiative would cost California taxpayers many millions of dollars.

The nonpartisan state Legislative Analyst's Office (LAO) undertook an estimate of the projected costs of Proposition 21 and concurred with opponents that the initiative would have a substantial adverse impact on the state budget. Many costs of implementing the reform were uncertain, depending on how much enthusiasm district attorneys around the state had for prosecuting accused youths as adults. The LAO report concluded, however, that several provisions were likely to carry costs exceeding $1 billion.[72] Although opponents of Proposition 21 pointed to these costs, a majority of California voters either paid no attention or thought that they were justified as a means of enhancing public safety, given what was perceived to be the substantial threat of juvenile crime.

Law Reform as Moral Panic

The adoption of Proposition 21 by California voters represented a major reform of that state's juvenile justice policy; it substantially expanded the category of youths who could be prosecuted as adults by lowering the minimum age and increasing the range of eligible crimes, and it shifted authority to make this decision from courts to prosecutors. It is sobering to consider that the process by which these potentially transformative changes were undertaken had many features of a moral panic, a particular form of irrational collective action that has long interested sociologists. Incidents as disparate as the seventeenth-century Salem witch trials, contemporary episodes of public alarm over illegal drug use (in the 1960s and 1980s), and child sexual abuse (in the 1980s and 1990s) all bear the hallmarks of moral panics.

In a moral panic, the public, the media, and politicians reinforce each other in an escalating pattern of intense and disproportionate concern in response to a perceived social threat posed by a particular group of individuals. These individuals are viewed with fear and hostility; they are deviants who aim to harm society, and they threaten the moral order—"the enemy," as Erich Goode and Nachman Ben-Yehuda described them in their authoritative analysis.[73] Although sometimes the targeted enemy poses an imaginary threat (the Salem "witches," for example), more often a moral panic focuses on individuals who do real harm, such as sexual abusers or members of criminal street gangs. The targeting of juvenile gangs in the campaign to pass Proposition 21 was effective because gangs had been perceived as a threat for many years, and supporters of the initiative could arouse fear through a media campaign with little difficulty. The Field Poll described earlier indicates that the public's fear of gangs translated into punitive attitudes and support of Proposition 21. But what distinguishes a moral panic from an effort to deal with a pressing social problem is the gap between the perception of the problem and the reality. In a moral panic, the seriousness of the threat and the number of offenders are greatly exaggerated. This clearly describes the adoption of Proposition 21 by a public who inaccurately thought that youths were responsible for most crime and that juvenile crime was on the rise.

The California experience with Proposition 21 was typical of the way that a dynamic interplay among the media, politicians, and the public can create and sustain a moral panic as it runs its course. The role of the media is key: alarming stories fuel public concern about a danger by focusing intensively on the deviant perpetrators, reporting their activities and presenting specific incidents as representative of a broader peril. Cognitive psychologists have clarified the mechanisms by which media attention directed at a particular threat (such as crime) affects perceptions about the magnitude of the danger. Research indicates that individuals use heuristics, or rules of thumb, to process the vast amounts of information they receive and assess the importance of particular data. The research also suggests that although these shortcuts are very useful they can lead to systematic biases. One such cognitive bias is the *availability heuristic,* which leads us to overvalue vivid experiential data that can be readily brought to mind and to discount the importance of abstract information. Thus, a person who experiences a car crash caused by a car's brake malfunction may give this accident more weight than abstract statistics about the excellent safety record of that particular make of car. Availability leads individuals to judge the risk of an event that is readily imaginable to be more probable than one that is remote or not easily contemplated.[74] It is easy to see how television news stories depicting horrendous murders may assume disproportionate salience to a viewer evaluating the threat of crime—as compared with abstract crime statistics. The campaign for passage of Proposition 21 drew on these fears, vividly reminding the public of the random violent acts perpetrated by juvenile gangs and reinforcing the notion that the threat was imminent and serious.

Distorted perceptions of risk in a moral panic are not simply a matter of *individual* misperception. The fear becomes contagious and magnified as claims about the threat are repeated and reinforced in public discourse—a dynamic that involves not just the media, but also community members and politicians. As individuals talk to their neighbors, friends, and associates about a publicized threat (a news story about a gang shooting, for example), the perception that the danger is real is likely to be reinforced and to gain momentum, as each re-telling makes the threat more salient. Scholars have called this dynamic process an *availability cascade.*[75] The media, recognizing the public's concern, continues to focus on the peril, amplifying the threat. Public consensus (or consensus by a sizable group of the public) emerges that "something must be done" to stop the deviants—and that the problem in part is due to insufficient government efforts to control the wrongdoing. California voters, one may conclude, were primed to fear gangs by years of exposure to stories of drive-by shootings and terror in the streets. The intense media campaign to pass Proposition 21 drew on these fears and made them once again highly salient.

Politicians are key players in moral panics, generating and reinforcing public fears and promising solutions. This response is almost inevitable when horrendous highly publicized incidents occur. In Arkansas, for example, Governor Huckabee and other politicians began to call for legislative reform immediately after the Jonesboro shootings.[76] Politicians and the media work hand-in-hand to generate and reinforce the fears of citizens. Politicians use media appearances and interviews as an important means of rallying public concern, reminding the audience of the threat and promising responsive initiatives. Responses inevitably involve the social control apparatus of society—tougher law enforcement efforts and legislative reform. Ironically, because the threat that government officials promise to address is exaggerated, their efforts to fix the problem are often later perceived by the public as having been successful.

California politicians played a key role in initiating and promoting Proposition 21, as our earlier account suggested. Governors Wilson and Davis led the campaign for passage and both governors amplified and fueled the voters' fears of gang violence before and during the campaign. Governor Davis stated plainly his view that his popularity with California voters was linked to his advocacy of Proposition 21—despite the opposition of his party.[77] In other states, as well, governors have been instrumental in promoting legislative reform of juvenile justice policy. For example, Governor George Allen led the charge to reform Virginia law in the mid-1990s.[78] As chief executives of state government, governors occupy bully pulpits from which they can hold forth on the urgency of the threat of juvenile crime and to advocate for tougher legislation. What is somewhat unusual about California is that politicians seem to have *precipitated* the moral panic that led to the dramatic legislative reforms of Proposition 21 by intentionally arousing latent public fears.

Moral panics are volatile phenomena. Intense public fears dissipate eventually, or even quickly, and public attention is diverted to other issues. (The volatile nature of moral panics is suggested by the public rejection of Governor Davis in a recall election conducted in the aftermath of California's energy crisis, just a few years after he successfully led the campaign to pass Proposition 21.) Panics that focus on crime seem to recur periodically in response to new incidents or to political rhetoric focusing on the problem. These episodes have a lasting impact, however, when they become institutionalized through legislative reform. Long after public fears of juvenile crime have subsided, punitive policies that are enacted into law determine how the justice system deals with youths charged with crimes. At that point, politicians may be reluctant to endorse corrective policy changes, however sensible, that might be portrayed by their opponents as "soft" on crime.

Race and Public Attitudes toward Youth Crime

Understanding the recent reforms of juvenile justice policy as moral panics to some extent solves the puzzle of why the public and its elected officials have so readily abandoned deeply embedded paternalistic attitudes toward youth to collectively view young offenders as "the enemy"—despite a declining crime rate. One more issue must be addressed, however, and that is the extent to which racial and ethnic biases influence public and political attitudes toward juvenile crime—and contribute to support for punitive policies. In California and elsewhere, minority youths are disproportionately represented among the population of young offenders and are more likely to be sanctioned as adults than are white youths.[79]

Explanations for this disparity are complex. Most analysts conclude that it reflects both higher offending rates among minority youths and differential responses to minority and white youths by justice system officials—including police, prosecutors, judges, and corrections officers.[80] Whatever the source of the phenomenon, it probably contributes to an assumption by many people that young criminals are mostly minority youths. This view likely has been reinforced by the media's disproportionate focus on minority offenders, and particularly on gangs, that for the most part are organized on the basis of racial and ethnic identity. As we have seen, the campaign to pass Proposition 21 explicitly played on Californians' fear of gang violence in a state in which virtually every citizen was familiar with the Crips and Bloods, probably the most notorious African American gangs.

The extent to which racial prejudice has influenced attitudes about juvenile crime is uncertain. Most people today are not likely to acknowledge racial bias and may be guarded when researchers raise the topic to probe racial attitudes; thus, the most accurate studies likely are those that study racial attitudes indirectly. Some studies find no evidence of racial bias (often contrary to the hypothesis of the researchers).[81] However, others support the view that many people hold conscious and unconscious racial stereotypes that are linked to punitive attitudes toward young offenders. Much of this research focuses on participants in the justice system and is aimed at the overall goal of comprehending the extent to which racial attitudes or stereotypes contribute to disproportionate confinement of minority youths. One such study found that probation officers tended to attribute the criminal behavior of African American youths to internal factors (such as character and attitude), while the conduct of white youths was more likely to be attributed to external factors (such as the social environment). Minority youths were also deemed to deserve more punishment.[82]

Another study found that police and probation officers who were unconsciously primed to assume that a young offender in a crime vignette was African American were harsher in their judgments of culpability and deserved punishment than those who received neutral primes, an effect that was observed regardless of the race of the officer.[83] This research suggests that African American youths are perceived (both by whites and individuals of other races) as being more dangerous and more deserving of punishment than comparable white youths.

It seems at least plausible that racial stereotypes and attitudes have played a role in overriding conventional paternalistic views toward children in shaping opinions about youth crime. Adults, particularly those who are not themselves members of minority groups, may not respond to young offenders with the protective attitudes typically directed toward children if they do not identify delinquent youths with their own children. (If this is so, it is not surprising that most studies suggest that African Americans generally are more likely than whites to favor leniency toward young offenders.)[84] The demonizing of young super-predators as the enemies of society is easier to understand if people assume that most youths involved in criminal activity belong to a disfavored or "alien" group. Thus, conscious or unconscious racial attitudes may facilitate the hostile targeting of young offenders as deviants and evildoers that has characterized the moral panics of the past decade or more.

What Lessons Can We Take from Proposition 21?

The story of the campaign to adopt Proposition 21 offers an unsettling picture of the politics of contemporary juvenile justice law reform. Few would advocate that society undertake important changes in legal policy through such a process. A moral panic, possibly contaminated by racial bias, driven by distorted media depictions of youth crime and (often) by politicians opportunistically pursuing political ends is a dangerous and troubling basis for sweeping institutional reforms. The upshot of the campaign was the adoption by California of laws, now a part of the state code, that significantly expand the category of youths who can be subject to criminal court jurisdiction. Even after the public has turned to other concerns and the moral panic has dissipated (as they always do), its impact will be felt long into the future through its institutionalization in legislation.

How representative is California's experience with Proposition 21 of the juvenile justice reforms enacted since the late 1980s? At one level, California is unusual in that sweeping legal change was accomplished by voter referendum. The dynamic among the public, politicians, and the media that characterizes a moral panic was more explicit, in some sense, than it is with conventional legislative reform; in this case, the voting public was directly involved in the process. Experiences in other states, however, indicate that arousing public furor over juvenile crime and support for punitive legislation is not difficult, particularly in response to high-profile juvenile crimes that become the focus of media attention. Even without this trigger, a media campaign focusing on youth crime can generate public outrage and political pressure to adopt more stringent laws. The pattern of law reform has varied to some extent in different settings, but in states as diverse as New York and Arkansas, there are common components in the process: an outraged and fearful public, politicians eager to exploit this fear, and media that focus on crime to sell newspapers and attract viewers.[85] Too infrequently is the process one of careful deliberation and consideration of the costs and benefits of punishing juvenile offenders more severely. Although a defective process does not necessarily result in deficient policies, the climate of the recent reforms gives little basis for confidence in the development of contemporary youth crime policies.

The picture becomes even more troubling in light of evidence that public opinion about juvenile crime is far more complex than it appears to be during periods of moral panic. As we will explain in the concluding chapter, although politicians insist that the public demands harsh policies, many studies suggest that the public supports the rehabilitation of most young offenders—when attitudes are probed during periods of "repose" and when opinion polls are objectively constructed and precisely worded. Indeed, several recent surveys have found support for more lenient juvenile justice policies, suggesting that as juvenile crime has declined, public enthusiasm for the punitive reforms has cooled considerably.

The upshot is that a primary justification for the enactment of tough youth crime policies turns out to be weaker than proponents claim. To be sure, the public has often responded to high-profile murders or anti-crime campaigns like Proposition 21 with what has appeared to be passionate support for tougher juvenile justice policies. The research evidence suggests, however, that punitive public opinion is likely to dissipate when the crisis passes and a residual paternalism toward young offenders reemerges. If this is so, the public may demand tough policies in the short term, but not support them over time.

This account of the troubling politics of juvenile justice reform and of the volatile nature of public opinion in this area argues for a careful examination of the substance of contemporary policies. The fact that the law reform process has been deeply flawed and that the policies themselves are anomalous as a form of legal regulation of minors does not answer the question of whether the criminalization of juvenile justice is *substantively* deficient as legal policy. In the chapters that follow we deploy the empirical framework of the developmental model to examine the regulation of juvenile crime from two perspectives. First we examine the policy issues within a framework of criminal law principles and doctrines; second we probe the merits of the proponents' assumption that punitive policies toward young offenders promote social welfare.

CHAPTER 5

Immaturity and Mitigation

The case for retribution is not as strong with a minor as with an adult. Retribution is not proportional if the law's most severe penalty is imposed on one whose culpability or blameworthiness is diminished, to a substantial degree, by reason of youth and immaturity.

—Roper v. Simmons, 553 U.S. 541 (2005)

Public attitudes toward adult punishment of juveniles are complex; even youths who commit the most horrendous crimes evoke ambivalent (or conflicting) responses. Consider, for example, Lionel Tate, whose case we discussed in Chapter 1. Lionel was twelve years old when he killed Tiffany Eubanks, his six-year-old neighbor. Although his murder conviction and life sentence were eventually set aside on the ground that his competence to stand trial should have been evaluated,[1] many observers thought that a more important issue in the case was whether a twelve-year-old offender should be held fully responsible for his crime and subject to the same punishment that an adult would receive. The interest in Lionel's case and the uneasy reaction to the sentence imposed by the court reflected an intuition that Lionel, although he did something terrible, was just not as culpable as an adult counterpart and, because of his youth and immaturity, did not deserve to be punished as harshly.

118

Many people had a similar response to seventeen-year-old Lee Malvo, the sniper who, with his forty-two-year-old partner John Mohammed, killed several people in multiple shootings in the Washington, D.C., area in October 2002. Malvo, who acknowledged that he pulled the trigger in several of the killings, was charged with capital murder in Fairfax, Virginia. The Justice Department had dictated that he be tried first in Virginia, rather than Maryland where he was charged with another killing, because, at that time, juveniles could be subject to the death penalty in Virginia but not in Maryland.[2] However, the Virginia jury declined to sentence Malvo to death, despite the fact that he was clearly guilty of a horrendous and seemingly random murder (and, as the jury well knew, was involved in a killing spree that had spread terror in the Washington area). What distinguished Malvo from his partner, John Mohammed, who already had received the death penalty for another murder in Prince William County, Virginia, was Malvo's youth and his relationship with the older man, who was like a father to him.[3] To many people (including the jury, one might speculate), Malvo's acts were reprehensible, but he was not as culpable as his adult partner.

As a general matter, the criminal law recognizes that culpability, or blameworthiness, is an important factor in determining fair punishment; it also recognizes that two defendants who cause the same harm (killing another person, for example) can vary in their blameworthiness and in the punishment they deserve.[4] The jury's decision in Lee Malvo's case and the controversy surrounding Lionel Tate's sentence should remind us that the regulation of juvenile crime is not just a subcategory of the legal regime governing minors, our focus in Chapters 3 and 4. It is also subject to the principles and doctrines that define the criminal law. In this chapter, we examine juvenile justice policy in this framework and explore the question of how lawmakers should think about adolescent immaturity in determining the boundaries of fair criminal punishment for this category of offenders.

Focusing on Culpability

In policy discourse on youth crime, questions about the culpability and criminal responsibility of young offenders have received surprisingly little attention. As the recent wave of punitive law reforms has swept many youths into the criminal justice system, it is somewhat surprising that modern lawmakers and policy analysts have focused little on questions of whether adolescent immaturity affects blameworthiness and appropriate punishment.[5] The single important exception is the juvenile death penalty, an issue that we will address later in the chapter.

We cannot offer a full explanation of why this issue has received so little attention—in contrast, for example, to questions of how mental illness affects blameworthiness and criminal responsibility, which has been the focus of elaborate doctrinal development and theoretical analysis by scholars for more than 150 years. Although mental disorder and immaturity (insanity and infancy) are often classified together as excuses based on endogenous incapacity, immaturity has been ignored in the literature of criminal responsibility.[6] In part, this doctrinal and conceptual void can be traced to the segregation of young offenders for most of the twentieth century in a separate justice system grounded in rehabilitation, in which blame and punishment had no place—at least in theory.[7] The architects of the juvenile court and their successors for many years insisted that the disposition of delinquents was *not* governed by the criminal law, on the ground that young offenders were children who bore no criminal responsibility.

The Problem of Binary Categories

More broadly, the problem can be traced to the binary classification scheme that characterizes the regulation of children and youths, including juveniles involved in crime.[8] The use of binary categories under which adolescents are either children or adults has contributed to simplistic understandings of adolescent criminal responsibility. If delinquent youths indeed were blameless children, as the Progressive Era reformers insisted, then of course they lacked responsibility and should receive no criminal punishment. On the other hand, if young criminals are adults, as they have been characterized recently, of course they are fully liable for their crimes, because it is assumed that adults bear responsibility for their criminal conduct. This crude categorization of young offenders has persisted, even though many modern youth advocates are considerably more sophisticated than the early reformers. It has had a pernicious effect on the public debate about juvenile crime, because it has contributed to an often unspoken assumption that the only alternative to punishing juveniles as adults is no punishment at all.[9] The debate proceeds as though the policy options are limited to a choice between child and adult status—questions about how *adolescent* immaturity should count in criminal punishment are seldom addressed.

To describe the problem somewhat differently, the simplistic application of criminal law concepts to juvenile offenders has effectively limited the universe of doctrinal options to *excuse* and *full responsibility*. In legal parlance, excuse means complete exculpation; a defendant who is excused is not accountable for the harm she caused and should receive no punishment. Not surprisingly, defenses that excuse persons altogether from responsibility for criminal conduct are very narrowly drawn—only severe mental impairment or extraordinarily coercive circumstances qualify.[10] Thus it is also not surprising that policy-makers and the public reject the idea that adolescent offenders should be excused from criminal liability.

The Importance of Mitigation

But the criminal law does not view blameworthiness in such categorical terms. The concept of *mitigation* plays an important role in the law's calculation of blame and punishment, although it gets little attention in the debate about youth crime. Mitigation applies to persons engaging in harmful conduct who are blameworthy enough to meet the minimum threshold of criminal responsibility but deserve less punishment than a typical offender would receive. Through mitigation, the criminal law calculates culpability and punishment along a continuum and is not limited to the options of full responsibility (the presumption for typical adult offenders) or excuse (the disposition of children). As we will see, mitigation is woven into the fabric of criminal law doctrine.

Mitigation is also at the heart of our developmental model. Our analysis of the culpability of young offenders within the broader framework of criminal law doctrine and theory leads us to reject both the traditional model, under which young offenders (effectively) were excused from responsibility, and the contemporary approach that often holds youths fully responsible for their crimes. Instead, we conclude that a justice regime grounded in mitigation corresponds to the developmental reality of adolescence and thus is compatible with the law's commitment to allocating punishment fairly on the basis of blameworthiness.

That seems like a rather abstract benefit, but it is an important one. The history of juvenile justice policy is a cautionary tale about the costs of policy-makers' failure to pay careful attention to the link between adolescent development and criminal responsibility, or to tailor criminal punishment to the blameworthiness of young offenders. As we have seen, the fictional premise of the rehabilitative model—that young offenders were blameless children—contributed to the discrediting and downfall of the traditional juvenile court. Substantial costs are also evident in contemporary policy. Modern reforms of youth crime policy have been enacted through a highly politicized process, driven by distorted public perceptions of the threat of juvenile crime and possibly by illegitimate racial attitudes. On our view, these deficiencies are symptomatic of policy-making unfettered by the conventional limits on punishment embedded in the criminal law. The principle of proportionality, to which we now turn, constrains criminal punishment and can function as a check on the political process. Understanding the link between immaturity and culpability within a framework of standard criminal law doctrines and policies is the first step toward more rational policy-making.

Proportionality and Blameworthiness

The starting point of our analysis is *proportionality,* the bedrock principle that is the foundation of legitimate state punishment. Simply put, proportionality holds that criminal punishment should be measured by two criteria: the harm a person causes and her blameworthiness in causing that harm. The law recognizes that different wrongful acts cause different levels of harm through a complex system of offense grading under which more serious crimes (rape, for example) are punished presumptively more severely than less serious crimes (shoplifting, for example).[11] Beyond this, two people who engage in the *same* wrongful conduct may differ in their blameworthiness. A person may be less culpable than other criminals—or not culpable at all—because he inadvertently (rather than purposely) causes the harm, because he is subject to some endogenous deficiency or incapacity that impairs his decision-making (such as mental illness), or because he acts in response to an extraordinary external pressure—a gun to the head is the classic example. Less blameworthy offenders deserve less punishment, and some persons who cause criminal harm deserve no punishment at all. The principle of proportionality operates in the criminal law through a complex regime of doctrines and policies, including sentencing policies, under which culpability and deserved punishment are calculated on the basis of the seriousness of the harm, traits of the offender, and circumstances surrounding the offense.

The function of proportionality in the criminal law is to provide a guide for legislatures and a yardstick by which courts can assess punishment schemes; in this way, proportionality potentially constrains illegitimate political forces in dictating criminal punishment. For example, the Supreme Court in *Coker v. Georgia* invoked proportionality in prohibiting the use of the death penalty as punishment for rape. Some southern states allowed this sentence, which commentators have suggested was generally imposed only on black men who raped white women.[12]

To be sure, proportionality does not require precise calibration of punishment; at best, it operates as a crude constraint on legislatures and a moral admonition that criminal sentences should be based on harm and culpability. But conforming to a norm of proportionate punishment reinforces the legitimacy of the criminal justice system in important ways. Indeed, scholars such as Paul Robinson and John Darley have argued that only a system that is based on fair and proportionate punishment will have the moral credibility to maintain public respect and function effectively as a regime of crime control.[13]

Theories of Mitigation and Excuse

The criminal law starts with a strong presumption that adult criminal actors are fully responsible for their wrongful acts—and that they deserve full punishment. But, as we have suggested, the law sometimes departs from this position when actors engage in harmful conduct but are less blameworthy than the typical criminal. What makes the conduct of one person less blameworthy than that of another person who causes the same harm—an insane killer and his sane counterpart, for example? Answering this question is the key to understanding the sources of excuse and mitigation in criminal law.

Philosophers and criminal law scholars have written a great deal about criminal responsibility and the assignment of blame, and the question we ask can be answered at many levels. At the most abstract level, two broad theories are offered by scholars to explain the basis on which the criminal law evaluates blameworthiness in offenders.[14] The first is sometimes called *choice theory;* it has many variations and complexities, but a simplified description would go something like this: A person who causes criminal harm is a fully responsible moral agent (and deserves full punishment) if, in choosing to engage in the wrongful conduct, she has the capacity to make a rational decision and a "fair opportunity" to choose *not* to engage in the harmful conduct.[15] Thus, choice theory explains that in evaluating blameworthiness, the focus is whether the actor's choice to commit the crime was rational and also whether it was an exercise of free will. On this view, the actor whose thinking is substantially impaired or whose freedom is significantly constrained is less culpable than the typical offender and deserves less punishment—how much less depends on the extent of the impairment or coercion.

The second theory is sometimes called *character theory.* This theory links culpability to a strong inference that a criminal act is the product of the actor's bad character. To the extent that this inference does not hold, the actor's culpability is reduced or negated.[16] On this view, the blameworthiness of a criminal act varies depending not simply on the quality of the actor's choice but also on the meaning of the act as an expression of the actor's character. Thus, a character theorist would argue that an insane person's crime is an expression of his mental illness and not his bad character. Similarly, a lawbreaker who offends in response to a threat of injury is not culpable if a person of good character would likely succumb to the same pressure. Under this theory, one justification for punishing a first offender less severely than someone who has offended multiple times is that the criminal act of the first offender is more likely to derive from something other than bad character.

Both of these theories are invoked to explain the complex doctrinal apparatus through which the criminal law evaluates blameworthiness in determining liability and punishment. Character theory is more controversial than choice theory because it appears to invite an assessment of blame using criteria only indirectly linked to the criminal conduct.[17] Nonetheless, character theory explains some areas of doctrine and practice that are otherwise puzzling. Doctrines of excuse and mitigation often seem to require not only that the actor's reason and will were overborne, but also that the reaction was not morally deficient, that is, a person of good character would react similarly. Thus, a person who is provoked to kill will qualify for a mitigation defense only if a reasonable person would have lost control under the same circumstances.[18]

Our purpose is not to take sides in an academic debate but to provide a basis in the criminal law for evaluating adolescent culpability. Both of these theoretical frameworks support the conclusion that young offenders are less culpable than adults. In a framework that focuses only on choice, young law violators are less culpable because they are poorer decision-makers with more constrained opportunities to avoid criminal activity than adults. If bad moral character is the ultimate source of criminal culpability, then ordinary adolescents are less culpable than typical adult criminals because their identities are in flux and their characters unformed.[19]

Who Qualifies for Mitigation or Excuse?

We turn now to the task of translating theory into doctrine and practice. Under American criminal law, two very different kinds of persons can show that their criminal conduct was less culpable than that of the "typical" offender who deserves full punishment—those who are very different from ordinary persons due to impairments that contributed to their criminal choices and those who *are*

ordinary persons whose offenses are responses to extraordinary circumstances or are otherwise aberrant conduct.[20] Although it seems
paradoxical, adolescents, in a real sense, belong to both groups. In
the first group are individuals with endogenous traits or conditions
that undermine their decision-making capacity, impairing their
ability to understand the nature and consequences of their wrongful acts or to control their conduct. In modern times, this category
has been reserved mostly for offenders who suffer from mental illness, mental disability, and other neurological impairments. (At
common law, infancy was also an excusing condition of this type,
but this defense became obsolete with the establishment of juvenile
courts.)[21] The criminal law defenses of insanity, diminished capacity, extreme emotional disturbance, and involuntary act recognize
that psychological and biological incapacities can undermine
decision- making in ways that reduce or negate the culpability of
criminal choices.

Individuals in the second group are ordinary persons whose
criminal conduct is less culpable because it is a response to extraordinary external circumstances: These cases arise when the actor
faces a difficult choice, and her response of engaging in the criminal
conduct is reasonable under the circumstances, as measured by the
likely response of an ordinary law-abiding person in that situation.[22] Thus under standard self-defense doctrine, a person who
kills a threatening assailant is excused from liability if a reasonable
person in his place would have felt that his life was in danger. Similarly, the defenses of duress, necessity, and provocation are available to actors who can explain their criminal conduct in terms of
unusual external pressures that constrained their ability to choose.

An ordinary person also can offer another kind of culpability-
reducing evidence if he can show that the wrongful conduct was
aberrant or "out of character" in light of the actor's good reputation
and previous conduct as an upstanding citizen—in other words, that
the crime was not the product of the actor's bad character. Some

might view this category as a weaker version of the other two—a pronounced contrast between a person's established character and his bad conduct suggests that unusual circumstances or momentary dysfunction drove him to offend. However, reputation and character evidence that confirms the aberrant nature of the offense can be introduced at sentencing to mitigate punishment under many statutes, without regard to proof that the external circumstances were extraordinary or that the actor was impaired.[23]

The Role of Mitigation in Criminal Law

To complete our lesson in criminal law, we return to the distinction between excuse and mitigation and take a closer look at the role of mitigation. The line between mitigation and excuse is an important one because it marks the boundary of criminal responsibility: the difference between guilt and innocence. In the assessment of culpability, however, the differences are a matter of degree. Most mitigating conditions are of the same kinds as those that excuse. For example, mental illness that distorts the actor's thinking but is not severe enough to support an insanity defense (an excuse) can reduce the grade of an offense or result in a less punitive disposition.[24] Similarly, a person who robs a bank in response to a coercive threat that is not sufficiently compelling to excuse his conduct under duress defense may qualify for mitigation at sentencing.[25] Evidence that the crime was out of character is somewhat different from incapacity and coercion, in that it may be a source of mitigation but never functions as an excuse.

The substantive criminal law incorporates calibrated measures of culpability. For example, *mens rea* doctrine grades culpability on the basis of the actor's intentions and awareness of the risk-creating circumstances. The law of homicide operates through a grading scheme under which punishment for killing another person—the most serious harm one person can inflict on another—varies dramatically depending on the actor's blameworthiness.[26] Thus, the actor who kills intentionally is deemed less culpable if he does so without premeditation because his choice reveals less consideration of the harmful consequences of his act, and the actor who negligently causes another's death is guilty of a less serious crime than one who intends to kill. A person who kills in response to provocation or under extreme emotional disturbance may be guilty only of manslaughter and not of murder.[27] Under standard homicide doctrine, mitigating circumstances and mental states are translated into lower grade offenses that warrant less punishment.

Mitigation also plays a key role in sentencing for a range of offenses in addition to homicide. A defendant can introduce evidence relating to a broad range of factors to persuade the court that she deserves a more lenient sanction than the norm. Factors under state sentencing guidelines can be grouped roughly in the three mitigation categories described above. First are endogenous factors relating to the quality of the actor's *decision-making capacity*. These include impaired cognitive or volitional capacity due to mental illness or retardation, extreme emotional distress, youth, lack of sophistication, susceptibility to influence, or evidence that the crime was unplanned and spontaneous.[28] Typical mitigating factors relating to *coercive external circumstances* include duress, provocation, perceived threat, extreme need, and domination.[29] The third category recognizes mitigation when the criminal act was *out of character* for the actor.[30] For example, a reduced sentence might result if the crime was a first offense or an isolated incident; if the actor expressed genuine remorse or tried to mitigate the harm; if he had a history of steady employment, fulfillment of family obligations, and good citizenship; or, more generally, if the criminal act was aberrant in light of the defendant's established character traits and respect for the law's values. Under this category, the actor's settled identity as a moral person is deemed relevant to the assessment of blame.

Adolescent Development and Culpability

In Chapter 2, we described aspects of psychological development in adolescence that are relevant to youthful choices to get involved in criminal activity and that may distinguish young offenders from their adult counterparts. We now turn to the task of considering these developmental factors within the conventional criminal law framework for assessing blameworthiness. The unsurprising conclusion is that adolescent offenders, due to developmental immaturity, are presumptively less culpable than adults, but, with the exception of the very small number of offenders who are children, their crimes should not be excused. Each of the mitigating conditions generally recognized in the criminal law—diminished capacity, coercive circumstances, and lack of bad character—are relevant to criminal acts of adolescents; collectively they lend support to a justice regime grounded in mitigation for this category of offenders.

As a preliminary matter, a culpability line should be drawn between children and adolescents. Very few children commit crimes, and those who do should be excused from responsibility—as they presumptively were at common law. Excusing children from responsibility is compatible with the conventional drawing of the responsibility boundary in criminal law. Children differ dramatically from adults (and from adolescents) in their decision-making capabilities because their capacities for processing information and for considering and comparing the consequences of alternative choices are not yet developed.[31] Even in the nineteenth century, an era not famous for leniency toward young offenders, courts applying the infancy defense recognized intuitively what science confirms—that the cognitive decision-making capacity of children is so different from that of adults that they are appropriately grouped with actors suffering from severe mental disability. What this would mean in practice is that children below a jurisdictional age designated by policymakers would be subject only to purely rehabilitative interventions and not to criminal punishment. What this would mean in practice, as we discuss in Chapter 8, is that children who represent a threat to public safety, like mentally disordered persons, could be confined on civil commitment grounds to residential placements but not in correctional facilities.

Diminished Decision-Making Capacity and Mitigation

The adolescent who commits a crime rarely is so deficient in his decision-making capacity that he cannot comprehend the immediate harmful consequences of his choice or its wrongfulness, as might be true of a mentally disordered person or a young child. Yet, in ways that we have described in Chapter 2, the developmental factors that drive adolescent decision-making predictably contribute to criminal choices based on immature judgment. A quick review may be helpful. Although, in the abstract, youths in mid-adolescence have cognitive capacities for reasoning and understanding that may approximate those of adults, teenagers are less experienced and likely less competent at using these abilities under stress in real-world contexts—on the street, for example.[32] Perhaps more importantly, adolescents, even at age sixteen and seventeen, are immature in their psychosocial and emotional development, and this likely affects their decisions about involvement in crime in ways that distinguish them from adults. Due to their psychosocial immaturity, teenagers are more susceptible to peer influence than are adults and more inclined to conform their behavior to that of their peers. Youths also differ from adults in risk preference, tending to focus more on rewards and less on risks in making choices. Adolescent capacity for risk *perception* is close to that of adults in laboratory studies, but teenagers' abilities in this area are diminished in social contexts.[33] They also tend to focus on short-term rather than long-term consequences (and may be less capable of anticipating future consequences), and they are more impulsive and volatile in their emotional responses.[34] Recent brain research has informed our understanding of the biological underpinnings of these attributes. Adolescent brains are still developing in regions that control planning, impulse regulation, the anticipation of future consequences, and the reasoned calibration of risk and reward.[35]

It seems inevitable that these developmental influences in combination play an important role in youthful choices to engage in criminal activity. Consider the following scenario.[36] A teenager is hanging out with his buddies on the street, when, on the spur of the moment, someone suggests holding up a nearby convenience store. The youth does not really go through a formal decision-making process, but he "chooses" to go along, even though he has mixed feelings. Why? First and most important, he is concerned that his friends will reject him if he declines to participate, a negative consequence to which he attaches substantial weight in considering his options. Second, he simply does not think of ways to extricate himself, as a more mature person might do. This may be because he lacks experience, because he makes the choice so quickly, or because he has difficulty projecting the course of events into the future and considering the consequences of his choice beyond the immediate situation. The "adventure" of the hold-up and the possibility of getting some money are exciting. These immediate rewards, together with peer approval, weigh more heavily in his decision than the remote possibility of apprehension by the police. He probably never considers the long-term costs of conviction of a serious crime.

Research on youthful criminal activity offers some empirical support for this speculation. For example, unlike adult criminals, teenagers usually commit crimes with peers, suggesting that peer influence plays a role in criminal involvement during adolescence.[37] Researchers have also linked desistance from crime in late adolescence to improved future orientation (which may incline individuals to focus on the long-term consequences of risky conduct) and to changing patterns of peer relationships.[38] The scenario is also consistent with the general developmental research on peer influence, risk preference, impulsivity, and future orientation. As a general proposition, it is well documented that teenagers are inclined to engage in risky behaviors that reflect their immaturity of judgment.

We cannot directly study teenagers' actual decision-making "on the street," but it seems very likely that the psychosocial and emotional influences shaping adolescents' decision-making more generally contribute to their choices about criminal activity as well. These influences on decision-making are *normative*, as psychologists use this term—that is, typical of adolescence as a period and developmental in nature. They undermine decision-making capacity in ways that are accepted in the criminal law as mitigating culpability. Thus, youthful criminal choices may share much in common with those of adults whose decision-making capacities are impaired by emotional disturbance, mental illness or retardation, vulnerability to influence or domination by others, or failure to understand fully the consequences of their acts.

Although, in general, lawmakers have paid minimal attention to the mitigating character of adolescents' diminished decision-making capacities, some legislatures and courts have recognized that immature judgment reduces culpability. Many state sentencing statutes include youth or immaturity as a mitigating factor. Courts have also acknowledged that young criminals are less culpable due to their immature decision-making capacity. Most notably, from its earliest consideration of the constitutionality of the juvenile death penalty (a subject to which we will return shortly), the Supreme Court has focused on this rationale for mitigation. In *Thompson v. Oklahoma*, Justice Stevens focused on the immature judgment of adolescents—albeit not precisely in the language of developmental psychology—in explaining why imposing capital punishment on a fifteen-year-old killer would violate the principle of proportionality:

[L]ess culpability should attach to a crime committed by a juvenile than to a comparable crime committed by an adult. The basis of this conclusion is too obvious to require extensive explanation. Inexperience, less intelligence, and less education make a teenager less able to evaluate the consequences of his or her conduct while at the same time he or she is more apt to be motivated by mere emotion or peer pressure than is an adult.[39]

Situational Mitigation and the Context of Adolescence

That immaturity is mitigating as a type of diminished capacity may be, in Justice Stevens' words, "too obvious to require extensive explanation." But many adolescents do not get involved in crime. Many factors besides psychosocial immaturity contribute to adolescent criminal involvement. Among the most important is social context, which is linked to another source of mitigation in criminal law that sheds further light on key differences between adolescents and adult criminals.

Under standard doctrine, mitigation is available to adults who engage in criminal conduct in response to coercive external circumstances if an ordinary (i.e., reasonable) person (one with typical adult psychological capacities and moral values) who was subject to the same unusual pressures might have responded similarly. Ordinary adolescents who live in high-crime neighborhoods are subject to intense social pressures and often to tangible threats that induce them to join in criminal activity; in some contexts, coercion may be so extreme that only unusual youths resist the pressure. Jeffrey Fagan and others have described how powerful social norms within urban adolescent male subcultures promote violent crime. Sanctions enforcing these norms are severe; a youth who seeks to avoid confrontation when challenged by a rival may lose social status and be ostracized by peers or even be vulnerable to physical assault.[40] Not surprisingly, research suggests that when families move from high-crime to low-crime neighborhoods, adolescents are less likely to get involved in violent crime.[41] But teenagers usually are not in a position on their own to extricate themselves from their schools or their neighborhoods. They are financially dependant on their parents and legally subject to parental authority. Because they are minors, a web of legal restrictions on their liberty prevents adolescents from doing what we rightly would expect of an adult in this situation—to move to another location where there is less pressure to get involved in crime.

These circumstances are similar in kind to those involved in claims of duress, provocation, necessity, or domination by codefendants. They do not excuse young offenders from criminal responsibility, but they are appropriately deemed mitigating of culpability. When adolescents cross the line to legal adulthood, the formal disabilities of youth are lifted; young adults can avoid the situational pressures they face by removing themselves from the "criminogenic" setting. Moreover, pressures to get involved in crime ease as normal maturation influences young adults to move beyond the risky activities of youth. Thus, adults have no claim of situational mitigation on the grounds that they are restricted to a social setting in which avoiding crime is very difficult.[42]

Although the "reasonable person" standard applied to situational mitigation is typically based on the response of an ordinary adult, it is also instructive to analyze the culpability of juveniles in response to extraordinary circumstances by using as a baseline the reactions of ordinary adolescents. Mitigation based on "diminished capacity" is available to individuals who differ substantially from the adult norm. In our analysis of this issue, adolescents were grouped with mentally impaired persons. It is also important to recognize, however, that adolescents in fact are *not* a small group of abnormal individuals, but a large cohort of ordinary persons who happen to be in a particular developmental stage in which their tools for dealing with external pressures are less effective than are those of adults. For example, normal adolescents may lack the life skills and psychosocial capacities that would allow them to resist peer pressure to engage in criminal activity in some social contexts.[43] The psychological attributes that they bring to their experiences increase the challenges they face as compared to those faced by adults. Thus, as a few courts have recognized, the standard "reasonable adult" baseline may not fully accommodate responses to external pressures that are reasonable for adolescents.[44] A normative-adolescent baseline clarifies that the criminal choices of many adolescents (like those of ordinary adults who claim situational mitigation) can be explained in terms of exogenous pressures rather than individual moral deficiency or abnormality.

Development, Character, and Culpability

A third mitigating condition is also important in assessing the culpability of typical young wrongdoers. As we have indicated, at sentencing an offender can sometimes introduce evidence of good character, negating the inference that his bad act reflects bad moral fiber. Here mitigation applies to the crimes of young offenders as well—not because of their good character *per se*, but because their characters are unformed. As Chapter 2 explained, an important developmental task of adolescence is the formation of personal identity, a slow process of exploration and experimentation through which the youth separates from her parents and evolves toward an autonomous adult self. During adolescence, identity is fluid; values, plans and beliefs are tentative as teens struggle to figure out who they are. This process for many youths includes involvement in risky activities, including, perhaps, involvement in crime.

Our point is that the criminal conduct of most teenagers is grounded in transitory developmental processes that are constitutive of adolescence, such as immature judgment and normative experimentation with risky behaviors.[45] The vast majority of delinquent youths will outgrow their antisocial tendencies and will mature into persons who do not reject the law's values.[46] In part this is because the developmentally linked values and preferences that drive adolescent criminal choices change in predictable ways with maturation. Thus, the criminal act of the normative adolescent does not express his bad character and an important component of culpability in the typical criminal act—the connection between the bad act and morally deficient character—is missing in his conduct, just as it is in the adult who provides evidence of good character.

The fact that antisocial activity in adolescence typically is not indicative of bad character also raises important questions about the validity of "juvenile psychopathy," a diagnosis that increasingly is used in determining dispositions of young offenders. Psychopaths are individuals whose antisocial behavior is reflective of a presumably ingrained constellation of personality traits characterized by callousness, indifference to others, deceitfulness, and an absence of remorse or shame for harmful acts.[47] This label is perhaps the quintessential designation of "bad character"; it signifies that the individual's antisocial behavior is due to fixed aspects of his personality, an assumption that is difficult to defend as applied to individuals whose identity is still developing.[48] For this reason, the American Psychiatric Association mandates that the diagnosis of antisocial personality disorder (a disorder characteristic of most psychopaths) not be made prior to the age of eighteen.[49] Although the notion that some juvenile offenders are actual or "fledgling" psychopaths has become increasingly popular in legal and psychological circles, and some courts order assessments of psychopathy when sentencing juveniles, no data exist on the stability or continuity of psychopathy between adolescence and adulthood. Indeed, some psychopathic traits (impulsivity, irresponsibility, and egocentrism, for example) are characteristic of psychosocially immature, but otherwise perfectly normal, youths.[50] In the absence of solid research evidence that juveniles with psychopathic traits (e.g., juveniles who are callous, manipulative, and antisocial) actually *become* adult psychopaths, it is unwise to use this label when describing an adolescent.

We should make a final point about adolescent character formation and culpability. Although most impulsive young risk takers mature into adults with different values, some adult criminals are impulsive, sensation-seeking risk-takers who discount future consequences and focus on the here-and-now. Are these adolescent-like adults also less culpable than other adult offenders and deserving of reduced punishment? Our analysis of identity development in adolescence clarifies why the answer is clearly "No." Unlike the typical adolescent, the predispositions, values, and preferences that motivate the adult offenders are not developmental but characterological, and they are unlikely to change merely with the passage of time. Adolescent traits that contribute to criminal conduct are normative of adolescence, but they are not typical in adulthood. In an adult, these traits are often part of the personal identity of an individual who does not respect the values of the criminal law and who deserves punishment when he or she violates its prohibitions.

In sum, adolescents are different from adults in their decision-making capacities in ways that are more subtle than the differences between adults and children. Nonetheless, even sixteen- and seventeen-year-old teenagers are immature in their neurological, psychosocial, and emotional development and are still in the process of forming their personal identities. Moreover, until they are legal adults at age eighteen, adolescents are constrained in their freedom to extricate themselves unilaterally from social contexts in which avoiding participation in crime is difficult. These features of adolescence distinguish young offenders from their adult counterparts in ways that are recognized as mitigating under standard criminal law doctrines and principles. They are the building blocks of a legal framework grounded in mitigation under which adolescents are treated as a separate category.

Categorical or Individualized Mitigation?

Once it is accepted that immaturity is a mitigating condition, it is necessary to grapple with the important policy choice of whether it should be considered on an individualized basis or as the rationale for dealing with young offenders as a separate category based on age. In other criminal law contexts, individual defendants typically must show that they deserve leniency on the basis of diminished capacity, extraordinary circumstances, or good character. Traditional juvenile justice policy, in contrast, employed a categorical approach, dealing with (almost) all juveniles in a separate more lenient system; this approach continues under contemporary law, in a somewhat diluted form. As the boundary between the juvenile and the adult systems becomes more porous, however, evaluation of immaturity as a mitigator increasingly takes place (if at all) on a case-by-case basis in a transfer hearing, at sentencing, or sometimes informally in the charging decision.

The uniqueness of immaturity as a mitigating condition argues for the adoption of (or renewed commitment to) a categorical approach in the context of youth crime policy. Mitigating conditions and circumstances affect adult criminal choices in varying and idiosyncratic ways; thus individualized consideration of mitigation claims is appropriate. In contrast, the capacities and processes associated with adolescence are characteristic of individuals in a relatively well-defined group, whose development follows a roughly predictable course to maturity and whose criminal choices are affected predictably in ways that are mitigating of culpability.

Although variations exist among individuals in this age cohort, coherent boundaries based on developmental knowledge can delineate a minimum age for adult adjudication, as well as a period of years beyond this when a strong presumption of reduced culpability applies. The use of an age category is justified because the presumption of immaturity can be applied confidently to most persons in the group. Moreover, a categorical presumption of immaturity offers substantial efficiencies over an approach in which immaturity is assessed on a case-by-case basis, particularly since mitigation claims would be a part of virtually every criminal adjudication involving a serious crime by a juvenile.

Adopting a mitigation framework does not mean that all youths are less mature than adults in their decision-making capacity or that the personal identity of all juveniles is unformed. Some individuals exhibit mature judgment at an early age (although most are not offenders), and for others, antisocial tendencies that begin in childhood continue in a stable pattern of criminal conduct, and these tendencies ultimately define their adult characters.[51] Adult punishment of mature youths might be appropriate if these individuals could be identified with some degree of certainty. But we currently lack the diagnostic tools to evaluate psychosocial immaturity reliably on an individualized basis or to distinguish young career criminals from ordinary adolescents who, as adults, will repudiate their reckless experimentation. As a general matter, litigating maturity on a case-by-case basis is likely to be an error-prone undertaking, with the outcomes determined by factors other than psychological immaturity—such as physical appearance or demeanor.

A categorical approach that constrains decision-makers dealing with young offenders represents a collective pre-commitment to recognizing the mitigating character of youth in assigning blame. Otherwise, immaturity often may be ignored when the facts of a particular case engender a punitive response; indeed, immaturity is likely to count as mitigating only when the offender otherwise presents a sympathetic case. Young criminals who hurt other people are often repugnant—hardly childlike or seeming to deserve protection. A tension exists between the typical conception of immaturity (which suggests innocence and dependency) and its embodiment in a violent young lawbreaker. Vivid images of the juvenile's crime may lead the decision-maker to discount his immaturity. In contrast, the craziness of mental illness and criminal violence are compatible images, and decision-makers who accept the mitigating character of mental disorder in the abstract are less likely to be distracted in the individual case.

The fact that immaturity as mitigation is a somewhat delicate construct in practice is a critical concern for another reason. As Chapter 4 explains, research evidence indicates that racial and ethnic biases influence attitudes about the punishment of young offenders.[52] Thus, we should worry that decision-makers may be particularly inclined to discount the mitigating impact of immaturity in minority youths. The integrity and legitimacy of any individualized decision-making process is vulnerable to contamination from racist attitudes or from unconscious racial stereotyping that operates even among those who lack overt prejudice.[53] The upshot is that a strong presumption that mitigation applies categorically to juvenile offenders avoids both innocent errors and more pernicious influences that may distort individualized determinations.

A categorical approach is also compatible with the law's approach to regulating minors in other contexts. As we described in Chapter 3, children and adolescents are dealt with categorically for almost all purposes, despite variations in maturity of minors who are subject to paternalistic restrictions and protections. Thus, seventeen-year-olds are not offered the opportunity to demonstrate individual maturity or competence for purposes of voting, executing contracts, or obtaining standard medical care, nor are demonstrably immature youths of this age restricted from obtaining drivers licenses. The difference between the mitigation category that we propose and the general regulatory approach, of course, is that the category adopted in the juvenile justice context is more narrowly tailored than the standard binary categories of childhood and adulthood; it is designed to conform to the developmental reality of adolescence.

There is much to support a categorical approach to mitigation based on immaturity. This is not to say, however, that youths should never be subject to adult punishment. A policy that treats immaturity as a mitigating condition is viable only if public protection is not seriously compromised. Young offenders can threaten public safety, and tolerance of youthful misconduct, as we have seen, is tenuous at best. More important, *both* proportionate punishment and public protection are key aspects of the criminal law, and both must be accommodated. As we discuss in Chapter 8, public safety concerns dictate that some young recidivists who inflict a large amount of social harm must be incapacitated as adults. Although this response may undermine proportionality to some extent, in practice the sacrifice is likely to be modest. The small group of youths who are recidivist violent offenders are generally older teenagers and are more likely than other adolescent lawbreakers to be young career criminals of settled dispositions.[54]

Mitigation and the Juvenile Death Penalty

Although few observers would argue that youths should never be subject to adult criminal penalties, the question of whether a death sentence is ever appropriate punishment for a crime committed by a juvenile was the subject of a heated public debate in this country for many decades. The death penalty is the ultimate punishment, reserved for only the most culpable killers. Thus, the dispute centered on whether youths whose crimes occur before their eighteenth birthday should ever be in that category. All but a handful of countries around the world (Iran, Nigeria, and Congo, for example) exclude juveniles from the death penalty.[55] Until 2005, however, nineteen American jurisdictions authorized the use of this punishment for sixteen- and seventeen-year-olds, although only a few juveniles in a handful of states had actually received a death sentence in recent years.[56] In 2005 the U.S. Supreme Court effectively settled this debate—at least as a matter of law—holding in *Roper v. Simmons* that the juvenile death penalty categorically violates the prohibition of cruel and unusual punishment under the Eighth Amendment of the U.S. Constitution.[57]

Simmons was not the first occasion on which the Court examined whether imposing the death penalty for crimes committed by juveniles violates this standard. In *Thompson v. Oklahoma* in 1988, the Court prohibited the use of the death penalty on offenders aged fifteen and younger. Applying the standard used to evaluate Eighth Amendment claims—whether a particular punishment offends "emerging standards of decency in a mature society"[58]—*Thompson* emphasized that youthful immaturity reduces culpability.[59] But a year later, in *Stanford v. Kentucky* the Court upheld a statute authorizing the use of capital punishment for youths age sixteen and seventeen.[60] The Court agreed to revisit the issue in *Simmons* two years after it held in *Atkins v. Virginia* that imposing the death penalty on mentally retarded persons violated the constitutional standard, overruling an earlier opinion decided at the time of *Stanford*.[61] *Simmons* came to the Court after the Missouri Supreme Court found that state's juvenile death penalty statute unconstitutional under *Atkins*.[62]

The Court offered several bases for its conclusion that the juvenile death penalty is unconstitutional (including evidence of a growing public consensus opposed to the punishment as demonstrated by legislative change). The heart of *Simmons*, however, is a proportionality analysis, in which the Court, in large part relying on our previously published work, adopted the developmental argument for mitigation that we have outlined in this chapter.[63] The Court found that executing Chris Simmons and others who committed crimes as juveniles would violate the Eighth Amendment because adolescents under the age of eighteen, due to their immaturity, are not among the "worst offenders" for whom the punishment of death is reserved.[64] This did not mean, of course, that Simmons was exonerated—despite the scathing comments of Justice Scalia in his dissenting opinion, criticizing the *Simmons* majority for (in his view) finding that juveniles lack responsibility. Like others who confuse mitigation and excuse, Justice Scalia seemed to forget that mitigation in this context meant that Simmons, having escaped the death penalty, would spend the rest of his life in prison.[65]

In truth, Chris Simmons was probably not the youth that child advocates would have chosen to challenge the death penalty. He was seventeen years old when he and a friend broke into a woman's house and then brutally murdered her by taping her up and throwing her into a nearby river. Some testimony suggested that Chris panicked when the victim recognized him, although he was also reported to have expressed interest earlier in killing "someone" a few weeks earlier.[66] In general, Chris was not a person likely to arouse much sympathy, despite his intact family and the absence of a criminal record.

Justice Kennedy, writing for the majority, did not focus on Simmons himself; instead he described three features of adolescence that distinguish young offenders from their adult counterparts in ways that mitigate culpability—features that are familiar to the reader at this point. The first is the diminished decision-making capacity of youths, which contributes to a criminal choice that is "not as morally reprehensible as that of adults" because of its developmental nature. The Court pointed to the tendency of adolescents to engage in risky behavior and noted that immaturity and an "underdeveloped sense of responsibility" often result in "impetuous and ill-considered decisions" by youths. Second, the Court pointed to the increased vulnerability of youths to external coercion, including peer pressure. On the Court's view, this vulnerability, together with the more limited control that adolescents have over their environment (which restricts their ability to escape from a criminogenic setting) mitigates their culpability.[67] Finally, *Simmons* emphasized that the unformed nature of adolescent identity made it "less supportable to conclude that even a heinous crime was evidence of irretrievably depraved character."[68] Adolescents are less blameworthy than adults, the Court suggested, because the traits that contribute to criminal conduct are transient (that is, developmental), and because most adolescents will outgrow their tendency to get involved in crime as they mature. Although the Court did not elaborate, we have seen that each of these attributes of adolescence corresponds to a conventional source of mitigation in criminal law.

The Court in *Simmons* defended its categorical rule excluding juveniles from the death penalty against the challenge by dissenting justices that mitigating evidence of immaturity should be presented instead on a case-by-case-basis (the existing practice at the time). Adopting several of our arguments, Justice Kennedy noted the potential for error in distinguishing incipient psychopaths from youths whose crimes reflect "transient immaturity," and he expressed concern that the brutality of the offense might often overwhelm consideration of youth and immaturity.[69] (Indeed, the prosecutor had argued to the jury that Chris Simmons' youth was not mitigating, but *aggravating*.)[70] The Court acknowledged that like all categorical rules, the exclusion might be applied to some mature youths. Justice Kennedy noted, however, that society draws the line between childhood and adulthood at age eighteen for many purposes—and concluded that it should be the minimum age for death penalty eligibility as well.[71]

The death penalty is unique as a context in which lawmakers have paid serious attention to the question of how adolescent immaturity affects the culpability of young offenders. In capital murder cases, the assessment of blameworthiness occupies an extreme pole on the culpability continuum: the difference between a death sentence and life in prison. However, as we have shown, the mitigation analysis applies generally to the criminal punishment of young offenders. One lesson that can be drawn from *Simmons* is that contemporary reformers err in their argument that differential treatment of juveniles may be appropriate for minor crimes but not for serious offenses. The importance of recognizing the reduced culpability of a young offender is at least as important when the stakes are high.

Implementing a Mitigation-Based Model: Some Preliminary Thoughts

A substantial gap separates contemporary youth crime policy from one that is grounded in mitigation. Although juvenile justice reforms over the past generation have incorporated accountability into regimes that formerly were grounded (ostensibly) only in rehabilitation, this has usually been done in a piecemeal manner and often in response to political pressure. Moreover, lawmakers have seldom attempted reforms directed at tailoring dispositions to the culpability of young offenders. In most states, proportionate dispositions are not the norm in juvenile court.[72] More important, the trend of the past generation has been toward holding youths fully responsible for their crimes both in juvenile court (through sentences extending into adulthood) and in criminal court. Today, juveniles can be subject to adult adjudication and punishment for a broad range of crimes, including some, such as car theft and drug transactions, that appear to be quintessential adolescent behavior. Young criminals can also be tried as adults for first offenses that may well be experimental behavior that would not be repeated.[73]

Scientific evidence supports the analysis that most adolescents are less mature than adults in ways that distinguish their criminal choices and that this youthful immaturity mitigates culpability. However, most young law violators also are not children, and their immaturity does not excuse them from criminal responsibility. Thus, the evidence supports a system of crime regulation under which adolescents are dealt with as a separate legal category—neither children nor adults. As we pointed out in earlier chapters, this is an unusual move. For most legal purposes, adolescents are dealt with as children; occasionally they are classified as adults. Seldom do lawmakers recognize adolescence as a distinctive stage. But we have also seen that good reasons support adopting an intermediate category in the realm of crime regulation. In this context, classifying juveniles as children, the approach of the traditional regime, has been a failure. Further, our mitigation analysis clarifies that punishing young offenders as adults offends the core criminal law principle of proportionality. Unlike either of these alternatives, a mitigation-based model of juvenile justice under which adolescence constitutes an intermediate legal category is solidly grounded in criminal law theory and doctrine. Thus, it provides a legitimacy that neither the traditional rehabilitative model nor the recent full-responsibility reforms can claim.

Categorical recognition of the mitigating impact of immaturity can provide the conceptual framework for a separate justice system for juveniles, but it does not in itself dictate a particular set of institutional arrangements. Various responses, including a systematic sentencing discount for young offenders in adult court, might satisfy the demands of proportionality.[74] Ultimately, the case for a separate mitigation-based justice system for the adjudication and disposition of juveniles rests not only on proportionality, but also on evidence that such a system is the best means to minimize the social cost of youth crime. In the chapters to come, we show that a separate mitigation-based system can accommodate the seemingly conflicting goals of protecting public safety and responding to the attributes of this unique group of wrongdoers, without abandoning basic principles of criminal law.

CHAPTER 6

Developmental Competence and the Adjudication of Juveniles

Lionel Tate, the Florida youth described in Chapter 1, was fourteen years old when he stood trial as an adult on murder charges for killing his six-year-old neighbor. Throughout the trial, Lionel's defense attorneys were concerned about whether he understood the proceedings and the consequences of being convicted of murder, and they were troubled by his rejection of the state's offer of a plea agreement under which he would have received a three-year sentence in a juvenile facility. Against his attorney's advice, Lionel had acquiesced to his mother's insistence that he reject the plea offer; in her view, he had done nothing wrong.

As the trial to determine his guilt or innocence proceeded, Lionel's behavior reinforced his attorneys' concerns. He sat at the defendant's table doodling and drawing pictures, seeming to pay no attention to the proceeding that would determine his fate. One of his attorneys reported that there was no interaction between Lionel and his legal representatives. He "hasn't listened to one word and had no idea what's going on."[1] The attorney raised his concerns with the judge, asking that an evaluation of Lionel's competence to stand trial be conducted. The judge declined to order a competence evaluation, and the trial proceeded to conclusion; as we reported earlier, Lionel was convicted of murder and sentenced to life in prison.

149

Lionel, one of the youngest persons ever to be sentenced to life in prison, appealed his conviction on several grounds, including the claim that the harsh sentence was cruel and unusual punishment, given his youth. What persuaded the appellate court that the conviction could not stand, however, was the trial judge's rejection of the petition by Lionel's attorney for an evaluation of his client's competence to assist counsel and make a decision about the state's plea offer. Although Lionel's mother (who presumably was competent) effectively made the decision to reject the plea, a more mature defendant than Lionel might have been better situated to assess his options with the aid of his attorney, free of his mother's undue influence, and to make a self-interested decision. The court pointed to Lionel's youth (and even younger mental age, given his below-average IQ) and his lack of experience with the criminal justice system in holding that, due to the failure of the court to order an assessment of Lionel's competence, the conviction must be overturned.[2]

Lionel's case highlights an issue that we have not yet addressed in our developmental analysis of juvenile justice policy. Thus far our analysis has focused mainly on how adolescent immaturity affects youthful decisions to engage in criminal activity, and the extent to which it mitigates culpability under the principle of proportionality. In this chapter, we shift our attention to the adjudication process and examine whether and how developmental immaturity affects the ability of juveniles to function as criminal defendants—that is, to understand the criminal charges against them and the proceedings they face and to assist their attorneys.[3]

We saw in Chapter 5 that the principle of proportionality is deeply embedded in the criminal law as a means of promoting fair *punishment*. The principle of due process is also critically important in the administration of justice, to ensure that criminal *proceedings* incorporate the basic elements of fairness. It was on due process grounds that the Supreme Court held in *Pate v. Robinson* in 1966 that criminal defendants must be competent to stand trial, giving constitutional status to a requirement that was already well established in American law.[4] As applied to adults, the competence requirement has been the basis for excluding from adjudication those defendants whose severe mental illness or disability undermines their comprehension of the proceedings and ability to assist their attorneys.

The application of the competence requirement to juveniles charged with crimes has a more complex history than does its application to adults; it is a story that has unfolded in three stages. The first stage extended through the era of the traditional juvenile court, in which the competence requirement had no place. The second stage began after the Supreme Court announced in *Gault* in 1967 that juvenile proceedings must comply with due process, and many courts adopted the requirement of adjudicative competence as a means of protecting mentally ill and retarded youths from adjudication.[5] The third (and current) stage began in the early 1990s, with the legal reforms that have resulted in the adjudication of more, and younger, juveniles in criminal courts and in longer sentences in the juvenile system. In this context, the issue of what we call *developmental competence* has surfaced. A concern that began to emerge in the mid-1990s is that some youths facing charges in criminal court, or harsh sanctions in juvenile court, may not be competent to participate in their defense—not because of mental disability or illness, but because of immaturity. Although this issue was largely invisible as the reforms unfolded, it is one that lawmakers are beginning to recognize must be addressed.

This chapter examines the impact of immaturity on adjudicative competence and seeks to resolve some of the surprising challenges that requiring developmental competence raises for legal doctrine and practice. The challenges are created by the relatively large number of youths whose competence may be questionable, due to their immaturity, under the legal standard applied to adults, who may not become competent in response to interventions (such as medication) that usually are effective with adults suffering from mental illness, but that will not "cure" normative immaturity. How shall these youths be tried for their offenses? Should they be tried at all? We argue that incorporating developmental competence into legal doctrine and practice can be accomplished without excessive institutional disruption only if different standards of competence apply in criminal versus juvenile proceedings. This approach allows youths who are incompetent to stand trial under the adult standard to be tried in a juvenile court, which would not be possible if a single standard were applied.

Before turning to our examination of trial competence, it is worth underscoring again the distinction between competence and culpability—two very different constructs that are often confused, even by those with expertise in criminal law. Adjudicative competence refers to the ability of an individual to function effectively as a defendant in a criminal or delinquency proceeding. In contrast, determinations of culpability focus on the defendant's blameworthiness in engaging in the criminal conduct and on whether and to what extent he will be held responsible. Although many of the same incapacities that excuse or mitigate criminal responsibility may also render a defendant incompetent, the two issues are analytically distinct and separate legal inquiries, and they focus on the defendant's mental state at two different points in time (the time of the crime and the time of the court proceeding).

The Competence Requirement and Constitutional Doctrine

The reason that competence is required of defendants in criminal proceedings is simple: when the state asserts its power against an individual with the goal of taking away his liberty, the accused must be capable of participating in a meaningful way in the proceeding against him. If a defendant is so mentally ill or disabled that he cannot participate adequately, then the trial lacks fundamental fairness that is required as a part of due process under the Fourteenth Amendment to the U.S. Constitution. This is the reasoning of the U.S. Supreme Court in holding that criminal defendants must be competent to stand trial.[6]

Courts agree that the competence requirement serves three basic functions—all of which are important to the fairness of the trial. First, this requirement preserves the dignity and integrity of the proceedings, which would be compromised if an uncomprehending defendant faced an accusing state (in the form of the prosecutor) in a proceeding in which his liberty was at stake. Second, the requirement reduces error and promotes accuracy, making a wrongful conviction less likely. An incompetent defendant may be unable to challenge prosecution witnesses, offer exculpatory evidence, or raise defenses that a person with better comprehension would assert. Finally, the competence requirement safeguards the defendant's autonomy-based right to participate meaningfully in the proceeding, a core value of due process in this setting. Although defense attorneys often raise concerns about a defendant's competence to stand trial, such concerns are not in themselves a defense. All participants in a criminal trial have an interest in the defendant's competence, and the issue can be raised by the judge or prosecutor as well as the defendant.

In 1960 the Supreme Court announced a legal standard for trial competence in *Dusky v. United States* that has since been adopted uniformly by American courts.[7] According to *Dusky,* when the issue of a defendant's competence is raised in a criminal trial, the court's determination should focus on "whether the defendant has sufficient present ability to consult with his lawyer with a reasonable degree of rational understanding—and whether he has a rational, as well as factual, understanding of the proceedings against him." Thus, there are two parts to the competence requirement: the defendant must be able to consult with her attorney about planning and making decisions in her defense, and she must understand the charges, the meaning, and purpose of the proceedings, and the consequences of conviction.

The Trial Competence of Juveniles: A Brief History

The requirement that criminal defendants be competent to stand trial had no place in delinquency proceedings in the traditional juvenile court. In a system in which the government's announced purpose was to rehabilitate and not to punish errant youths, the procedural protections accorded adult defendants—including the requirement of adjudicative competence—were thought to be unnecessary.[8]

This all changed with *In re Gault* (discussed in Chapter 4), which led to an extensive restructuring of delinquency proceedings to conform to the requirements of constitutional due process.[9] Although the Supreme Court has never considered whether due process requires that juveniles in delinquency proceedings be competent to stand trial, many state courts have addressed this issue. With the sole exception of Oklahoma, all have held that the requirements of due process and fundamental fairness are satisfied only if youths facing charges in juvenile court are competent to stand trial.[10] In reaching this conclusion, courts have offered little analysis, but some have emphasized the value of accuracy and suggested that the right to counsel would be greatly diminished if the youth could not communicate with her attorney or were unaware of the nature of the proceedings.[11]

Courts incorporating the adjudicative competence requirement into delinquency proceedings have generally assumed that the incapacities of juveniles are analogous to those of their adult counterparts; the cases almost all have involved youths who were mentally ill or disabled. A few courts have suggested in passing that immaturity might exaggerate the challenges faced by incompetent juveniles, but developmental competence *per se* has received little attention in the case law.

On reflection, the absence of attention to developmental competence is not surprising. After all, the purpose of having a separate juvenile court and justice system was so that youths, *because* of their immaturity, would receive different treatment than would adult criminal defendants. The idea that immaturity in itself should be a basis for exclusion from a delinquency adjudication might seem somewhat incoherent—or at least inconsistent with the rationale for a separate system. As courts went about the business of deciding which adult procedural rights should apply in delinquency proceedings, they continued to assume that the juvenile court was different from the criminal justice system in its purposes and in the severity of its sanctions. Courts considering due process claims emphasized these differences and evaluated procedural protections in part on the basis of their compatibility with the unique purposes and character of the juvenile court.[12]

What happened to the occasional juvenile who was transferred to criminal court and tried as an adult? In that situation, whether a defendant's immaturity might affect his competence was clearly relevant, but, here again, developmental competence received little attention in the post-*Gault* period. A few statutes, such as Virginia's, require the judge in a transfer hearing to determine that the juvenile is competent to stand trial as a predicate to transfer; this could invite inquiry into the youth's immaturity.[13] Generally, however, the prohibition against trying incompetent defendants has not been adapted to exclude immature youths from transfer on this basis. Moreover, little evidence suggests that criminal court judges ordered evaluations of transferred youths to assess their competence to stand trial. This may not be so surprising when we remember that, until the 1990s, younger adolescents could not be transferred under most statutes. The occasional sixteen- or seventeen-year-old defendant may not have raised much concern because it was assumed that he was mature enough to participate in a criminal proceeding.

In sum, until the 1990s, the issue of juveniles' trial competence involved a straightforward incorporation of a procedural protection that was relevant to a relatively small number of mentally impaired adult defendants into delinquency proceedings, where it was assumed to apply similarly to a small number of mentally incapacitated youths. The issue of developmental competence did not become salient during this period—either in juvenile court, which was designed to deal with immature youths, or in criminal court—because most youths who were tried as adults were older adolescents.[14]

The Punitive Reforms and Developmental Competence

The punitive regulatory reforms that began in the late 1980s changed the situation dramatically by increasing the punishment stakes facing many young offenders and by eroding the boundary between the adult and juvenile systems. These developments inadvertently transformed the issue of adjudicative competence from a minor procedural reform in delinquency proceedings into a major institutional challenge and introduced developmental incompetence as a construct that demands attention.

The importance of this issue was not recognized immediately, however. As legislatures across the country began to enact laws that dramatically altered the landscape of juvenile crime policy, the procedural issue of whether youngsters charged with crimes might be less able to participate in criminal proceedings than adult defendants was not central to the policy debates.[15] Nor, with a few exceptions, was this issue considered by legislatures toughening sanctions in juvenile court.[16] Until the mid-1990s even critics of the reforms seldom pointed out that the new laws presumed that young defendants could function adequately in their criminal trials.

Given that developmental incompetence largely escaped the attention of courts and policy-makers until recently, it is worth asking directly whether the constitutional prohibition against criminal adjudication of incompetent defendants must be applied to this form of incapacity. The answer is surely "yes." The competence requirement is functional at its core, speaking to questions about the impact of cognitive deficiencies on trial participation.[17] Functionally it makes no difference if the defendant cannot understand the proceeding she faces or assist her attorney due to mental illness or to immaturity. In either case, the fairness of the proceeding is undermined. In short, the same concerns that support the prohibition against trying criminal defendants who are incompetent due to mental impairment apply with equal force when immature youths are subject to criminal proceedings.

The issue of developmental incompetence began to surface as reform policies were implemented and increasing numbers of immature youths faced prosecution in criminal court. The story of Lionel Tate and other highly publicized cases involving very young defendants focused national attention on the issue.[18] These cases highlight the challenge that now confronts policy-makers: how to respond to the reality that immature youths may be less capable trial participants than adults and that some may be unable to comprehend adequately the meaning and consequences of criminal proceedings or to assist their attorneys in their defense. Jurisdictions across the country are beginning to come to terms with the challenges of how to assess developmental competence and how to respond when a young defendant is found incompetent on the basis of immaturity.[19]

The punitive reforms present a more subtle challenge in the context of delinquency proceedings; as we have suggested, the juvenile system was explicitly designed to deal with immature youth. But today, juvenile courts impose severe sanctions; in some states today, a twelve-year-old can face a twenty-year sentence in a delinquency proceeding.[20] Under these conditions, a juvenile's capacity to comprehend the jeopardy he faces and his ability to assist his attorney is as important as it would be in a criminal trial.

Adolescent Development and Trial Competence

In the context of the recent changes in juvenile justice policy, it has become important to have a better understanding of how the capacities of children and adolescents to participate in criminal proceedings compare with those of adults. In pursuit of this end, we first examine the specific abilities that are required for adjudicative competence under the legal standard. We then turn to the research comparing the abilities of juveniles and adults—focusing particularly on a large study that we conducted with colleagues on these issues.

A Taxonomy of Competence-Related Abilities

Three broad types of abilities are implicated under the *Dusky* standard for competence to stand trial: (a) a factual understanding of the proceedings, (b) a rational understanding of the proceedings, and (c) the ability to assist counsel.[21] Although *Dusky* directs courts to consider these types of abilities, it provides no clear guidance about their relative importance or about the level of competence required for each. Courts applying the standard are directed to weigh each factor, but otherwise they exercise substantial discretion in deciding "how much competence is enough." Examining each component of competence under the *Dusky* standard and considering how the capacities of juvenile defendants are likely to compare with those of adults is instructive.

Factual understanding focuses on the defendant's knowledge and awareness of the charges and his understanding of available pleas, possible penalties, the general steps in the adjudication process, the roles of various participants in the pre-trial and trial process, and his rights as a defendant.[22] Courts assessing factual understanding are concerned with capacity rather than actual understanding to the extent that these can be distinguished; thus, a defendant's deficits in this realm will rarely be the basis of a finding of incompetence to stand trial, as long as she has the capacity to learn from relatively brief instruction.[23] Intellectual immaturity in juveniles may undermine factual understanding, especially given that youths generally have less experience and more limited ability to grasp concepts such as rights.[24] Juveniles also may be more likely than adults to have extensive deficits in their basic knowledge of the trial process, such that more than brief instruction is needed to attain competence.

The *rational understanding* requirement of *Dusky* has been interpreted to mean that defendants must comprehend the implications, relevance, or significance of what they understand factually regarding the trial process.[25] Deficits in rational understanding typically involve distorted or erroneous beliefs that nullify factual understanding.[26] For example, an immature defendant may know that he has a right to remain silent, yet believe that the judge can take this "right" away at any time by demanding a response to questions.[27] (When asked what he thought the "right to remain silent" meant, the twelve-year-old son of one of the authors said, "It means that you don't have to say anything until the police ask you a question.") Intellectual, emotional, and psychosocial immaturity may undermine the ability of some adolescents to grasp accurately the meaning and significance of matters that they seem to understand factually.

Finally, the requirement that the defendant in a criminal proceeding must have the *capacity to assist counsel* encompasses three types of abilities.[28] The first is the ability to receive and communicate information adequately to allow counsel to prepare a defense. This ability may be compromised by impairments in attention, memory, and concentration, deficits that might undermine the defendant's ability to respond to instructions or to provide important information to his attorney, such as a coherent account of the events surrounding the offense. These capacities continue to improve through age sixteen, according to studies of cognitive development.[29] Second, the ability to assist counsel requires a rational perspective regarding the attorney and her role, free of notions or attitudes that could impair the collaborative relationship. For example, some young defendants develop a belief that all adults involved in the proceeding are allied against him, perhaps after seeing defense attorneys and prosecutors chatting together outside the courtroom. Third, defendants must have the capacity to make decisions about pleading and the waiver or assertion of other constitutional rights.[30] These decisions involve not only adequate factual and rational understanding, but also the ability to consider alternatives and make a choice in a decision-making process. Immature youths may lack adequate capacities to adequately process information and exercise reason in making trial decisions, especially when the options are complex and their consequences far-reaching. Moreover, emotional and psychosocial immaturity may influence youths to make impulsive or shortsighted choices that reflect immature judgment.[31]

The MacArthur Juvenile Adjudicative Competence Study

As juveniles' competence to stand trial began to emerge as an important issue in the mid-1990s, the need for a comprehensive study comparing the abilities of adolescents and adults in this realm became apparent. Before this time, a few small studies had looked at particular capacities in juveniles that were important at different stages in the justice process. However, no comprehensive research had compared the specific capacities of juveniles and adults that are directly implicated in assessments of adjudicative competence. In response to that need, under the auspices of the MacArthur Foundation Research Network on Adolescent Development and Juvenile Justice, we and our colleagues conducted a large-scale study designed to examine empirically the relationship between developmental immaturity and the abilities of young defendants to participate in their trials.[32] The study did not aim to evaluate adolescents' competence to stand trial explicitly, because this ultimately is a legal judgment. Rather, the purpose of the study was to determine how and to what extent adolescents and adults differ in abilities implicated under the *Dusky* standard. The study also probed age differences in psychosocial influences on decision-making in the legal process.

The study included 927 youths (age eleven through seventeen) and 466 young adults (age eighteen through twenty-four) in four communities in the United States. The adult and youth groups each included two subgroups matched for age, gender, and ethnicity: participants involved in the justice system and "community" participants (individuals from the same neighborhoods without justice system involvement). The youth participants were divided into three age categories: 11–13 (20 percent of the youth sample), 14–15 (37 percent), and 16–17 (43 percent).

Along with an intelligence test and a measure of symptoms of mental illness, we administered two standardized interviews designed to assess abilities relevant to adjudicative competence. The first, the MacArthur Competence Assessment Tool-Criminal Adjudication (MacCAT-CA), is an interview that was developed by other researchers independent of this study specifically to assess individuals' understanding of charges, penalties, pleas, and the roles of trial participants, as well as their ability to communicate relevant facts to counsel and to reason about a plea offer.[33] The MacCAT-CA had previously been administered by the researchers who developed it to large numbers of adult defendants (in jails) whose competence was not questioned, as well as to individuals in forensic psychiatric facilities who had recently been found incompetent to stand trial. We used the norms derived from that study to set a cut-off score indicating "impairment."[34] The second interview (the MacJEN) was designed by our research team to assess psychosocial maturity in various aspects of legal decision-making.

Based on participants' responses to the MacCAT-CA interview, we found that competence-related abilities improve between the ages of 11 and 16. On average, youths aged 11 to 13 demonstrated significantly poorer understanding of trial matters, as well as poorer reasoning and recognition of the relevance of information for a legal defense, than did 14- and 15-year-olds, who in turn performed significantly more poorly than individuals aged 16 and older. There were no differences between the 16- and 17-year-olds and the young adults. The study produced similar results when adolescents and adults were categorized according to their scores above and below the cut-off scores indicating impairment. Nearly one-third of 11- to 13-year-olds and about one-fifth of 14- and 15-year-olds, but only 12 percent of individuals 16 and older evidenced impairment at a level comparable to mentally ill adults who had been found incompetent to stand trial with respect to either their ability to reason with facts or understand the trial process.

Not surprisingly, intelligence test scores (IQ) were also significantly related to responses in the interview, with low IQ youths in the younger age groups being particularly likely to show significant impairment. For example, among youths with an IQ from 60 to 74, 55 percent of 11- to 13-year-olds and 40 percent of 14- and 15-year-olds were significantly impaired. These results are especially important because a greater proportion of detained youths were in the lower IQ ranges (and thus are at greater risk for incompetence) compared with community youths, a finding consistent with much other research.[35] However, although intelligence was a significant factor in accounting for individual performance, the relation between age and performance was significant independent of intelligence. For example, while detained youths on average were much lower in IQ than the community youths, differences across age groups were apparent in both the detained and community samples. Individual performance did not differ significantly by gender, ethnicity, or, in the detained groups, as a function of the extent of individuals' prior justice system experience. This last finding is important, because it indicates that there are components of immaturity independent of a lack of relevant experience that may contribute to elevated rates of incompetence among juveniles.

The MacJEN interview was designed to probe how psychosocial influences affect decision-making by assessing participants' choices in three hypothetical legal situations involving a police interrogation, consultation with a defense attorney, and the evaluation of a proffered plea agreement.[36] Significant age differences were found in responses to police interrogation and to the plea agreement. First, youths, including 16- to 17-year-olds, were much more likely to recommend waiving constitutional rights during an interrogation than were adults, with 55 percent of 11- to 13-year-olds, 40 percent of 14- to 15-year-olds, and 30 percent of 16- to 17-year-olds choosing to "talk and admit" involvement in an alleged offense (rather than "remaining silent"), but only 15 percent of the young adults making this choice. (Defense attorneys uniformly would agree that admitting involvement in the crime, unless advised to do so by counsel, is almost always a choice that is not in the defendant's interest.) There were also significant age differences in response to the plea agreement. This vignette was styled so as not to clearly favor accepting or rejecting the state's offer, which probably accounted for the fact that young adults were evenly divided in their responses. In contrast, 75 percent of the 11- to 13-year-olds, 65 percent of the 14- to 15-year-olds, and 60 percent of the 16- to 17-year-olds recommended accepting the plea offer. Together, these results suggest a much stronger tendency for adolescents than for young adults to make choices in compliance with the perceived desires of authority figures.

Analysis of participants' responses to the vignettes also indicated differences between the youngest age group and older subjects in risk perception and future orientation. Participants were asked to explain their choices, including their perceptions about positive and negative consequences of various options; questions probed the subjects' assessment of the seriousness of risks (the perceived negative consequences) and the likelihood of risks materializing. Analyses indicated age differences on all of these dimensions of "risk perception," with the 11- to 13-year-olds less able to see risks than 16- to 17-year-olds and young adults. Similarly, fewer 11- to 13-year-olds mentioned the long-range consequences of their decisions than did older adolescents, suggesting differences in future orientation consistent with those we described in Chapter 2.

Our study's findings are consistent with those of earlier studies that examined various dimensions of youths' functioning in the justice system. For example, an important study of youths' and adults' capacities to understand Miranda rights in the early 1980s found that, compared with adults in the criminal justice system, 14-year-olds in juvenile detention were less able to understand the meaning and importance of *Miranda* warnings.[37] Other studies using smaller samples also have found age differences across the adolescent years with regard to knowledge of legal terms and the legal process in delinquency and criminal proceedings.[38] Finally, a series of studies found significant age differences across the adolescent years in "strategic thinking" about pleas; older adolescents were more likely than younger subjects to make choices that reflected calculations of probabilities and costs based on information provided.[39]

In light of what is known about psychological maturation in early and mid-adolescence, these findings and those of our adjudicative competence study are not surprising. Indeed, given the abilities required of defendants in criminal proceedings, it would be puzzling if youths and adults performed similarly on competence-related measures. This research provides powerful and tangible evidence that some youths facing criminal charges may function less capably as criminal defendants than do their adult counterparts. This does not mean, of course, that all youths should be automatically deemed incompetent to stand trial any more than would a psychiatric diagnosis or low IQ score. It does mean, however, that the risk of incompetence is substantially elevated in early and mid-adolescence; it also means that policy-makers and practitioners must address developmental incompetence.

The Uniqueness of Developmental Incompetence

The scientific evidence we have described presents a challenge to courts and legislatures—how to comply with the requirements of constitutional due process by ensuring that youths who are incompetent as a result of immaturity are not subject to adjudication in either criminal or juvenile court. A modest response would be to amend existing statutes to clarify that immaturity, as well as mental illness and retardation, can be the basis of a competence assessment and determination. Predictably, as developmental incompetence gains recognition, attorneys and judges will become attuned to discerning these incapacities in immature youths in the trial context and take steps to protect them. Courts applying the *Dusky* standard can then determine whether individual youths are competent and exclude those who are not until their competence is demonstrated, just as they would in the case of a defendant whose incompetence was due to mental illness or retardation.

A few jurisdictions appear to have adopted this approach,[40] but standing alone it may not be sufficient—in part because, without other adjustments, the disruptive impact on the justice system could be substantial. This is because developmental incompetence is different from mental illness and disability in two ways that create unique challenges.

First, the number of younger teenagers whose competence is questionable is likely to be quite large. A relatively small percentage of seriously impaired adult defendants are referred for competence evaluations, and an even smaller percent are found to be incompetent to stand trial. In contrast, our research indicates that the competence of a substantial percentage of teens under the age of sixteen may be uncertain under the legal standard applied to adults. This suggests that competence is potentially an issue for most youths in this age category who face criminal prosecution. The research also suggests that, under the *Dusky* standard, a substantial percentage of younger adolescents in *juvenile* court may be at risk for incompetence. The challenge is to handle this reality in a way that is consistent with due process without overwhelming the system with a flood of competence petitions—both in criminal court and juvenile court.

The second difference between immaturity-based impairments of competence and the traditional variations is that the standard disposition provided to incompetent adult defendants may not be appropriate or effective for many youths whose incompetence is due to immaturity. Adults who are found to be incompetent to stand trial are typically committed to mental health facilities for brief periods to be restored to competence through programs that include instruction (sometimes called "competence training") and psychotropic medication to alleviate psychotic symptoms.[41] This regimen is usually effective and most defendants are restored and returned to court in a few months. The Supreme Court held, in *Jackson v. Indiana,* that the state cannot hold incompetent defendants indefinitely trying to make them competent, because indeterminate long-term confinement of an individual not yet convicted of a crime violates constitutional due process.[42] In response, many states provide for a statutory period (often six months or a year) for restoration after which these defendants must be released and the charges dropped.[43]

This framework may be ill suited for dealing with developmental incompetence, however. Although some youths may become competent with instruction about the trial process, their attorney's role, and other matters necessary for adequate participation, others (particularly those who are deficient in reasoning ability) simply will not attain competence until they have time to mature psychologically. If this period of maturing extends into the future for a year or more, "waiting for maturity" becomes problematic on due process grounds under *Jackson*. Although child advocates (or defense attorneys) might be satisfied with the dismissal of charges against immature youths who cannot be made competent within a relatively brief period through instruction, this solution is unlikely to be acceptable to those who are concerned about public safety or about young offenders' accountability for criminal conduct.

Consider, for example, the case of a twelve-year-old who is charged with armed robbery and aggravated assault as a result of an incident in which he and his friends allegedly ran away with an elderly woman's purse after assaulting her with a tire iron. Because of his extreme immaturity, the youth does not understand the seriousness of the charges against him or the consequences of being convicted of these crimes, and it is highly unlikely that these deficits can be remedied in the near future. If the judge finds him to be incompetent to stand trial, neither long-term confinement nor dismissing the charges will be a satisfactory disposition. The former violates constitutional due process and the latter sacrifices public safety and allows him to escape responsibility.

The upshot is that simply revising statutes to add developmental immaturity as a source of incompetence is likely to impose an unacceptable burden on the courts and on society—both because of the large number of youths whose competence may be uncertain under *Dusky* and because attaining competence through maturation may be an unacceptably long process. Both criminal and (particularly) juvenile courts are likely to be flooded with petitions for competence evaluations, and large numbers of youths could be found incompetent, with no satisfactory disposition available for many of them. Under the heavy burden that this will impose on the justice system, the constitutional requirement of competence is likely to be given lip service without providing any substantial protection for immature youths.

The Case for Dual Competence Standards

What we propose in the pages that follow are doctrinal and institutional adjustments and policy reforms that respond to the challenge posed by developmental competence. Our aim is to suggest ways that the law can protect youths who are at risk for incompetence and whose developmental incapacity is not quickly correctable, while limiting the burden on the system.

First consider how the issue could be dealt with in criminal court. In this context, under *Dusky* every defendant must have a rational understanding of the proceedings and be able to provide meaningful assistance to his attorney. The research suggests that the risk of incompetence in these respects is elevated for youths under the age of sixteen and very high for those under age fourteen. Thus, competence is potentially a concern whenever juveniles under age sixteen face adjudication in criminal court—both those who are transferred and those who are charged directly as adults.

How can lawmakers respond to this concern? One possible legal response is to require an evaluation of competence for all youths below some minimum age; whether that age is sixteen or younger is a legislative judgment. A variation of this approach is the Virginia transfer statute requiring a finding of competence before a youth is transferred.[44] But the research on juvenile competence might also be relevant to a legislative judgment about the minimum age of adjudication in adult court. Many states have set this bar very low, usually without considering that many youths of the minimum age may not be competent. A legislature might well decide, in the interest of efficiency and fairness, to draw the jurisdictional line for criminal court eligibility at an age at which competence will not be an issue in every case. Thus, for example, if the minimum jurisdictional age were sixteen, as was true until the 1990s in many states, developmental incompetence would rarely be an issue. In states that set the minimum age at thirteen or fourteen, however, attorneys and judges should be alert to the possibility that younger teenagers may have impairments in competence due to developmental immaturity.

What should be the disposition for youths found incompetent to proceed in criminal court? Certainly, the first option is to provide remedial instruction to assist them to attain competence. But what about those juveniles who need more time to mature than the standard statutory period allows? Legislatures might sensibly conclude that the most appropriate disposition for these youths is adjudication in a juvenile delinquency proceeding. For example, consider our hypothetical twelve-year-old robber. If the criminal court judge decides that he is incompetent and cannot be made competent in the short term, both public protection and accountability argue in favor of juvenile court adjudication.

But how can a youth who is incompetent to stand trial in criminal court be competent to stand trial in a delinquency proceeding? Our proposed solution to the problem of dealing with these juveniles—adjudication in juvenile court—is possible only if criminal and juvenile courts apply dual standards of competence. What that means is that the judge in a delinquency proceeding applies a less demanding competence standard than the judge in a criminal proceeding, such that a youth found incompetent to stand trial as an adult under the *Dusky* standard might well be competent to face adjudication in juvenile court. Such a regime largely resolves the quandary faced by courts and lawmakers dealing with immature youths charged with serious crimes.

Although some child advocates will take issue with this proposal, the alternative of retaining a uniform competence standard for criminal and juvenile courts is unlikely to be satisfactory—to say the least. First, under a uniform standard, juveniles who are incompetent to be tried as adults (and cannot be made competent in a reasonable time) would also be unable to participate in delinquency proceedings. In effect, this means that some youths who are deemed the most dangerous by legislatures, judges, and prosecutors—those who are being charged as adults—could not be tried at all. Under a uniform standard, the robbery and assault charges against our hypothetical twelve-year-old likely would have to be dismissed. For a public concerned about safety and accountability, this outcome would be unacceptable.

Second, the use of dual competence standards is the best means to avoid what otherwise could be profound disruption of juvenile delinquency proceedings. Although few young teenagers are charged as adults, many face adjudication in juvenile court, an institution that was developed, after all, to respond to the criminal activity of immature youths. Our research suggests that the evenhanded application of adult competence criteria in juvenile and criminal courts may well result in the disqualification of a substantial percentage of youngsters from adjudication in *any* court. This outcome is jarring in light of uncontroversial premises of juvenile court jurisdiction. Many people oppose trying young juveniles in adult court, but few would argue that youngsters who have been charged with crimes should not be adjudicated at all. Thus, as a policy matter, a strong case can be made for a relaxed juvenile court competence standard under which immature youths found incompetent in criminal court could be tried in delinquency proceedings.

As a purely conceptual matter, the adoption of dual standards is quite feasible because competence, unlike many procedural protections, is a matter of degree. The legal boundary between competence and incompetence is located along a continuum by legal authorities on the basis of a mix of policy concerns. Thus, in theory, lawmakers could require a higher level of competence in criminal court than *Dusky* mandates—the capacity, for example, to independently make all key trial decisions.[45] That the Dusky standard is not more demanding reflects an implicit balancing of defendants' rights and interests against the public's interest in bringing criminals to justice. The upshot for our purposes is that the competence thresholds for delinquency and criminal proceedings can be fixed at different locations on the basis of different policy demands in the two legal settings.

Dual Standards under the Due Process Clause

The feasibility of adopting dual standards does not answer the critical legal question of whether the application of less demanding competence criteria in juvenile court delinquency proceedings satisfies the mandates of due process. Post-*Gault* courts have ruled consistently that youths in delinquency proceedings must be competent, but they have differed regarding the threshold for competence in this setting. Some courts have assumed that the *Dusky* standard should simply be incorporated into delinquency proceedings, while others have emphasized that juveniles should be assessed by "juvenile rather than adult norms."[46] These latter courts, while not elaborating on the meaning of "juvenile norms," have stressed that youths in delinquency proceedings cannot be expected to have the same level of comprehension as adults.[47] This approach amounts to an implicit recognition that the distinctive purposes of the juvenile court may warrant a less exacting standard, which, these courts assume, violates no constitutional norm. However, because a central feature of the legal framework that we endorse is a regime of dual standards, and because that feature is likely to be somewhat controversial, it is important to demonstrate that this approach satisfies the requirements of due process.[48]

The principle of fundamental fairness is the broad constitutional standard under which courts evaluate procedural challenges in both criminal and delinquency proceedings. Applying this standard, the Supreme Court has made clear that the U.S. Constitution does not require wholesale incorporation of adult procedural rights into delinquency hearings. The Court has held that some important safeguards in criminal proceedings, such as the right to a jury trial and the right to bail, would undermine the purposes of the juvenile justice system and that they are not essential to due process in this setting.[49]

The Court has offered no test to guide the determination of whether a contested procedural protection is required by fundamental fairness. However, several themes can be extracted from its examination of due process claims in delinquency proceedings. First, the Court has emphasized that a procedural safeguard that is likely to be "disruptive of the unique nature of the juvenile process" may not be required in juvenile court.[50] This deference rests on the assumption that a delinquency proceeding is different from a criminal trial in ways that serve the interests of youths facing charges in juvenile court.[51] This qualifying condition leads us to conclude that a second consideration is important in analyzing whether a particular procedural protection is required: A relaxed juvenile court competence standard is constitutionally sufficient only if delinquency proceedings differ substantially from criminal trials in their aims and punishment stakes. Finally, the Court has focused on whether a contested procedural safeguard is important for accurate fact-finding.[52] Based on this concern, we conclude that a relaxed juvenile court competence standard must generally satisfy the purposes of the competence requirement as applied in this setting.

As to the first consideration, the earlier discussion makes clear that the imposition of the adult competence standard is likely to seriously disrupt delinquency proceedings and burden the administration of justice in this context. A relaxed standard will deter a flood of petitions for competence evaluations and hearings that would divert financial and human resources to a process that most would agree should have limited importance in juvenile court. Moreover, as we have explained, if many younger defendants are found incompetent under the adult standard, government efforts to protect the public from youth crime, to hold young offenders accountable, and to provide them with rehabilitative services will be undermined. A doctrinal regime under which many younger teenagers—particularly those charged with serious crimes—might be immune from prosecution probably would be rejected as unacceptable and ultimately would undermine the legitimacy of the juvenile court. A tailored juvenile court competence standard can function to exclude only the very small number of youths whose extreme immaturity makes even juvenile court adjudication inappropriate.

Despite the potentially disruptive impact of a uniform competence standard, dual standards are constitutionally acceptable only if delinquency proceedings differ substantially from criminal trials in ways that reduce the need for the level of procedural protection afforded defendants in criminal court. The interests of defendants facing criminal punishment justify the existing competence requirement and serve as a baseline for evaluating the interests of juveniles in delinquency proceedings. In other contexts, the Court has made clear that the state's purposes in restricting liberty and the impact on affected individuals are key to evaluating the requirements of procedural due process. For example, in *Addington v. Texas,* the Court held that where the state's purpose in confining an individual is not punishment but treatment for mental illness, the procedural requirements of criminal proceedings can be relaxed.[53]

On our view, a relaxed competence standard satisfies constitutional due process only if delinquency proceedings are distinguished from criminal trials in two important ways. First, the punishment a youth receives in a delinquency proceeding must be significantly less severe than the sentence that an adult counterpart would receive. If youths in delinquency proceedings do not face the same jeopardy that criminal defendants face, they may not need the same procedural protections. Traditionally, juvenile dispositions have been shorter in duration than criminal sentences and have not extended into adulthood or directly affected adult status or opportunities. Only if these conditions hold is a relaxed competence standard appropriate.

Second, a relaxed standard may be justified if the purposes of the juvenile proceeding are broader than that of a criminal trial. Both criminal and juvenile proceedings aim to punish offenders, deter crime, and protect the public. However, the juvenile system, traditionally at least, also has been committed to treatment and to offering dispositions that enhance the likelihood that delinquent youths will become productive adults. The Supreme Court has emphasized this distinction in declining to require some procedural protections in delinquency proceedings, and it is important in the justification of a relaxed competence standard.

In sum, whether a juvenile court proceeding is sufficiently different from a criminal trial to justify relaxing the constitutionally required competence standard depends in part on institutional features of the juvenile justice system. If youths facing adjudication in juvenile court are subject to dispositions that are more lenient than criminal punishment and that are aimed in part at promoting their welfare, then the stakes they face are lower than, and different from, those facing criminal defendants. Under these conditions, the need for adult procedural safeguards to protect their interests is less compelling, and a relaxed competence standard may be justified. On the other hand, to the extent that juvenile proceedings and criminal trials are alike in their consequences and purposes, then accused youths should receive the same protections as criminal defendants.

What Competence Criteria Should Be Applied
in Juvenile Court?

Assuming (for now) that the institutional preconditions noted above are met, we have suggested that a relaxed competence standard must also satisfy the underlying purposes of the criminal competence requirement: the promotion of dignity, accuracy, and defendant participation. What exactly should this standard be, and how would it differ from the adult *Dusky* standard? Richard Bonnie and Thomas Grisso have proposed a sensible and workable juvenile court competence standard under which the accused youth must have a basic understanding of the charges, the proceeding, and the roles of the principal participants—including his own role as a defendant—and the capacity to communicate with his attorney.[54] This standard satisfies the purposes of the competence requirement. At the same time it is one that most youths facing delinquency charges will be capable of meeting, including those who are incompetent under *Dusky*.

A bit more elaboration on the operation of the proposed juvenile standard may be useful. A youth faced with a serious delinquency charge must understand why he faces a deprivation of liberty and the possible extent of that confinement. But, because the consequences are less far-reaching than those of a criminal proceeding, a lesser ability to foresee remote consequences would be sufficient. The youth must also understand that his attorney is to advocate for him, that the prosecutor aims to convict and punish him, and that the judge will decide whether he committed the crime based on the evidence. But he need not understand how advocacy is translated into practice in a way that would be required of an adult, and he may play a more passive role in relation to his attorney in planning his defense. The juvenile need not have the ability to weigh the value of defense strategies or to advise counsel accordingly. But he must have the capacity to provide his attorney with an account of relevant events and to answer questions so that the attorney can plan and execute a defense. He must also be able to understand information provided by his attorney and evidence offered by witnesses. In delinquency proceedings, attorneys will often have an additional burden of explanation and solicitation of assent in planning a defense. It seems likely, however, that in practice attorneys already play this role with younger clients, whose questionable competence heretofore has not been expressly acknowledged.

This relaxed standard satisfies the purposes of the competence requirement sufficiently to protect the interests of youths in delinquency proceedings—assuming the preconditions of lesser sanctions and a commitment to youth welfare are met. The dignity and integrity of the proceedings are preserved if youths are not confused about the jeopardy they face or bewildered at the purpose and nature of the proceedings. Accuracy is satisfied if a young client can describe relevant events to her attorney and understand evidence offered in the proceedings; this communicative role also satisfies the purpose of promoting participation by the youthful client. Finally, the youth's autonomy-based right to participate in the proceeding is satisfied if he comprehends the charges and the hearing's purposes, can follow—at least in a rudimentary way—the evidence presented by witnesses, and can communicate with his attorney.

Many attorneys and judges are unsophisticated about developmental psychology and would benefit from guidelines for evaluating and enhancing the capacities of immature youths to participate in delinquency proceedings.[55] Such guidelines might include advice, grounded in an understanding of normative psychological development, on interviewing young clients and explaining trial-related concepts, as well as measures for evaluating the comprehension of young defendants. If attorneys take seriously the goals of promoting their young clients' meaningful participation, most youths should be capable of participating in delinquency proceedings with sufficient competence to satisfy due process requirements and principles of fundamental fairness.

Dealing with Incompetent Youths in Delinquency Proceedings

Even under a relaxed standard, some youths will not be competent to face adjudication in a delinquency proceeding. This number is likely to be very small, particularly in jurisdictions that adopt a *minimum* age of eligibility for adjudication in delinquency proceedings, as we recommend in Chapter 8.[56] Of the eligible youths who lack competence in delinquency proceedings, some can acquire the requisite understanding through age-appropriate instruction—a variation of the "competence training" described earlier. However, immature youths who do not respond sufficiently to instruction or cannot learn to communicate with their attorneys in a reasonable time period cannot be adjudicated fairly.

Although no single dispositional response will deal with every youth in this category, several options are available that together will resolve most cases adequately. Under the conventional child welfare authority of the state, interventions are appropriate when children exhibit problem behaviors that interfere with their healthy development and that their parents do not remedy.[57] Thus, mental health, social service, and educational dispositions are likely appropriate for most of these youths. For some youths, mental illness may be a contributing factor to incompetence or to the delinquent conduct; they may be candidates for mental health interventions, including admission to inpatient facilities. Others may become involved in criminal activity due to inadequate supervision or guidance from their parents. In these situations, intervention by social service agencies may be appropriate to provide services to the family to correct problems that have contributed to the child's delinquent behavior. If parents cannot provide adequate care and oversight, removal of the child from the family and placement in foster care sometimes may be necessary. Educational programs may also be indicated, including, in some cases, individualized programs mandated under federal law for students with disabilities.[58] Finally, in the rare case, dismissal of the charges with no other action will be the right response. The lesson is that dealing with this small category of incompetent youths creates little threat of a systemic crisis, in sharp contrast to the potential disruption of both juvenile and criminal proceedings that is likely to occur if a uniform standard is applied.

Juvenile Dispositions under a Constitutionally Adequate Regime

We have argued that dual standards will satisfy the demands of due process if dispositions in delinquency proceedings are less punitive than criminal sentences and have broader purposes that include promoting the welfare of young offenders. These conditions may pose a challenge for lawmakers today, created by the recent trend toward harsher juvenile justice sanctions. The recent reforms, by raising the punishment stakes in delinquency proceedings and by emphasizing retribution over rehabilitation, undermine the justification for relaxed procedural safeguards. Let's examine the implementation of these requirements in the context of contemporary juvenile justice policies.

First, youths who do not meet adult competence standards cannot be subject to sanctions that approximate adult punishment or carry consequences into adulthood. This would include blended sentences, sex offender registration, and the use of juvenile records in adult sentencing, including sentencing under three strikes laws.[59] Moreover, to justify a relaxed competence standard, the juvenile court dispositions imposed on these youths should be briefer in duration than adult sentences. Because youths of questionable competence are likely to be younger teenagers, even dispositions within juvenile court jurisdictional boundaries could approximate adult sentences in duration. If so, the jeopardy facing youths in delinquency proceedings would be similar to that of adult defendants, and the justification for a relaxed competence standard would not hold.

A relaxed competence standard can be justified more readily if the system's goals transparently include the promotion of youth welfare, through correctional programs that are tailored to juveniles' distinctive needs. A key purpose of programs in the juvenile setting is to prepare youths for productive, noncriminal adult lives and not simply to punish and incapacitate them as lawbreakers. A programmatic focus emphasizing education, job training, and the acquisition of life skills, together with investment in clinical and family support networks aimed at facilitating the transition to life outside of the correctional system, define the distinctive purposes of the juvenile system in ways that support a relaxed competence standard.[60]

In executing the constitutional mandate of more lenient dispositions and distinct programmatic goals, jurisdictions committed to punitive policies may opt for a "limited" response, under which only those youths who fail to meet the adult competence standard are insulated from punitive sanctions and offered educational and skill-building programs in the juvenile system. This response will require the separation of youths who meet the *Dusky* standard from those who do not for the purpose of determining dispositions. Under this approach, the juvenile justice system effectively would become a two-tier institution, within which dual competence standards are applied and youths are assigned to different dispositional regimes in part on the basis of their developmental competence. Although assignment might be based presumptively on age, juvenile court competence hearings likely would become commonplace, as attorneys would be obliged to raise the issue in questionable cases. This would result in considerable administrative costs.

An alternative approach is to undertake broader reforms of the juvenile system. The constitutional challenge to adjudicate only competent defendants will not in itself lead lawmakers to undo punitive policies or embrace major changes that alter the character of the modern juvenile system. However, as the mandate of trial competence gains attention in policy debates, those who have reservations about the recent legal trend on the basis of its general unfairness or its social cost may well conclude that this challenge is yet another reason to re-evaluate the wisdom of punitive policies and to reassess the purposes and programs of the juvenile justice system.

Together, Chapters 5 and 6 clarify that contemporary youth crime policy undermines essential commitments of the criminal law and criminal justice policy. In Chapter 5, we saw that adult punishment of juveniles threatens proportionality, a principle embedded in the criminal law that is at the heart of a fair justice system. Chapter 6 shows that the adjudication of immature youths in criminal proceedings may violate the principle of due process and that the recent legal trend toward criminal prosecution and punishment of juveniles has unintentionally created a procedural challenge of constitutional proportion. Substantive and procedural fairness are important to the legitimacy and stability of any system of state-sponsored punishment, and neither has received adequate attention in the reforms of juvenile justice policy over the past generation.

CHAPTER 7

Social Welfare and
Juvenile Crime Regulation

Timothy Kane, a fourteen-year-old Florida boy, was playing video games with some friends on Super Bowl Sunday in 1992, when a couple of older youths suggested that they all break into a neighbor's house. Tim later reported that he went along because he did not want to stay behind alone—and he did not want to be called a "fraidy-cat." Upon entering the house, the boys were surprised to find the elderly neighbor, Madeline Weisser, and her fifty-five-year-old son, John Bolton, at home. While Tim hid under the dining table, Alvin Morton, age nineteen, shot and killed Mr. Bolton and, with the help of seventeen-year-old Bobby Gamer, stabbed and killed (and almost decapitated) Ms. Weisser. Tim was tried as an adult and convicted of felony murder for his role in the crime. He received a life sentence with a possibility of parole in twenty-five years, a sentence he is currently serving in a Florida prison.[1]

In Chapter 5 we examined youth crime policy through the lens of criminal law proportionality analysis and concluded that young offenders deserve less punishment for their criminal acts than their adult counterparts and that mitigation should be the hallmark of fair juvenile justice regulation. On that basis, Tim's life sentence was excessive punishment for a fourteen-year-old whose psychosocial immaturity appears to have led to his involvement in the crime—and who did not participate in the killing itself. In truth, however, whatever supporters of punitive policies might think of Tim's case, they will probably not be persuaded by the general argument for mitigation; fairness alone is not likely to carry the day in determining the shape of youth crime policy. For supporters of the recent reform trend, the most pressing concern in responding to juvenile crime is to protect the public from dangerous young criminals. This then is a consequentialist justification for policies under which more youths are dealt with in the adult system and offenders in the juvenile system are incarcerated for longer periods of time. Advocates argue that society's interests are promoted by tough incarceration policies because these measures will reduce juvenile crime. Less crime means fewer potential victims, more citizens who can walk the streets without fear, and, ultimately, lower expenditures on law enforcement and prisons.

The claim that tough policies will reduce crime is critical to the social welfare justification for more punitive sanctions. Although the argument seems straightforward, it turns out to be hard to evaluate. For example, juvenile crime has declined over the past decade, but the causes are complex and the impact of the recent legal changes on this trend is unclear. As we will see, studies that have examined the impact of punitive policies on youth crime report mixed results, offering little solid support for the claim that declining crime rates are due to the enactment of harsher laws.

Evaluating whether the recent reforms promote social welfare also requires consideration of other factors. First are the direct budgetary impacts of tough laws, which are substantial, as legislatures and government agencies are beginning to recognize.[2] Resources spent on building and staffing correctional facilities needed to incarcerate more juveniles for longer periods are not available for other social uses. Second, even assuming that tough sanctions can reduce juvenile crime, at some point the additional dollars expended may not offer enough benefit to be justified. Economists explain that while some amount of incarceration yields substantial benefits in terms of decreased crime, those benefits decrease (that is, fewer crimes are avoided) for each unit of increased incarceration.[3] Third, if less costly correctional dispositions are effective at reducing recidivism in some juvenile offenders, incarcerating those youths may not be justified on utilitarian grounds. Finally, included in the calculus are the intangible effects of dispositional interventions and facilities on the future welfare of young offenders. Correctional policies and programs that either reduce or enhance the likelihood that youths who come into the justice system will lead satisfying lives impact social welfare.

In this chapter we examine empirical evidence that can inform our thinking about how to design crime policies that best promote social welfare. This evidence is varied; it includes studies of the economic costs of various sanctions, the deterrent effects of statutory change, recidivism rates in the adult and juvenile systems, and the effectiveness of different kinds of programs. No single body of research provides a clear answer to our question, but the complex empirical account that emerges indicates that broad use of adult sanctions with juveniles does not promote social welfare and that a mitigation-based approach is justified on pragmatic as well as retributive grounds. The research, on our view, supports that adult punishment and longer incarceration in the juvenile system have contributed somewhat to a reduction in juvenile crime, largely through incapacitation. But the costs are high and the benefits likely are limited to a far smaller group of young offenders than are subject to harsh penalties under current law.[4] Moreover, extensive research indicates that less costly sanctions in the juvenile system, including community-based programs, are effective at reducing recidivism.[5]

Our social welfare analysis is informed by the scientific account of adolescence and youth crime described in earlier chapters. An important lesson of the research described in Chapter 2 is that most young lawbreakers are normative adolescent offenders whose criminal activities are linked to developmental forces and who can be expected to "mature out" of their antisocial tendencies. There is no reason to assume that these youths are headed for a career in crime unless correctional interventions inadvertently push them in that direction. The research also shows that social context is critically important to the successful completion of developmental tasks that are essential to the transition to conventional adult roles associated with desistance from crime. For young offenders, correctional programs shape that social context and can enhance or inhibit psychosocial maturation.

Today, many teens without prior records are swept into the adult criminal justice system, by any account a harsh developmental environment. Even in the juvenile systems in many states, young offenders are incarcerated for long periods in prison-like facilities. Developmental knowledge reinforces the conclusion that, as applied to normative teenagers, the claimed social benefits of harsh punishment are inflated and some of the costs are ignored or undervalued. Even if fairness to young offenders were deemed unimportant and the only consideration in formulating juvenile justice policy were to promote society's interest, the enthusiasm for imposing harsh sanctions on young offenders is misguided.

Youths behind Bars: The Expanding Net

Before we examine the costs and benefits of the recent legal reforms, we should take a closer look at the implementation of the new laws. How have they changed the way juveniles are actually being processed and punished? As a result of the reforms, a large number of youths who previously would have been under the exclusive jurisdiction of the juvenile court are potentially subject to processing and punishment as adults. This does not mean, however, that all or even most youths who *could* be subject to criminal prosecution today are tried and punished as adults. In some states, the tough reforms seem to have had surprisingly little effect on the adjudication and disposition of young criminals. For example, emerging evidence suggests that California's Proposition 21 (discussed in Chapter 4) has had a more modest impact on prosecutorial and judicial practices than was predicted by either supporters or opponents.[6] In many states, however, the impact of tougher laws has been substantial. In the 1990s and beyond, many states categorically lowered the age of criminal court jurisdiction for a broad range of serious crimes, and a few states lowered the general jurisdictional age from eighteen to seventeen or sixteen. Even as the reform trend has slowed generally, Rhode Island for a brief period in 2007 lowered the general jurisdictional age for criminal court jurisdiction from eighteen to seventeen. In this way, groups of juveniles have been reclassified categorically as adults for purposes of criminal prosecution.[7]

More information is available about youths who are tried as adults as a result of discretionary judicial transfer than about those who are subject to criminal prosecution under legislative waiver or automatic transfer statutes. The number of youths transferred by judges fell from a high of 12,000 in 1996 to about 7,000 in 2002, the most recent year for which we have figures.[8] The percentage of transfer cases involving violent offenses against persons was slightly higher than that for property and drug offenses.[9] A large proportion of transferred teens are sixteen or seventeen years old; judges are less likely to transfer youths aged fifteen or younger, although the number of youths under age fifteen who were transferred doubled between 1985 and 2002.[10] African American juveniles are far more likely to be waived to adult court than their white counterparts. Statistics from the 1990s indicate that more than 60 percent of transferred youths were convicted of their offenses and, of those convicted, about 70 percent were incarcerated in prison or jail.

It is clear that a far larger number of youths under the age of eighteen are prosecuted and punished as adults under legislative waiver statutes (or automatic transfer) than are transferred by judges, but we lack good statistics on how many youths are subject to criminal court jurisdiction under these statutes.[11] Thirty-eight states mandate adult criminal prosecution for some categories of young defendants under the age of eighteen (based on the offense charged), and about a dozen set the age of general jurisdiction for adult criminal prosecution at age sixteen or seventeen. [12] According to recent estimates, each year about 250,000 teenagers, mostly sixteen- and seventeen-year-olds, are automatically subject to criminal prosecution and punishment under legislative waiver statutes or because juvenile court jurisdiction ends before age eighteen.[13]

Youths who are convicted in criminal court are more likely to be incarcerated for their offenses, and, according to recent studies, are confined for substantially longer periods on average than those who are sentenced in juvenile court.[14] Much of the best empirical data on these issues (and generally on the impact of juvenile justice policies and practices) comes from the Washington State Institute for Public Policy, a research institute funded by the state legislature.[15] In one study, these researchers compared average minimum sentence lengths before and after the 1994 enactment of a Washington statute automatically transferring to adult court sixteen- and seventeen-year-old youths charged with certain violent crimes that previously had been subject to discretionary judicial transfer. The researchers found sentences to be 50 percent longer for crimes that met the automatic transfer criteria under the new law than under the judicial waiver regime, when fewer than 25 percent of youths charged with these crimes were tried as adults.[16] Fifteen percent of youths automatically transferred to adult court received sentences of five years or more, whereas no youths retained in juvenile court before 1994 received such sentences.[17] Because jurisdiction in the juvenile correctional system in most states ends by age twenty-one or earlier, some youths who are prosecuted as adults receive sentences many times as long as the maximum period of confinement in a juvenile facility. Recall Tim Kane, for example, the Florida boy who is serving a life sentence for felony murder; he would have been released after a few years (at most) from the juvenile system.

That is not to say that young offenders today are subject to lenient treatment in the juvenile system; delinquency dispositions have also become harsher under the recent legal reforms. Youths are more likely to be confined in secure juvenile facilities and for longer periods than a generation ago. According to another Washington study, confinement rates in that state's juvenile system increased by 40 percent during the 1990s—during a period when serious crime rates fell by 50 percent. In the late 1980s out of every 1,000 youths in Washington, 2.5 youths were confined in juvenile facilities; a decade later the confinement rate had increased to 3.5 youths per 1,000.[18]

The best available evidence indicates that the punitive reforms have resulted in substantial increases in the incarceration of juveniles, both in the adult criminal justice system and in the juvenile system. In an era in which juvenile crime rates have declined, more young lawbreakers are subject to incarceration and for longer periods, due to the combination of legislative waiver laws and tougher sanctions in the juvenile system.

The Economic Costs of the Punitive Reforms

The debate about the merits of the punitive reforms has focused primarily on whether tough sanctions reduce juvenile crime and, to a lesser extent, on their impact on young offenders. Interestingly, until recently, the economic costs associated with the increased use of incarceration of juveniles received relatively little attention in policy debates.[19] Economic expenditures are the most concrete costs of the policies we are examining, and much evidence supports that the impact on state budgets of the recent justice reforms has been substantial. The headline is that although juvenile crime has declined significantly since the early 1990s, the costs of responding to youthful criminal activity have risen substantially. According to a careful analysis of the costs and benefits associated with one state's policies responding to juvenile crime, serious juvenile crime declined by 50 percent between 1994 and 2001, while expenditures in the juvenile justice system over that same time period increased by 43 percent.[20]

This increase in spending is due largely to the expanded use of incarceration as the preferred (or required) sanction for young offenders. Longer sentences in both the juvenile and criminal systems and the use of incarceration in place of community sanctions add up to higher justice system costs. The cost of incarcerating a youth for a year in the juvenile system varies in different states, depending on labor costs and the quality and kinds of programs provided. The annual cost per youth ranges from $100,000 in California, to $40,000 or less in some other states.[21] A year of imprisonment in the adult system is less expensive than a year of incarceration in the juvenile system, in part because prisons are less likely to provide educational and counseling services and have a higher ratio of inmates to staff. Cost estimates per prisoner in adult facilities range from $25,000 to $40,000 per year.[22] But because criminal sentences generally are longer than juvenile dispositions, they often are costlier.[23] Tim Kane, for example, will cost Florida taxpayers at least $30,000 a year for twenty-five years or more in prison (assuming *no* Cost increases)—or a minimum of $750,000—for his participation in the break-in that resulted in his neighbors' deaths. Even if Florida spends twice as much per year on incarcerated juveniles as it spends on adult prisoners, the cost to taxpayers would have been a fraction of this amount if he had been adjudicated in juvenile court and sent to a juvenile facility for a few years.

The lower cost of incarceration in prisons than in juvenile facilities led one state, Rhode Island, to lower its jurisdictional age for criminal adjudication recently so that all seventeen-year-olds would be dealt with in the adult system.[24] Within months, however, the legislature reversed itself, recognizing somewhat belatedly that in the long term, this move would not reduce the cost of crime. This is so, in part, as we have seen, because sentences in the adult system are longer than juvenile dispositions. Rhode Island legislators also had overlooked the fact that the cost of housing a juvenile in an adult facility within the "Supermax" section of the prison (which was necessary to protect their safety) was more than twice that of housing an adult in the same institution ($100,000 versus $40,000). Moreover, as we will see shortly, some factors that lower the cost of confining adult prisoners—larger size, higher prisoner\staff ratio, and fewer educational and counseling programs—also contribute to making prisons aversive social contexts for adolescents that likely contribute to recidivism and inhibit the transition to normative adulthood. The additional costs expended on juvenile facilities contribute to making them superior developmental environments. Thus, putting juveniles who would otherwise be confined in the juvenile system into adult facilities may reap some transitory savings, but, as Rhode Island recognized, these are likely to be outweighed by the long-term costs.

The recent reforms have also generated increased procedural costs. In the juvenile system, many cases that would have been dealt with informally twenty years ago are subject to formal adjudication in juvenile court today.[25] Increased costs also are associated with prosecution and adjudication in criminal court. The procedural protections afforded defendants and the time expended by judges, attorneys, jurors and law enforcement agents combine to make criminal trials very expensive. Even when convictions are based on plea agreements, the costs are far greater than are those of delinquency proceedings, which, even in the post-*Gault* era, tend to be more informal, briefer, and simpler.

Is social welfare enhanced by the increased government expenditures on youth crime regulation? The opportunity costs of tougher laws may be substantial. The costs of juvenile justice administration will be paid either through higher taxes or by shifting funds from other programs. Because governors and legislatures are often reluctant to raise taxes, they may cut allocations for public schools or social programs so that adequate funds are available for incarcerating juveniles.[26] We do not attempt to evaluate these trade-offs but instead examine two questions that must be answered affirmatively if the public expenditures on juvenile crime are to be justified from the perspective of social welfare: First, are the economic costs of incarceration policies (together with other indirect costs that we will explore shortly) offset by greater public benefits in terms of reduced crime? And second, are these policies more effective at accomplishing this goal than alternative, less costly policies?

Do Harsh Sanctions Reduce Juvenile Crime?

Several kinds of benefits may follow if youth crime policies based on expansive use of incarceration are effective in accomplishing the goal of reducing youth crime. First, economists undertaking cost-benefit evaluations of crime policies include the benefit to potential victims of crimes that are not committed. Fewer crimes will reduce these costs, including (depending on the crime) lost possessions, physical pain, psychological distress, lost productivity, medical expenses, and lost lives. Second, a reduction in crime enhances the well-being of citizens generally. It seems likely that people attach a monetary value to feeling safe as they go about their lives—for example, they may be willing to pay more for housing in safe neighborhoods than in otherwise comparable high-crime neighborhoods. Third, desistance from a life of crime (or never getting involved in criminal activity in the first place) offers intangible value to youths in terms of their future well-being and productivity. Put differently, teenagers who are deterred from involvement in crime (or from re-offending) may experience benefits from lives that are more likely to include educational achievement, stable employment, and rewarding intimate relationships than are the lives of young criminals.[27] Finally, state expenditures on the operation of the justice system should decline if crime is reduced (at least, if the system is administered rationally), including not only the costs of operating correctional facilities and programs but also the costs of law enforcement and criminal proceedings.

Thus a critical question is whether harsh sanctions represent an effective means of reducing crime, as proponents argue. To try to answer that question, we turn first to the "theory" underlying the punitive reforms—why proponents think tough policies will reduce crime. We then look at the evidence regarding whether the claims have merit.

Harsh Policies and Crime Reduction—The Case in Theory

Consequentialist justifications for imposing harsh sentences on juveniles focus on the goal of preventing future crime rather than on fair punishment for the past criminal act.[28] As first-year law students learn in their Criminal Law class, several preventive rationales are offered to justify criminal punishment. First, the threat of harsh sanctions may deter future crime generally by discouraging youths from ever getting involved in criminal activity.[29] Moreover, policies that emphasize incarceration also could serve a specific deterrence function, influencing juveniles not to re-offend. Here the idea is that the experience of being in prison is sufficiently unpleasant that youths will be motivated to stay out of trouble once they are released. Second, imprisonment prevents crime by incapacitating offenders. Young criminals who are locked up cannot be out on the streets committing crimes, a point that is particularly salient as applied to high-risk youths. Third, imprisonment could reduce future crime by rehabilitating young offenders so that they will mend their criminal ways—although, in truth, recent reformers have not emphasized rehabilitation.

Preventive rationales for criminal punishment need not be excessively punitive. Many modern theorists accept that deterrence is the primary justification for punishing criminals, but they may disagree about what *level* of punishment is appropriate on grounds of cost-effectiveness or compatibility with other values. For example, some legal theorists hold that prevention of crime is a legitimate justification for criminal punishment but argue that the appropriate amount of punishment is limited by the retributive principle of proportionality.[30] Politicians in the 1980s and 1990s, however, often seemed unconcerned with fairness constraints, arguing that harsh punishment of juveniles was necessary to contain the epidemic of youth crime.

The Traditional Regime and the Failure to Prevent Crime

This epidemic, according to supporters of the reforms, was caused largely by the lax response of traditional juvenile courts to youth crime, a response that, as we reported in Chapter 4, failed utterly to deter crime, or to incapacitate or rehabilitate young criminals. Critics viewed the juvenile court as a revolving door; the typical young offender received a slap on the wrist and was soon out on the street again engaging in criminal activity—until he got caught and returned to court—and on and on. Youths effectively were invited to engage in criminal activities by a regime that employed (virtually) unsupervised community probation as the standard sanction. A delinquency charge and adjudication carried no deterrent threat because youths knew that no serious consequences would follow.[31]

As we have suggested, the perception that juvenile court judges were unduly lenient was due as much to the naive rhetoric that surrounded the traditional regime as it was to the reality of the juvenile justice system. In fact, many youths who committed serious crimes were confined in secure correctional facilities. However, there is some merit to the critics' challenge that the system failed to deter youths from engaging in criminal activity. Much anecdotal evidence indicates that young criminals of a generation ago assumed that they were insulated from punishment by virtue of their status as juveniles, and this may have encouraged some to engage (or persist) in delinquent activities. Police officers reported that they were taunted during arrests by youths calling "I'm a juvie," as though this meant they had a free pass to engage in criminal activity. "Adult" members of criminal gangs frequently assigned to juveniles tasks that might result in arrest. Even Chris Simmons, whose death sentence the Supreme Court overturned in 2005, was reported to believe that as a juvenile he would be treated leniently.[32] Thus, it is hard to deny that the traditional juvenile system failed not only in its avowed mission of rehabilitation, but also in deterring crime and incapacitating young criminals.

Another factor reinforced the claim that legal reforms were necessary to protect the public from young criminals. In the 1990s, some observers predicted that, unless tough policies were enacted, the country would face an even larger wave of violent youth crime in the first decade of the twenty-first century as a sizeable cohort of children born in the early 1990s (the second baby boom) became teenagers. Several criminologists promoted this view, warning politicians and the public of a "coming generation of super-predators," youths without moral sensibilities who would roam the streets in gangs and terrorize the public with their violent, senseless rampages.[33] Thus, the policy goal of crime prevention took on an unprecedented urgency in the face of this putative overwhelming threat.

Do Lower Crime Rates Show that Harsh Policies Are Effective?

As evidence that the recent reforms have succeeded in achieving their crime-reduction goal, supporters point to the fact that juvenile crime has declined substantially since the early 1990s. On this account, youths who might be inclined to engage in criminal activity have been deterred because they now realize that real consequences will follow. Moreover, those juveniles who did not get the message are locked up (and presumably will learn from the experience to stay out of trouble in the future). So, to what extent does the decline in criminal activity among juveniles indicate that the reform policies are working?

Although crime rates should fall if tough sanctions in fact deter crime, criminologists who study both adult and juvenile crime emphasize that we cannot assume that changes in crime rates are caused by changes in penal policy affecting the harshness of punishment. Historical reviews indicate that crime rates fluctuate over time and that many factors contribute to the variations. Criminologists agree that crime rates fell (from extraordinarily high rates) for much of the nineteenth century and began to rise again in the mid-twentieth century. There is no agreement, however, about what explains this trend.[34] Changing crime rates may be influenced by demographic factors; some experts have suggested that crime rates are correlated with the percentage of teenagers and young men in the population at a given time.[35] Others point to cultural and religious influences. James Q. Wilson and Richard Herrnstein, for example, have argued that declining crime rates in the nineteenth century resulted from the period's religious revivalism and moral awakening that affected patterns of socialization of children in families, schools, and communities.[36] As mentioned earlier, some criminologists attribute the sharp rise in teenage homicide in the late 1980s to the easy availability of cheap guns.[37] (The crack epidemic is thought to be another contributing factor). Why were teenagers able to get firearms so easily? The explanation may lie partly in developments in technology and marketing and partly in the successful lobbying efforts of the National Rifle Association.

Crime rates are statistically complex; during any period, many factors can influence individual decisions to get involved in criminal activity that in the aggregate constitute crime rates. Changes in justice policies might be important, but assertions that declining juvenile crime rates demonstrate that punitive policies have been effective are naive—particularly in light of the fact that crime rates began to decline in many states before the legal reforms were enacted.

Does Deterrence Work? Evidence from the Research

Although broad claims about the causes of fluctuations in crime rates are speculative, social scientists have produced a large body of research (mostly focusing on adults) that probes the deterrent effects of criminal sanctions. Perceptual deterrence studies (based on self-report) provide the most direct evidence of the impact of anticipated punishment on individuals' decisions not to engage in criminal activity, but their reliability is uncertain and findings are mixed. Moreover, the extent to which expressed intentions predict behavior is unclear.[38] Other researchers focus on more indirect evidence, seeking to link changes in crime rates to particular statutory enactments or changes in law enforcement practices while controlling, to the extent possible, for other factors that influence crime rates.[39] These studies either examine crime rates immediately before and after a policy reform or compare crime rates in states that have adopted enhanced penalties with others that have not.

Experts on deterrence agree that simply having a system of law enforcement and criminal punishment has a general deterrent effect on crime—there would be a lot more crime if there were no criminal justice system.[40] However, as Daniel Nagin, a leading expert on deterrence research, has emphasized, getting useful information about the marginal deterrent impact of particular policy changes is an uncertain business.[41] Studies of the effectiveness of specific policies on criminal behavior have produced varied findings. For example, studies of three-strikes laws have found a crime-reduction effect in some states, but not in others, and some studies have found that criminal activity actually increased following the enactment of the enhanced penalties.[42] Some researchers have found an initial deterrent effect of new policies (such as drunk driving laws) that erodes over time.[43]

One explanation for the varied and inconsistent research findings is that many factors contribute to effective deterrence besides the severity of sanctions. Certainty of apprehension and punishment appears to be far more important to deterrence than severity of sanction; potential offenders who fear they will get caught are more likely to be deterred than those who think they will not.[44] If law enforcement is ineffective or harsh sentences under the new laws are imposed infrequently or unpredictably, potential offenders may view the risk of arrest and punishment as low, and enhanced penalties will have little deterrent impact. Of course, would-be criminals must also be aware of the increased sanctions in some general way for deterrence to work. Further, the punishment must represent a substantial threat to the individual, in terms of both loss of liberty and social stigma. If many associates are subject to the new sanctions, their deterrent effect may be diluted.[45] Finally, the added cost to the actor represented by the threat of punishment (along with other costs) must outweigh the anticipated gains of the crime. Ultimately, deterrence theory presumes a rational decision-maker who weighs the expected benefits of criminal activity against the risk and perceived consequences of apprehension and punishment. Conditions affecting this calculus may vary in different localities and among different groups of offenders, contributing to variability in the deterrent effect of new sentencing policies. For all of these reasons, we have no clear picture of how enhanced criminal sanctions, on their own, impact criminal activity.[46]

Even assuming that harsh criminal penalties generally have a deterrent effect on criminal activity, it is uncertain whether juveniles will respond similarly to adults. Two factors that might differentially affect the responses of youths would appear to be in tension with one another. First, because of their psychosocial immaturity, youths may be less responsive to the impact of criminal penalties than adults. The developmental influences on decision making that were described in Chapter 2—an inclination to take risks, a tendency to focus on immediate rather than future consequences, an orientation to potential rewards as opposed to costs, susceptibility to peer influence, and impulsivity—in combination may lead youths to discount or ignore the prospect of harsh punishment in their choices about criminal involvement. Approval by anti social peers may be a particularly important influence that undercuts the deterrent effect of severe sanctions. A self-report study of inner-city youths by Wanda Foglia found that the threat of legal sanctions had little impact on delinquent behavior but that peer behavior had a powerful impact, both through concern about social sanctions and through internalized norms.[47]

Although the psychosocial immaturity of adolescents may undermine the deterrent impact of severe sanctions, a second factor may enhance that impact. The breadth of the changes in the juvenile justice regime over the past generation may influence modern youths to consider the prospect of punishment in ways that delinquents in earlier generations did not. If youths thought they were insulated from criminal liability because of their juvenile status under the traditional regime, they now may be more likely to perceive that this is not so. As we have suggested, the *existence* of a justice system that punishes crimes has a general deterrent effect, even if the marginal deterrent effect of particular polices is uncertain. In the past, the rhetoric of rehabilitation surrounding the traditional juvenile court may have led youths to perceive a world effectively without legal accountability, a perception that the punitive reforms may well have altered.

A few studies have sought to gauge the deterrent effect of legislative waiver statutes that have lowered the age of criminal court jurisdiction in different states—with mixed results.[48] Simon Singer and his colleagues studied the impact of New York's statute categorically lowering the age of criminal court jurisdiction, and found no effect on juvenile crime rates over a ten-year period.[49] A study that compared Idaho, a state that adopted a legislative waiver statute, with Montana and Wyoming, which did not, found that crime rates rose in Idaho and declined in the neighboring states.[50] However, Stephen Levitt, an economist, found a link between juvenile crime rates and changes in the severity of punishment. Levitt examined juvenile crime rates over a fifteen-year period, from 1978 to 1992, analyzing changes when juveniles reach the age at which they become subject to criminal court jurisdiction. Levitt found that in states with lenient juvenile systems, rates for violent crime declined sharply at the jurisdictional age when youths faced adult sanctions, while crime rates rose when youths attained adult legal status in states with strict juvenile systems and more lenient adult regimes. Levitt concluded that the threat of harsh punishment has a substantial deterrent effect and that much of the increase in juvenile crime in the late 1980s and early 1990s can be attributed to lenient juvenile sanctions.[51]

Levitt's study is the most comprehensive effort to link changes in juvenile crime rates with the severity of sanctions in several jurisdictions. His finding that crime rates decline when youths move from a very lenient juvenile justice system into the adult system is not surprising; it is consistent with the intuition that youths who perceive that they are insulated from criminal liability generally as juveniles may be deterred when they confront a regime of tough sanctions. This is a variation of the uncontroversial assumption that the existence of a criminal justice system has some deterrent effect. The finding that crime rates increase rather dramatically when youths move from a tough juvenile system to a lenient adult system is more puzzling. We are unfamiliar with states in which criminal court sanctions systematically are more lenient than juvenile court dispositions, and Levitt does not identify which states he classifies in this way.[52]

In sum, the research on the deterrent effect of legal regulation on juvenile crime is sparse and gives no clear answer to the question of whether legislative waiver laws and other punitive measures reduce juvenile crime. The evidence that the reforms have contributed to the decline in crime rates through deterrence is weak. Although Levitt offers some indirect support for the idea that the transformation of youth crime policy has had a deterrent impact, most other researchers have not found support for the conclusion that particular punitive laws deter youths from engaging in criminal conduct.

Specific Deterrence: Do Punitive Laws Reduce Recidivism?

Some researchers have sought to measure the specific deterrent effect of the punitive reforms on juvenile crime by examining whether criminal prosecution and punishment reduces recidivism. Given that the recent legal changes have altered dramatically the risks facing youths who get involved in crime, it would be useful to know whether youths who experience harsh punishment then alter their future behavior. These offenders know about the risk of punitive sanctions, and they know that they may be caught and punished. Are they more likely to desist from criminal activity than are those who are dealt with more leniently? The answer should be "yes" according to deterrence theory—and advocates for adult punishment.

Research based on interviews of young offenders indicates that being tried in criminal court causes some youths to understand for the first time that their criminal conduct has serious consequences.[53] As a youth in one study explained, "When you're a boy, you can be put into a detention home. But you can go to jail now. Jail ain't no place to go."[54] However, it is not clear whether, or to what extent, this awareness affects actual involvement in crime; as we have suggested, youths who commit crimes often are not guided by a rational decision-making process. Another study found that youths who were interviewed upon release from prison reported intentions not to get involved in crime again, but follow-up analysis of recidivism rates suggested that they had not adhered to their plans.[55] Moreover, some researchers have found that youths in prison are less likely to forswear future criminal activity than their counterparts in juvenile facilities.[56] Lawrence Sherman and others have argued that juveniles who are punished as adults become defiant at the perceived injustice of the severe sanctions they have received and reject the system as illegitimate.[57] In short, it is not clear, based on these studies, whether youths who are tried and punished as adults learn the lessons that policy-makers aim to teach in a way that deters their antisocial conduct.

Another method of evaluating the specific deterrence effect of adult sanctions is to compare recidivism rates of youths prosecuted and punished in the adult system with those who are sanctioned as juveniles. Most studies undertaking this comparison have found higher recidivism rates among juveniles tried and punished as adults. However, some of these studies are seriously flawed by selection bias, in that the two groups of youths differed in *other* ways that may have affected recidivism. For example, transferred youths may have been involved in more serious criminal activity or have had more serious criminal records, and thus *ex ante* presented a higher risk of recidivism.[58] In other studies, differences in the length of the incarceration period make comparison difficult; re-offending often is measured from the date of confinement, but only happens after inmates are released.[59] But two studies in the 1990s tried with more success to control for these differences. One group of researchers led by Donna Bishop and Charles Frazier compared a group of 2,700 Florida youths transferred to criminal court, mostly based on prosecutors' discretionary authority under Florida's direct-file statute, with a matched group of youths retained in the juvenile system.[60] In another study, Jeffrey Fagan and his colleagues compared fifteen- and sixteen-year-olds charged with robbery and burglary in several counties in metropolitan New York and in demographically similar counties in New Jersey.[61] The legal settings differed in that New York juveniles charged with robbery and burglary, aged fifteen and older, are automatically dealt with in the adult system under that state's legislative waiver statute; in New Jersey, transfer is rarely used, and the juvenile court retains jurisdiction over almost all youths charged with these crimes.

Fagan found that youths convicted of robbery in criminal court were re-arrested and incarcerated at a higher rate than those who were dealt with in the juvenile system, but that rates were comparable for burglary, a less serious crime. The risk of re-arrest within three years of "street time" was 29 percent lower for the New Jersey youths convicted of robbery in juvenile court than for the New York juveniles who were processed in the criminal system. The study also examined the number of days until re-arrest and found a similar pattern; the youths sentenced for robbery in criminal court re-offended sooner than their juvenile court counterparts (457 days after first release for the criminal court offenders versus 553 days for juvenile court offenders). There was no difference between the two groups convicted of burglary. Recidivism was not affected by sentence length; longer sentences were not more effective at reducing recidivism than shorter sentences.[62]

The Florida study also supports the conclusion that juvenile sanctions may reduce recidivism more effectively than criminal punishment. This study measured only re-arrest rates and found lower rates for youths who were retained in juvenile court than for youths who were transferred. The follow-up period in this study was relatively brief—less than two years. During this period, 29 percent of the transferred youths were rearrested as compared to 19 percent of the youths in the juvenile system. The researchers also calculated yearly re-arrest rates, which was .54 arrests per year for the transferred group versus .32 for the retained youths. Transferred youths who were rearrested were apprehended sooner after their release than juvenile system youths who re-offended—135 days after release versus 227 days. Youths who were incarcerated in the adult system served longer sentences; the mean time was 245 days served versus 90 days served by those who were incarcerated in the juvenile system. As in the New York-New Jersey study, longer sentences did not have a deterrent effect.

Studies finding that adult punishment may actually contribute to recidivism in young offenders charged with violent crimes seem to undercut the claimed benefits of the recent reforms. The findings, however, should be viewed with caution. In both studies, the two groups of offenders (or the two settings in Fagan's study) may differ from one another in subtle ways other than in the sanction the youths received. These researchers have mitigated this problem far better than earlier studies; Fagan by comparing two jurisdictions within the same general metropolitan area that dealt with the same offenses differently and Bishop and Frazier by matching each youth with a counterpart on several variables, including criminal charges, number of prior referrals, and most serious prior offense. Nonetheless, it is possible that Florida prosecutors used other, more subtle distinctions not measured by the researchers as a basis of filing charges in criminal court, such that more antisocial youths were dealt with in the adult system. Moreover, as the researchers concede, the police may have monitored youths who had been in the criminal system more closely than others, resulting in a higher re-arrest rate. In Fagan' s study, New York prosecutors have charging discretion that may have affected the composition of the study cohort. For example, they may have charged fifteen-year-olds who seemed less culpable with lesser crimes than robbery, so that they would not be prosecuted as adults. Thus, the cohort of young robbers in that state may have been the more serious offenders. Because almost all youths in New Jersey are retained in the juvenile system, prosecutors would not have influenced the composition of the sample in this way.[63] Moreover, law enforcement may be more aggressive and effective in New York than in New Jersey, leading to higher re-arrest rates in the former jurisdiction.

Given the limitations of the research, it is fair to ask whether these studies are helpful in determining whether young offenders who are subject to tough sanctions are more or less likely to offend in the future. At a minimum, this research provides no support for the contention that criminal punishment will reduce recidivism effectively. Indeed, almost all of the rather sparse empirical evidence points to the conclusion that it does *not* have this effect. Absent randomized experiments, in which offenders convicted of the same crimes are randomly assigned to either adult or juvenile sanctions— experiments that few, if any, jurisdictions would permit—the findings from studies like those of Fagan and Bishop and Frazier are the best available research evidence, and they do not support the conclusion that sanctioning juveniles as adults deters young offenders from future offending.

Incapacitation: Lowering Crime Rates through Incarceration

Youths who are inclined to commit crimes are constrained from doing so if they are incarcerated. Although it is unclear whether harsh sanctions deter youths in general from criminal activity or reduce recidivism, imprisonment certainly can reduce crime through incapacitation.[64] Supporters of the recent reforms may point to this reality as powerful evidence that tough sanctions indeed reduce crime, despite the lack of evidence that young criminals are deterred. The unassailable logic is that the more time young criminals spend in prison, the less time they are on the street getting in trouble.

Although this prescription is logical, it is problematic as social policy. Incapacitation is effective (in the short term at least), but it is very costly as a means of preventing crime. Deterrence operates by influencing the choices of potential offenders, and thus, if it is effective, the overall economic and social cost of crime should be reduced; fewer prison cells are needed, fewer people become victims; and youths live their lives in more socially (and personally) beneficial ways. In contrast, as we have seen, confinement of youths for long periods in correctional facilities carries a high economic cost and other social costs as well—particularly if the specific deterrent effect is weak or incarceration itself contributes to re-offending. Almost all young offenders *will* be released at some point to rejoin society; thus the impact of incarceration on re-offending and generally on their future lives must be considered in calculating its costs and benefits.

The benefits of incapacitation adhere only in cases of youths who would otherwise be out on the street committing crimes. For some youths who have caused serious harm through their criminal activity, the risk of recidivism is high enough at the outset (based on prior record, for example) that the costs of extensive incapacitation may be justified on social welfare grounds. But many youths are not in this category, and as lawmakers expand the category of young offenders who are subject to harsh sanctions to include moderate-risk offenders (first offenders, for example), the marginal benefits of incapacitation decline. At some point, the cost of sanctions involving long periods of incarceration will exceed the benefits, particularly if these costs include increasing the risk of re-offending in the future.

The research that we have reviewed provides no clear answer to the question of how much the criminalization of juvenile justice policy has contributed to the declining crime rate of recent years. Our review leads us to conclude that the punitive reforms likely *have* had some effect, at least in the short term, through increased incapacitation (both in the adult and juvenile systems) and possibly through general deterrence as well. Theory and research on adults support the view that a justice regime that signals to youths that they will be held accountable for their misdeeds should deter crime more effectively than one in which they think their status as juveniles shields them from punishment.[65] It is not at all clear, however, whether the legal changes of the past generation are optimal or excessive as the means of bringing about changed perceptions, and the threat of excessive sanctions may yield little added deterrent benefit. A juvenile system grounded in accountability and certainty of sanction may shape perceptions in ways that influence behavior as effectively as the current regime, with a more modest budgetary impact and fewer collateral costs.

Beyond this, the evidence does not support the claims by supporters of the punitive reforms that juveniles will be deterred by tough sanctions or that the reforms are responsible for the decline in juvenile crime rates that began in the mid-1990s. In many states, such as California, juvenile crime rates had been steadily declining for many years before the legislature moved to pass tough laws in 2000. Moreover, although the research findings are mixed, most studies find no evidence that the enactment of automatic transfer laws discourages youths generally from getting involved in crime. Somewhat more surprisingly, perhaps, the research does not indicate that those young offenders who are sentenced to prison for violent offenses are less likely to offend upon release by virtue of that experience; indeed, the few studies that exist suggest that they have higher recidivism rates than their counterparts in the juvenile system and that sentence severity does not appear to affect recidivism. In short, the argument that public safety will be promoted if youths get "adult time for adult crime" has little empirical support. Given that this claim is at the heart of the consequentialist argument for harsh sanctions, the case for get-tough policies is far weaker than its supporters acknowledge.

A Tale of Two Systems: Correctional Programs
as Developmental Contexts

The dearth of evidence supporting the effectiveness of tough sanctions in deterring youthful criminal activity becomes less puzzling when we examine the response of young offenders to harsh punishment in light of developmental knowledge about adolescence discussed in Chapter 2. First, teenagers on the street deciding whether to hold up a convenience store may simply be less capable than adults, due to their psychosocial immaturity, of considering the sanctions they will face. Thus, the developmental influences on decision-making that mitigate culpability also may make adolescents less responsive to the threat of criminal sanctions. Beyond this, however, sanctions themselves may vary in their impact on the future developmental trajectories of adolescents in ways that affect recidivism. Research supports the conclusion that prison provides an aversive social context that is likely to inhibit youths from accomplishing developmental tasks of adolescence that are essential to the transition to conventional adult roles. In contrast, the juvenile system, despite its considerable shortcomings, potentially can provide a better environment for development. In general, scientific knowledge about adolescence reinforces the lesson of other research that a policy that aims to reduce recidivism will deal with most young offenders in the juvenile system.

Before we probe the impact of different correctional settings on young offenders, we should recall some of the lessons about adolescent development from Chapter 2. Adolescence is a formative period of development. In mid- and late adolescence, individuals normally make substantial progress in acquiring and coordinating skills that are essential to filling the conventional roles of adulthood. First, they begin to develop basic educational and vocational skills to enable them to function in the workplace as productive members of society. Second, they also acquire the social skills necessary to establish stable intimate relationships and to cooperate in groups. Finally they must begin to learn to behave responsibly without external supervision and to set meaningful personal goals for themselves. For most individuals, the process of completing these developmental tasks extends into early adulthood, but making substantial progress during the formative stage of adolescence is important.

This process of development toward psychosocial maturity is one of reciprocal interaction between the individual and her social context. As developmentalists put it, healthy social contexts provide "opportunity structures" that facilitate normative development—but social contexts can also undermine this process.[66] Several environmental conditions are particularly important, such as the presence or absence of an authoritative adult parent figure, association with pro-social or antisocial peers, and participation (or not) in educational, extracurricular, or employment activities that facilitate the development of autonomous decision-making and critical thinking. For the youth in the justice system, the correctional setting becomes the environment for social development and may affect whether he acquires the skills necessary to function successfully in conventional adult roles.

Normative teenagers who get involved in crime do so, in part, because their choices are driven by developmental influences typical of adolescence. In theory, they should desist from criminal behavior and mature into reasonably responsible adults as they attain psychosocial maturity. We have indirect evidence that many young offenders follow this process as predicted; the crime rate drops off sharply in late adolescence, and the research shows that desistance is often linked to achieving stable employment or a satisfying marriage.[67] Whether youths successfully make the transition to adulthood, however, depends in part on whether their social context provides opportunity structures for the completion of the developmental tasks described above.[68] The correctional environment may influence the trajectories of normative adolescents in the justice system in important ways. Factors such as the availability (or lack) of good educational, skill-building, and rehabilitative programs; the attitudes and roles of adult supervisors; and the identity and behavior of other offenders shape the social context of youths in both the adult and the juvenile systems. These factors may affect the inclination of young offenders to desist or persist in their criminal activities and may facilitate or impede their development into adults who can function adequately in society—in the workplace, in marriage or other intimate unions, and as citizens.

Prisons as Developmental Settings

In most states, youths in prison are dealt with like other inmates, receiving few (or no) special accommodations or programs in recognition of their developmental needs.[69] Many features of the prison experience make it a harmful environment for adolescent offenders.[70] First, prisons are generally much larger institutions than juvenile facilities. According to one estimate, more than 40 percent of prisons house more than 500 prisoners; many have an inmate population of more than 1,000.[71] Even the largest juvenile facilities— training schools—house on average about 125 youths, and other residential programs are far smaller.[72] Institutional size affects the experience of inmates in several ways; in large institutions, violence levels are higher, staff-inmate relationships are more impersonal, and the organizational structure is more rigid.[73] Researchers have found that recidivism rates among juvenile offenders increase with the size of the institution.[74]

The function of prison is to punish and confine criminals, and that purpose is reflected in the institution's organization and staffing. More than two-thirds of prison employees are uniformed guards and other security staff whose job is to maintain order and security by monitoring inmates. Although some educational and counseling programs may be provided, these services are not readily available, and are often provided by adjunct staff, and not integrated into prison life. Some states provide special instructional programs in prison for minors, but this is by no means the norm; full-day educational programs are rare.[75] One study reported that the teacher-to-student ratio in prison was 1 to 100, and that fewer than 40 percent of inmates received any academic instruction.[76] Counseling and therapeutic and occupational training staff generally are scarce in prison; fewer than 10 percent of prisoners in one study were involved in any kind of counseling program.[77]

These dimensions of prison organization shape the experience of youths incarcerated in the adult system in ways that seem likely to undermine healthy psychosocial development. First, adult authority figures are unlikely to exert a positive influence. Researchers report that correctional officers, whose job is to maintain security, have impersonal, authoritarian, and often hostile relationships with inmates. Not surprisingly, young prisoners, in turn, express hostility toward staff, who are perceived as being unconcerned about inmates' welfare and uninterested in helping young prisoners develop social skills, improve relationships, or deal with problems.[78] Further, many prisons provide minimal positive structure for inmates' daily lives, because they offer little in the way of education, occupational training, or rehabilitation. In these facilities, much time is spent in cells or in the prison yard with other prisoners, under the surveillance of guards on the perimeter.[79]

Frequent opportunities for interaction among prisoners together with distant relationships with staff combine to create an aversive developmental setting. Although youths are separated from adults in some prisons, and experts uniformly urge separation, this is not the practice in most facilities.[80] According to reports by young prisoners, experienced criminals teach them strategies and methods for engaging in criminal activity and avoiding detection.[81] Young inmates also are more likely to be victimized than are their counterparts in juvenile facilities or older prisoners; five times as many youths in prison report sexual assaults as do youths in juvenile facilities.[82] In some facilities, young prisoners who are targets of older predators are isolated for their own protection, apparently because isolating victims is easier than restraining attackers.[83] Most prisoners do not report victimization to prison officials; to do so is a serious violation of prison norms against snitching, and may only increase vulnerability to attack. Young prisoners often attempt to protect themselves from victimization by responding aggressively to threats, which in turn can result in disciplinary sanctions.[84]

In general, juvenile inmates engage in more misconduct and are subject to administrative segregation and disciplinary sanctions (such as exclusion from work assignments, programs, and good-time credits) far more often than are older prisoners. To some extent, the aggressive misconduct of young inmates probably reflects the reality that some youths in prison are tough, antisocial individuals—Moffitt's "life-course persistent" offenders. However, developmental influences may also be a factor. Being more sensitive to peer approval than are adults, adolescents may engage in aggressive conduct to prove their toughness and masculinity, and thereby attain higher peer status.[85]

In sum, the experience of imprisonment is more adverse for adolescents than for older prisoners. Unlike adults, adolescents are in a formative developmental stage that powerfully influences the future trajectory of their lives. Prisons function as apprenticeship programs for professional criminals. They also provide barren and hostile settings for developing essential capacities and skills that are necessary for the transition to conventional adulthood. Correctional staff—the available adult authority figures—are distant and hostile, and adult prisoners typically either threaten young prisoners or influence them to become more proficient criminals. In most facilities, little effort is made to prepare youths to function in the workplace as adults or to develop the interpersonal skills necessary to establish stable intimate relationships.

Moreover, the harmful effects of imprisonment follow young offenders after they are released in ways that amplify its negative impact on psychosocial development. A felony conviction is a stigmatic signal that carries legal disabilities, such as disenfranchisement and, until recently, exclusion from military service (which has been found to be another pathway to desistance for juvenile offenders).[86] Just as important are the informal handicaps that undermine the ability of young felons to move into conventional adult roles. Disclosure of a criminal record is mandatory in many settings, and often the criminal conviction will bar educational opportunities and meaningful employment. Further, a youth who has been in prison may find it much harder to develop social relationships with affiliates who are not involved in crime—regardless of his social skills. Thus, youths who serve time in prison are severely handicapped in their efforts to find meaningful legal employment or to marry or establish a stable intimate relationship, which are the two most important factors associated with desistance from involvement in crime.

Juvenile Facilities as Developmental Settings

Juvenile facilities are far from optimal as settings for healthy adolescent development under the best conditions, and some institutions for young offenders are almost indistinguishable from prisons. Some facilities, however, provide young offenders with programs, supervision, and supportive correctional environments that, in combination, are less likely to harm their prospects for becoming productive adults—and, at their best, may contribute positively to the transition from antisocial adolescent to normative adult. In other words, "typical" prisons and "adequate" juvenile facilities (which may not be typical) differ in several ways that may be important to their developmental impact on confined youths. These differences may shed light on the question of why youths who are imprisoned do not appear to be more effectively deterred than youths in the juvenile system despite the adverse nature of the prison experience.

Although the regulation of youth crime has become harsher over the past generation, juvenile facilities and programs in many states continue to recognize that convicted youths are adolescents with developmental needs. This perspective translates into an environment that is less purely custodial than that of typical prisons. In many juvenile facilities, a relatively large number of line staff perform educational and counseling duties. Ninety-five percent of training schools have a ratio of at least one teacher per fifteen youths, and two-thirds have one counselor for every ten youths.[87] Even in states that have embraced punitive reforms enthusiastically, the program and organization of juvenile facilities often is based on a developmental therapeutic model. For example, in Florida, where Tim Kane, whose story opened this chapter, is currently serving a life sentence in prison, the juvenile correctional programs (for which he would have been eligible had he not been transferred) are based on empirically validated cognitive behavioral principles that guide staff behavior and staff-resident interaction.[88] Residents' daily schedules include academic classes, skills training, counseling, and recreational activities.[89]

There is some evidence that these programmatic differences affect the social environment of youths in the juvenile system in ways that contribute positively to psychological development. Based on self-report studies, youths in juvenile facilities have far more positive attitudes about staff than do young prisoners. In general, the former group report that staff are concerned about their welfare, encourage them to participate in programs, and attempt to help them develop social skills and to solve problems.[90] Further, offenders in juvenile facilities are also more likely than youths in prison to say that they intend to avoid criminal activity in the future. When asked to evaluate programs, youths reported benefiting the most from long-term intensive programs in which they developed relationships with caring counselors, particularly programs that were directed at improving social skills and self-control. In effect, these youths reported that the staff in their facilities provided social conditions and experiences that research indicates facilitate the attainment of psychosocial competence. As we will see shortly, the characteristics of programs that youths found most helpful are those that researchers have correlated with reduced recidivism.

Youths in Community-Based Programs

Even under contemporary law, many youths (perhaps a majority) serve all or part of their delinquency dispositions in their communities, rather than in correctional facilities.[91] For some offenders, community dispositions may be optimal, providing a lower cost sanction than confinement in a correctional facility and offering a better context for navigating the transition to productive adulthood. In theory, at least, many normative adolescents will be better off if they are not removed from their families, schools, and communities. (Despite stereotypes of the contrary, research finds that many juvenile offenders do not come from terrible home environments.)[92] For nondelinquent youths, these social environments provide the opportunity structures for completing the developmental tasks that are the basis of psychosocial maturity. Residential facilities, even those that are organized to respond to adolescents' developmental needs, generally are not ideal developmental settings, particularly if youths are confined for long periods and prevented from acquiring important interpersonal and decision-making skills. Moreover, the dispositional goal for every delinquent youth is that she ultimately be able to function in the social context that constitutes her community.

An obvious problem with community sanctions for many delinquent youths is that their families, peer groups, neighborhoods, and schools may undermine rather than support healthy psychosocial development. As Chapter 5 explains, toxic social contexts contribute to youthful involvement in criminal activity, and unless something changes, they are likely to contribute to recidivism. Youths whose friends are involved in crime, whose parents are deficient, and whose schools are dangerous settings that lack resources may find it hard to stay in their communities and *not* get involved in criminal activity again. This suggests that community sanctions may be inappropriate for some high-risk offenders. It also suggests that an important goal of any community-based disposition must be to minimize the impact of negative social influences by providing delinquent youths with tools to deal in self-protective ways with their social environment and to facilitate and reinforce settings that promote healthy development.[93]

The goal of changing the interaction between the young offender and his social environment is also important for offenders returning to their communities after incarceration. A reentry period of structured supervision and support can enhance the youth's ability to function in his community in ways that minimize the likelihood that he will simply reconnect with antisocial peers and resume his involvement in criminal activity. The developmental benefits of programs in correctional facilities can be lost when youths return to their homes and neighborhoods, unless they receive support through the transition. Recent research indicates that juveniles who have been released from institutional placement are more likely to reoffend when they return to environments characterized by inadequate parents and, especially, by the presence of antisocial peers.[94] Increasingly, effective correctional programs include intensive community probation to ensure that interventions have a lasting impact.

If this developmental goal is adopted, community sanctions under a contemporary regime will be quite different from those employed by the traditional juvenile court, where loosely supervised probation was a standard disposition for less serious and first-time offenders. If offenders who are subject to community sanctions are not carefully supervised and if the criminogenic influences in their social environment are not addressed, many will not desist from criminal activity. Moreover, an important lesson of the deterrence research is that young offenders must understand that they will be punished for the harms they cause. The traditional juvenile courts, in meting out community probation (and little else) to many young offenders, failed to communicate this message and apparently achieved little deterrence. Some localities have found that sanctions that include not only therapeutic and skill-building programs, but also compensation to victims, community service, close supervision, and enforcement of probation conditions such as curfews and orders to avoid antisocial peers are effective in promoting accountability and reducing recidivism.[95]

Community dispositions continue to play a key role in contemporary juvenile crime policy, affecting many youths who a generation ago were processed informally and diverted from the justice system entirely.[96] Supporters of harsh sanctions are suspicious of community-based sanctions, in part because they assume that public protection requires incarceration of many young offenders. The extent to which this is true depends on the effectiveness of community-based programs in reducing recidivism. While traditional probation has not been successful at achieving this goal, contemporary programs that apply the developmental lessons we have described are far more promising, as we will see in the next section. If interventions in the community *are* effective at reducing re-offending with youths who otherwise would be confined, they may be superior on social welfare grounds, given that they are far less costly financially and less disruptive to young offenders' lives.

What Works with Young Offenders?

The evidence we have presented thus far generally supports a policy of retaining most young offenders in the juvenile system as more likely to promote public welfare than the contemporary approach of punishing many youths as adults. But juvenile correctional facilities and programs vary greatly. Some youths are incarcerated in prison-like training schools, while others receive loosely supervised community probation—neither of which is effective at changing antisocial behavior. An important question therefore is, what can the juvenile system offer young offenders that will be effective at reducing recidivism?

Until the 1990s most researchers who study juvenile delinquency programs might well have answered that the system had little to offer in the way of effective therapeutic interventions; the dominant view held by social scientists in the 1970s and 1980s was that "nothing works" to reduce recidivism with young offenders.[97] Today the picture is considerably brighter, in large part due to a substantial body of research produced over the past fifteen years showing that many juvenile programs, in both community and institutional settings, have a substantial crime-reduction effect; for the most promising programs, that effect is in the range of 20 percent to 30 percent.[98] Moreover, by applying meta-analysis, a quantitative method for coding, analyzing, and accurately combining and comparing the findings of many related studies (some of which do not produce statistically significant findings simply because their samples are too small to reveal any effects), researchers are able to accurately sort the types of interventions that are promising from those that are ineffective and to clarify the attributes of effective programs.[99] An increased focus on research-based programs and on careful outcome evaluation allows policy makers to assess accurately the impact on recidivism rates of particular programs to determine whether the economic costs are justified. In a real sense, these developments have revived rehabilitation as a realistic goal of juvenile justice interventions.

In general, successful programs are those that attend to the lessons of developmental psychology, seeking to provide young offenders with supportive social contexts and to assist them in acquiring the skills necessary to change problem behavior and to attain psychosocial maturity. In his comprehensive meta-analysis of four hundred juvenile programs, Mark Lipsey found that among the most effective programs in both community and institutional settings were those that focused on improving social development skills in the areas of interpersonal relations, self-control, academic performance, and job skills.[100] Some effective programs focus directly on developing skills to avoid antisocial behavior, often through cognitive behavioral therapy, a therapeutic approach with substantial empirical support.[101] For example, Aggression Replacement Training is a cognitive-behavioral intervention that focuses on anger control, pro-social skill development, and moral reasoning. Other interventions that have been shown to have a positive effect on crime reduction focus on strengthening family support. In Functional Family Therapy, for example, therapists work in youths' homes to improve emotional connections between parents and children and to strengthen parents' abilities to provide structure and limits for their children. This approach explicitly recognizes the importance of authoritative parenting for healthy development, as does Multidimensional Treatment Foster Care (MTFC), an intervention that has been found to be quite effective with high-risk and chronic offenders. MTFC places youths with trained and supervised foster parents for six to twelve months, while they also engage in family therapy with their own parents. This program involves close supervision and treatment in the home, school, and community; adult mentoring; and separation from delinquent peers.[102]

Another intervention that has been successful with violent and aggressive youths is multi-systemic therapy (MST), a community-based program that has been replicated and evaluated repeatedly for almost twenty years with many groups of juvenile offenders. MST is thoroughly grounded in developmental knowledge, combining cognitive behavioral therapy with an ecological approach that deals with individual youths in the multiple social contexts in which they live—their families, peer groups, schools, and communities, addressing the factors that contribute to criminal conduct across these settings. MST therapists work in teams with small caseloads of four to six families, providing intensive in-home services. The focus of treatment is to empower parents with the skills and resources needed to support their children in avoiding problem behaviors and to give youths the tools to cope with family, peer, and school problems that can contribute to re-involvement in criminal activity.[103] Controlled studies of MST have shown it to be among the most effective justice system treatments when it is practiced with fidelity to the developers' model. One study compared chronic and violent offenders receiving MST with a randomly assigned group who received the standard treatment of supervised probation, and found that MST reduced rates of both re-offending and incarceration in this group of high risk offenders. The MST youths had significantly lower recidivism rates over a fifty-nine-week period despite the fact that they remained in the community an average of seventy-three days more during that period than did youths in the control group.[104] Moreover, a two-year follow-up study showed that youths who received MST continued to re-offend at a substantially lower rate than those who got the standard dispositional treatment (although the rates for both groups were relatively high).[105]

Not all juvenile programs are effective at reducing crime. Two popular programs—military boot camps and "scared straight" programs in which youths are taken to adult prisons and lectured on the perils they face if they persist in their criminal ways—actually increase recidivism; young offenders who participate in these programs commit more crimes than other youths.[106] Moreover, even effective programs can fail if they are not well implemented. Some studies have found substantial variations in recidivism rates due to differences in the quality of staff and compliance with program protocols.[107] In one study, youths in Functional Family Therapy with incompetent therapists had higher recidivism rates than controls, while recidivism declined by 20 percent for those with competent therapists.[108] This variation suggests that general replication in the justice system of effective "model programs" may sometimes not produce the positive results that program developers achieve. Beyond this, the duration of treatment and amount of contact time are often positively correlated with effectiveness. Lipsey's meta-analysis found that those programs that exceeded the mean in these dimensions were more effective at reducing recidivism than briefer programs that involved less contact.[109] Finally, the age and risk presented by offenders may be important to programs' success. Some programs are more effective with older (and others with younger) youths, and some with high-risk (or low-risk) offenders.[110]

Many treatment programs in the justice system are more expensive than standard probation or parole, the alternative with which they often are compared. MST, for example, costs approximately $5,000 for each youth participating in the program. How can policy-makers decide whether the benefits of particular programs justify their cost to taxpayers? Recently state governments have begun to focus on the cost-effectiveness of criminal and juvenile sanctions and have enlisted economists to calculate whether the benefits of various programs, as measured by the value to taxpayers and crime victims of the programs' expected effect on crime, are greater than their costs. A comprehensive cost-benefit analysis of four hundred programs aimed at crime reduction found that several of the juvenile justice programs we have described offered taxpayers the best return for dollars invested—better than programs aimed at adult criminals and better than early childhood and school prevention programs (although the latter have other goals besides crime prevention).[111] For example, based on research showing that MST reduces recidivism by about 30 percent, taxpayers gain about $31,000 in subsequent criminal justice system savings for each program participant—or more than $6 for each dollar spent. When the value to potential crime victims is included, the benefit rises to $131,918, or $28 for each dollar spent. The cost-benefit ratio for Functional Family Therapy, Aggression Replacement Training, and Multidimensional Treatment Foster Care were also very favorable.[112] The bottom line is that a range of intensive programs in the juvenile system have proved effective if they are faithfully and competently implemented with appropriately targeted youths. These programs offer good value for taxpayers' dollars spent, and the benefits in terms of crime reduction far exceed the costs.

This promising research on programs in the juvenile justice system provides further evidence challenging the claim that punitive policies promote social welfare by reducing youth crime. As cost-conscious policy-makers are beginning to recognize in several states, it makes sense to include research-based programs as a key component of the legal response to juvenile crime. The fact that some of the most cost-effective interventions are community-based programs suggests that community sanctions can play an important role in a contemporary regime that is quite different from that of probation and parole in the traditional system. This not to say, however, that all young offenders should remain in the community. Even though some programs, such as MST, have been shown to reduce recidivism even in serious and chronic offenders, there may be good reasons to place in residential facilities some youths who commit serious violent crimes or who are repeat offenders. Very few studies of justice system programs to date have compared community-based sanctions with incarceration, and thus the impact of incapacitation on crime rates has rarely been included in the calculus. Some youths simply present too much of a recidivism risk to warrant their staying in the community. Moreover, the threat of incarceration may have an impact on general deterrence that would be diluted in a regime that seldom uses confinement as a sanction. However, community sanctions are appropriate dispositions for many youths, and others can benefit from community-based interventions as part of the transition from residential programs. For any state aiming to advance social welfare through its juvenile justice policies, extensive use of programs that have demonstrated effectiveness is a good investment.

In this chapter, we have examined youth crime policy through a consequentialist lens, a perspective from which the primary policy goal is to promote social welfare—and particularly to prevent future crime. Many supporters of punitive policies, adopting this view, argue that public safety requires the extensive use of incarceration (often in the adult system) for young offenders. We have found little empirical support for this claim or generally for the argument that the punitive reforms promote public welfare. Indeed, most of the evidence points to the conclusion that the social costs of criminalization outweigh the benefits. This evidence comes from several sources. First, extensive use of incarceration is expensive; juvenile justice expenditures have risen steeply as juvenile crime has declined. To an extent, the expenditures may have contributed to the decline, through the incapacitation of many young offenders. But the research evidence, although limited in its ability to permit causal inferences to be drawn, provides little support for the notion that tough sanctions function effectively to deter crime, either generally or in their impact on young offenders. Instead, the research supports the view that adult punishment of young offenders encourages re-offending and undermines the prospect of normative development; this tentative conclusion is reinforced by developmental knowledge about adolescence. Finally, the research indicates that treatment programs in the juvenile system grounded in developmental knowledge offer a cost-effective means of reducing recidivism. This evidence suggests that rehabilitation, discredited as the foundation of the traditional juvenile system, has a revitalized role to play in a contemporary regime that aims to promote social welfare.

CHAPTER 8

The Developmental Model and Juvenile Justice Policy for the Twenty-First Century

Fair punishment and cost-effective crime reduction are the cornerstones of successful youth crime regulation, and a juvenile justice regime grounded in developmental knowledge is more likely to realize these goals than either the traditional or the contemporary regulatory approaches. In earlier chapters, we argued that both the traditional rehabilitative model of juvenile justice and the contemporary regime have failed to measure up to the conventional demands of fairness and cost-minimization, in large part because both regimes fail to attend to the accumulated scientific knowledge about the nature and course of adolescent development.

Our developmental model is based on three key lessons taken from the scientific literature on adolescence. First, adolescents' choices to get involved in criminal activity are shaped by developmental forces that contribute to immature judgment, and thus are less culpable than are those of adults. Second, because of these developmental influences, normal adolescents, particularly those growing up in high-crime neighborhoods, may get involved in criminal activity, but most are likely to mature out of these inclinations. And third, because social context plays a key role in the accomplishment

223

of essential developmental tasks during adolescence, the correctional settings and interventions that constitute society's response to juvenile crime will likely affect whether delinquent youths make a successful transition to adulthood.

In this chapter we translate the developmental model of juvenile justice into a set of policy prescriptions that embody the model's lessons. What we offer is not a detailed blueprint for a model system but guidelines for reform that, if undertaken, would yield a system different in important ways from both the traditional rehabilitative model and the contemporary regime. The developmental model supports retaining a separate juvenile system with a far less permeable boundary with the adult system than exists under current law. It is a regime in which young offenders receive proportionate sanctions of determinate duration, executed in settings that facilitate the transition to healthy adulthood—whether in the community or in correctional facilities. The jurisdictional boundaries of a system grounded in developmental knowledge will differ from current boundaries, both in the minimum age of adult prosecution and in the maximum dispositional age. Finally, transfer to criminal court will be limited to a narrow category of recidivists charged with serious violent offenses, and judicial and prosecutorial discretion over transfer will be constrained to cases that fall within this group.

The chapter concludes by focusing on youths who represent a small percentage of young offenders but are at the heart of the policy discussion about juvenile crime: high-risk juveniles who seriously threaten public safety through repeated criminal activity. In contrast to the vast majority of juvenile offenders, their involvement in crime does not appear to be the product of adolescent immaturity; it has, instead, roots in neurological, psychological, familial, and environmental deficits. Many of these juveniles begin to engage in criminal conduct at an early age; unlike normative adolescent offenders, they are likely to continue their criminal activity into adulthood. Dealing effectively, but also fairly, with this group of young offenders is essential to the stability and legitimacy of a legal regime based on the developmental model.

Should We Abolish the Juvenile Court?

Conservative critics of the juvenile justice system have long wished for its demise, or at a minimum have sought to transform it into a forum for dealing with minor crimes.[1] More surprising, some critics of the *contemporary* (as well as the traditional) regime—experts who share many of our concerns—argue that the juvenile court should be abolished. These critics, most famously Barry Feld, claim that an "integrated system" for adults and juveniles that employs a "youth discount" in sanctioning young offenders will serve the interests of young offenders and society better than the current bifurcated system.[2] No state has actually moved to abolish its juvenile justice system; however, the provocative argument for abolition has received much attention in academic and policy circles and warrants serious consideration. It will not surprise the reader that we oppose an integrated justice system, but we think it worthwhile to spell out the argument for abolition of the juvenile court and explain why it is a bad idea.

The liberal argument for abolition focuses on some of the same procedural deficiencies in delinquency proceedings addressed by the Supreme Court in *In re Gault*. Modern abolitionists argue that juveniles continue to receive inadequate representation and procedural protection, despite the ruling in *Gault* extending to juveniles many of the procedural protections enjoyed by adults in criminal trials, including the right to an attorney. This concern has become more pressing as the purpose of the juvenile court has shifted overtly from rehabilitation to punishment.

Deficiencies in procedural protection exacerbate what critics decry as the capricious and biased quality of juvenile court dispositional and transfer decisions. In most states, dispositions are not determinate or subject to the constraint of proportionality; thus, judges have substantial discretion to order sanctions on the basis of qualities of the offender that are not directly linked to the offense. This can result in decisions influenced by racial and ethnic bias, such that minority offenders receive harsher sanctions than white youths.[3] The research also indicates that ethnic minority youths are more likely to be transferred to the adult system than are white teenagers charged with the same crimes and with similar offense histories, a disparity especially evident in cases of nonviolent offenses, such as drug-dealing.[4] An integrated criminal justice system abolishes transfer. Further, in the view of Feld and others, decisions by criminal courts, constrained by sentencing guidelines, are less vulnerable to racial prejudice or to other biases and preferences that judges may hold.[5]

The problem, according to Feld, is not simply that the juvenile court's mission has become indistinguishable from that of the adult criminal court but that the very premise of the rehabilitative model is fundamentally flawed. The traditional court claimed to be a social welfare agency, a role that Feld views as fundamentally incompatible with its punishment and social control mission. A court responding to criminal conduct cannot (and should not, he argues) be in the business of providing social services to juveniles; instead these services should be available to all children on the basis of need.

Why We Need a Separate Juvenile Justice System

Feld and others make powerful arguments that the juvenile court is a flawed institution, but the case for abolition is not persuasive, for at least two reasons. First, less draconian measures than abolition may go a long way to correct the problems that Feld discerns in the juvenile system. Second, the criminal court is unlikely to provide a setting for the adjudication and punishment of juveniles that will better serve either their interests or those of society than the juvenile system. On our view, maintaining a robust boundary between the two systems is essential to the satisfactory regulation of juvenile crime.

Consider the more limited procedural protections enjoyed by juveniles in delinquency proceedings. In fact, juveniles now enjoy many rights of adult defendants, including the right to an attorney, the right to confront witnesses, and the privilege against self-incrimination; only a handful of protections, like the right to a trial by jury, are not available in juvenile court in most states.[6] The tendency of juveniles not to exercise their rights, and particularly their tendency to waive their right to an attorney, is concerning, but it could be dealt with through restrictions on waiver.[7] It is true that many juvenile court judges are less deferential of procedural rights than are criminal court judges, but, at least in part, this is due to a residual paternalistic concern for the welfare of juveniles that often benefits youths in delinquency proceedings. Many judges view young offenders as different from adult criminals and embrace the goal of helping them change their lives, an objective much less common among criminal court judges. It is not surprising that procedural protections may be taken somewhat more seriously in a setting in which the government's straightforward aim is to punish the defendant and protect society.

On our view the broad discretion that prosecutors and judges enjoy under the current regime presents a more serious problem than the lack of procedural protection. In many states prosecutors can determine unilaterally whether youths charged with serious crimes will be tried as juveniles or adults. A judgment of this importance should not be delegated to officials who often are inclined to weigh the short-term benefits of incapacitation excessively and to discount the long-term costs. Further, as Feld and others note, the authority of juvenile court judges to make dispositional and transfer decisions on the basis of factors not directly related to the offense and the youth's prior record may contribute to decisions that are biased in unacceptable ways. Constraining prosecutorial and judicial discretion is important, but, as we suggest below, this can be accomplished without abolishing the juvenile system.

An integrated justice system, even one with sentences subject to a "youth discount," would offer few benefits to juveniles charged with crimes. First, juveniles likely will continue to be represented by less experienced and less competent attorneys, simply because the stakes they face—given the youth discount—would be lower than those confronting adult defendants. More important, we are skeptical that the government will be inclined to use the lessons of developmental psychology in responding to young offenders in a system directed primarily at punishment—even if juveniles are held in separate facilities.[8] Enthusiasm for developing and implementing programs that can reduce recidivism and promote healthy development is far more likely to be sustained in a regime in which juveniles are dealt with as a special category of offenders with particular developmental needs. Unlike Feld, we see no irreconcilable tension between crime control and social welfare, so long as interventions directed at delinquents offer the prospect of effectively reducing recidivism.

More generally, the cost of adapting the criminal justice system to provide a context for healthy development would be substantial— far greater than the cost of making needed adjustments in the juvenile system. Prisons are violent social settings, deeply embedded with norms of punishment, and characterized by suspicion and hostility between staff and inmates; this is not likely to change with an influx of young offenders. In contrast, the research evidence indicates that individuals who staff juvenile courts, probation departments, programs, and facilities are more likely to care about youth welfare and to understand and attend to the special developmental concerns of youths.[9] In general, if the goal is to promote healthy development, the institutional arrangements of the juvenile system are far more promising than those of the criminal system. The magnitude and cost of the changes in the adult system necessary to attain even minimal adequacy in this regard are likely to be extraordinary. To be sure, the juvenile justice system is in need of reform, but even in its current state and despite the recent punitive reforms, it is likely to do less harm to young people and generally more likely to reduce the cost of crime than the adult system.

A separate juvenile system is also more likely to maintain a regime of relatively lenient sanctions than is an integrated justice system with a policy of youth discounts. The existence of the juvenile court as a distinct institution signals that adolescents and adults involved in criminal activity are different and therefore should be subject to different treatment. The sentencing distinctions between juveniles and adults are far more likely to break down in an integrated system. Political pressure on issues relating to crime tends to function as a one-way ratchet in the direction of ever-stiffer penalties. Over time, the discount likely will become riddled with exceptions as objections are raised against applying the youth discount to certain crimes or offenders. A better choice is a regime that maintains a firm boundary between the juvenile and criminal systems and excludes from the juvenile court's jurisdiction only a small number of older youths charged with serious crimes.

Taking Proportionality Seriously
in Juvenile Court Dispositions

Under our developmental model, juvenile court dispositions should be proportionate in severity to the seriousness of the offense and the culpability of the offender. The principle of proportionality is the bedrock of a fair and legitimate justice system, and it is the basis of youth crime regulation grounded in mitigation that holds young offenders accountable for their crimes but presumptively subject to more lenient sanctions than their adult counterparts. Taking proportionality seriously, however, also means that dispositions in the juvenile system should be based on the harm of the criminal act and culpability of the actor.

This represents a reform of juvenile sentencing policy and rejection of policies and practices embedded in the rehabilitative model that, although limited by the dramatic reforms in recent years, persist in almost all states. The Progressive Era reformers who established the juvenile court (and their successors for many years) had no interest in proportionate punishment, insisting that delinquency interventions were not "punishment" at all but were for the purpose of treatment. Thus, judges based dispositions, in theory at least, on the rehabilitative needs and prospects of the individual youth. The juvenile court has changed in many ways over the years, but with very few exceptions, states have not adopted determinate sentencing.[10] Almost universally, judges retain the authority to make individualized dispositional decisions, although today sanctions are often much harsher than was once the case, and many serious cases are excluded altogether from juvenile court jurisdiction.

Broad discretionary authority is justified as a means of allowing courts to tailor dispositions on the basis of youths' amenability to treatment or risk of re-offending, but it is not compatible with a commitment to fairness. Discretion allows judges to ignore the mitigating effect of immaturity and to impose sanctions on the basis of personal characteristics that may be illegitimate as a basis for punishment—factors such as race, ethnicity, or socioeconomic status.[11] This means that a drug dealer can be punished more seriously than an armed robber. It also means that two individuals may commit a crime together but receive different sanctions based on personal characteristics. Both outcomes are problematic on fairness grounds.

The developmental model incorporates proportionality both by punishing young offenders less harshly than their adult counterparts generally and by imposing sanctions that are based at least roughly on the seriousness of the offense and the culpability of the offender. Proportionality is a crude principle; it does not require that dispositions be based on fine-grained assessments of harm and culpability. But at a minimum, immaturity and the harm of the offense should count, such that younger offenders should be punished less severely than older youths and punishment calibration should be based on the seriousness of the offense.

A youth's prior criminal record is also a legitimate consideration in determining proportionate dispositions. Following a standard practice in criminal court, first offenders should receive less severe sanctions than recidivists. Although leniency to first offenders is often justified on preventive grounds (recognizing that a first offender does not represent the same threat of future harm as a recidivist), it also is compatible with principles of fairness. A repeat offender may deserve more punishment because he has failed to learn his lesson or to feel remorse for earlier offenses.

The reality is that even today juvenile court judges do not ignore proportionality, even though they have the authority to exercise broad discretion in most states. Considerable evidence indicates that delinquency dispositions are based largely on the juvenile's present offense and prior record—just as sentences are in criminal court.[12] Our research group recently examined predictors of incarceration versus probation in juvenile court felony dispositions in two jurisdictions, Philadelphia and Phoenix.[13] In this study, we had access to a wealth of non-legal information about each offender, including demographic characteristics and measures of psychological functioning. We found, however, that the only consistent predictors of disposition were the seriousness of the current offense and the number of prior convictions. None of the other factors, including race, had a significant impact on the decision to release a juvenile back into the community versus sending him to some sort of secure placement.[14]

Proportionality and Social Welfare

Fair punishment is not the only goal of juvenile justice policy. Policy-makers also aim to reduce juvenile crime in a cost-effective manner. Scientific knowledge about normal adolescent development, together with other criminological research, confirms the intuition that dispositions may vary greatly in their impact on the future lives of young offenders, influencing whether they return to the streets or follow more productive paths when their sentences are complete. In any given case, the available evidence may suggest that a particular disposition—whether a community program, confinement in a juvenile facility, or imprisonment—is likely to reduce the cost of crime and thus be optimal from a social welfare perspective. This raises an important question: Is a regime based on proportionate punishment compatible with this quite different goal of promoting social welfare?

In most cases, we think the answer is "yes." Fairness concerns dictate the duration of a youth's sentence and the extent to which he is deprived of liberty, on the basis of harm and culpability, while social welfare goals determine the content of the programs that he receives and the correctional context. What happens to the youth during the period that he is in state custody can be of critical importance to his future prospects and to the social cost of his criminal conduct, whether his sentence involves minimal constraint or a long period of confinement.

Sometimes, to be sure, fairness and social welfare may conflict. For example, it may appear that a youth would benefit from a more restrictive intervention than is warranted on the basis of the seriousness of his offense—perhaps to extricate him from a social setting in which he seems likely to get in more serious trouble. Under the traditional rehabilitative model, this kind of argument justified intervention (including confinement) for status offenses, such as truancy and curfew violations. Alternatively, we could imagine a case in which a relatively severe disposition is warranted on the basis of the seriousness of the crime but *not* on social welfare grounds. Perhaps the young offender has committed a crime that usually would result in incarceration (armed robbery or aggravated assault, for example), but the likelihood that he will re-offend is low and his family is ready to participate in community-based treatment. In this case, the social costs of incarceration may outweigh the benefits. Should this youth receive a proportionate sentence or one that is most likely to promote social welfare?

The question of whether a juvenile offender's sanction ought to include institutional placement or be limited to a community sanction will sometimes expose a tension between social welfare considerations and proportionality. Little evidence supports the *rehabilitative* effectiveness of institutional placement for juvenile offenders; indeed, some research indicates that the aggregation of antisocial juveniles in group settings may have the unintended effect of increasing delinquency, by fostering bonds among delinquent peers.[15] This may explain why some popular approaches to institutional placement, such as "boot camps," increase re-offending.[16] In contrast, some community-based treatment programs, especially those that involve offenders' families are both effective at reducing crime and cost-effective.[17] However, institutional placement may be appropriate on proportionality grounds for serious offenses, even for relatively low-risk offenders. The issue is even more complex in that public safety considerations may warrant the secure placement of *some* individuals convicted of a particular serious crime, but not others. For example, what if the low-risk offender can safely remain in the community, but his co-defendant cannot?[18] Should high-risk and low-risk youths receive the same sentences for their similar crimes?

Hard questions about accommodating social welfare concerns without sacrificing fairness are not unique to the juvenile system; they also arise routinely in criminal sentencing.[19] In that context, courts struggle to impose fair punishment while attending to crime prevention concerns. Although some criminal law theorists would disagree, excessive punishment would seem to be a greater affront to proportionality and fairness than insufficient punishment.[20] In other words, punishing a youth less harshly than he deserves as a means of promoting his welfare and reducing the social cost of his crime may be more acceptable than imposing a harsher sentence than he deserves in the interest of incapacitation and public protection. However, an important element of fairness is to treat similar cases similarly; thus, we are not sanguine about a regime in which one armed robber is sent to a secure correctional facility while another receives a community sanction based on a court's judgment about risk and amenability to rehabilitation. This is particularly worrisome to the extent that racial and socioeconomic biases may play a subtle, perhaps even unconscious, role in sentencing. Indeed, even unbiased judges may make sentencing decisions on the basis of criteria that are legitimate but likely to affect minority youths and those who are socioeconomically disadvantaged more adversely than others. For example, judges may view community sanctions as more appropriate for youths with involved parents to supervise and participate in programs. This (probably valid) consideration may disfavor poor and minority offenders who may be more likely to come from single-parent households or families in which supervision is lax. These concerns lead us to conclude that a presumption favoring proportionate punishment is justified, and that in hard cases, fairness should trump social welfare.

We recognize that policy-makers may reach a different conclusion, and that these are difficult choices. Fortunately, cases involving normative adolescent offenders that truly present a conflict between fairness and social welfare are likely to be infrequent. In general, the research evidence supports the greater use of community sanctions in dispositions for juveniles than for adults on grounds of social welfare—but *also* on grounds of proportionality. Moreover, proportionality does not require precisely measured punishment and is satisfied by a sentencing regime that authorizes a range of sanctions for a given offense, so long as the range is relatively narrow. Modest sentence variations based on social welfare concerns acknowledge the multiple goals that must be accommodated in a satisfactory and stable system, without undermining fairness excessively. A regime committed to the recognition of adolescents as a distinct category and to a presumption that juveniles should be punished more leniently than adults embodies the principle of proportionality far better than the contemporary regime. Reforms that reinforce and maintain a sturdier boundary between juveniles and adults will generally serve the interests of justice, even if sanctions are not rigidly calibrated on the bases of harm and culpability.

Drawing the Jurisdictional Boundaries

Among the most important policy decisions in the regulation of youth crime are the designation of the jurisdictional age boundary between the juvenile and adult system and the determination of which juveniles can be tried as adults. We examine these issues below. But first we should address a preliminary jurisdictional issue: What should be the minimum age of *juvenile* court jurisdiction? In our view, that age should be ten. Children age nine and under are truly children in terms of their psychological development and can not properly be held accountable for their crimes in a system committed to proportionality. Under our developmental model, punishment is among the appropriate purposes of delinquency adjudication; we reject an approach aimed solely at rehabilitation. The criminal choices of children under age ten, due to their cognitive and psychosocial immaturity, are simply not culpable enough to subject them to even minimal criminal responsibility or, accordingly, to state-imposed punishment. Moreover, below age ten, children are likely to lack competence to stand trial even under a relaxed juvenile court standard. (See Chapter 6.)

This does not mean that the state is powerless to intervene when, as occasionally will happen, youngsters below the minimum jurisdictional age engage in criminal activity. As we discuss later in this chapter, the state has the authority to intervene when children engage in harmful conduct and their parents are unable or unwilling to exercise appropriate control. For children under the age of ten, however, such interventions are grounded in the state's *parens patriae* authority to promote the child's welfare.

Deciding where to draw the chronological age boundary between adolescence and adulthood for purposes of justice policy is a more complex challenge than setting the minimum age of juvenile court jurisdiction because several concerns are important but may not point in the same direction. The first is psychological development; the line should be drawn with attention to the process of maturation, ideally shielding immature youths from adult prosecution and punishment while holding mature individuals fully accountable. This factor turns out to be somewhat complex, however, because, as we have explained, the relevant psychological abilities and capacities do not develop in lockstep fashion, but progress at different rates. Thus, logical reasoning and information-processing capacities that are most relevant to competence to stand trial and related matters mature steadily through pre-adolescence and early adolescence, reaching adult levels around age fifteen or sixteen. In contrast, psychosocial capacities that influence involvement in criminal activity, such as impulse control, future orientation, or resistance to peer influence (as well as the regions of the brain that regulate these phenomena), mature primarily in middle adolescence, continuing into late adolescence and even into early adulthood. Consequently, a sixteen-year-old may have the logical reasoning abilities of an adult and the impulse control or susceptibility to peer pressure of a teenager. Thus, a jurisdictional boundary separating minors from adults based on studies of logical reasoning and basic cognitive abilities would classify adolescents as adults at a younger age than a boundary based on research on psychosocial development or brain maturation. Beyond this, there is a great deal of individual variation in maturation rates; some youths are adultlike at age fifteen, while others are still immature in early adulthood. Adolescence and adulthood are not tidy developmental categories; the transition to adulthood is a gradual process. The upshot is that science does not dictate any specific age as the appropriate threshold for adult adjudication and punishment.

Societal values and goals are also important, of course. Public safety will play a role in setting the jurisdictional boundary, sometimes weighing in favor of extending criminal court jurisdiction to youths who are not fully mature but have caused grievous harm and pose a serious threat of future criminal activity. Fairness principles strongly support restrictions prohibiting the criminal prosecution of pre-teenagers and young adolescents, but by mid-adolescence, mitigation claims are weaker and occasionally may be trumped by other priorities. But social welfare goals also support extending juvenile court dispositional jurisdiction so that some serious young offenders can be held accountable in correctional settings that maximize the likelihood of successful transitions to adult roles.

An appropriate balancing of the relevant factors will result in a regime based on three age categories. In the first group are youths whose immaturity across multiple domains of functioning warrants their categorical treatment as juveniles. Based on the available research evidence, we think this boundary setting the *minimum* age of adult adjudication should be at age fifteen.[21] This is closer to the traditional juvenile court boundary than the jurisdictional line set in many states today, which typically is lower than age fifteen. Although generally we do not advocate a return to the traditional rehabilitative model, our analysis of the available scientific evidence leads us to conclude that traditional law was correct in this regard. We recognize that an occasional fourteen-year-old may possess near-adultlike maturity, but this would be unusual, and individualized assessment poses a substantial risk of error. A boundary of age fifteen protects against adult prosecution of youths who are likely to be both significantly less culpable than their adult counterparts and substantially more vulnerable to the harsh context of adult prison.

A second category of individuals, those who commit crimes after their eighteenth birthday, should be dealt with as adults. Age eighteen is the presumptive marker between childhood and adulthood, the age of majority for most legal purposes, and it should also be the presumptive age of adult status for purposes of criminal adjudication. In almost forty states, juvenile court jurisdiction ends at age eighteen, the same age at which an individual becomes an adult for purposes of voting, executing a lease or contract, and consenting to medical treatment.[22] Although studies of brain development indicate that continued maturation takes place until at least age twenty-five or so, policy-makers would not likely endorse treating individuals who offend in their early twenties as juveniles, nor should they. These criminals are mature enough to be held fully accountable, and public safety requires that they be punished as adults.

The age group in the middle, and the one that poses the most difficult challenges to policy-makers and practitioners, is comprised of fifteen- to seventeen-year-olds. This is a transitional period for so many important aspects of psychological development that there is likely to be much variation—not only among individuals of the same chronological age but also *within* individuals, in that development in different domains of psychological functioning proceeds at different rates. We recommend that the juvenile court presumptively retain jurisdiction over individuals in this age group because, collectively, they deserve mitigation on the basis of immaturity. Just as important, the juvenile system is more likely to provide a social setting and programs tailored to the developmental needs of mid-adolescents. However, to maintain the stability and legitimacy of the juvenile system and to accommodate society's interest in crime reduction, mechanisms must be provided through which some youths in this age group who are charged with serious crimes can be transferred to the adult system. This determination should be made on the basis of their presenting offense and criminal record.

Extending Juvenile Court Dispositional Jurisdiction

Although age eighteen is the appropriate boundary of juvenile court jurisdiction for purposes of *adjudication,* the jurisdictional age for *dispositions* should extend into early adulthood, optimally until age twenty-four or twenty-five.[23] Youths who engage in serious criminal conduct at age sixteen or seventeen usually should be dealt with as juveniles, on both mitigation and social welfare grounds. However, if age eighteen marks the end of juvenile court jurisdiction altogether, there often may not be time for sufficient punishment. This is problematic on proportionality grounds; it would be perverse for older youths to receive less punishment than their younger counterparts, whose dispositions will not be cut short by the jurisdictional age boundary. More likely, a uniform jurisdictional age boundary for adjudication and disposition will result in many older youths being classified as adults, eroding the boundary between the juvenile and the criminal systems. Indeed, the only realistic alternatives to extending the jurisdiction for juvenile court dispositions well beyond age eighteen are automatic transfer to criminal court of older juveniles charged with especially serious violent crimes or "blended sentencing," under which juveniles are sanctioned in the juvenile system and may be transferred to adult prison when they reach the age of eighteen.[24] In our view, extended jurisdiction is superior to either of these alternatives.

In the discussion of the criteria for transfer below, we will artic-ulate our opposition to automatic transfer solely on the basis of the presenting offense, but a few words on blended sentencing are in order. This alternative, conceived as a policy for dealing with youths convicted of serious crimes, has several problematic fea-tures. Most versions of blended sentencing provide for an assess-ment of the offender's progress and the likelihood of recidivism at age eighteen, the point of transfer from the juvenile to the adult system. Youths found to represent a low risk of re-offending may receive probation at that point, while other youths are sent to the adult system. Critics have argued, correctly we think, that this scheme represents "the worst of both worlds" for juveniles, com-bining the less protective due process rights of the juvenile court (the forum of adjudication) with the more punitive sanctions of the adult system, where at least a portion of the sentence is carried out.[25] Moreover, discretionary judicial assessments on which adult punishment is based carry the possibility of bias and may disad-vantage minority offenders. Finally, for some young offenders, nei-ther prison nor release from confinement at age eighteen is an appropriate sanction for their offenses. A sixteen-year-old youth may deserve incarceration that extends beyond his eighteenth birthday, but not necessarily the sanction of confinement in an adult prison.

Extended jurisdiction in the juvenile system can provide suitable dispositions for such youths and, generally, has several advantages over blended sentencing. First, it acknowledges immaturity as a mitigating factor. Punishment should be based on the offender's culpability *at the time of the offense;* thus, the fact that a youth, be-cause of the seriousness of his crime, deserves a sanction that ex-tends into adulthood does not mean that the conditions of punishment when he reaches adulthood should be those imposed on individuals who offend as adults. Second, extended jurisdiction provides the option of imposing real sanctions involving lengthy periods of incapacitation on older juveniles who commit serious offenses. Thus, public safety can be promoted through proportionate sentences that have the advantage of avoiding the exposure of young offenders to the potentially harmful effects of the adult correctional system. Since developmental factors play a role in the criminal activity of many of these youths, it seems desirable to punish them in a setting that is more likely than adult prison to reduce the risk of recidivism and promote the transition to healthy adulthood when they are released into society.

The benefits of extending juvenile court dispositions into adulthood can be realized fully only if the juvenile system develops a variety of programs and facilities that are appropriate for individuals at different stages of adolescent development. As any parent recognizes, the developmental needs of thirteen-year-olds are quite different from those of young adults in their twenties. These differences could be accommodated by separating adolescents according to educational age categories: middle school, high school, and post-high school. This scheme has the advantage of grouping juveniles on the basis of their stage of psychological development and their educational level, permitting both more efficient delivery of academic and vocational services and smoother transitions back into the community upon release from institutional placement.

When Should Juveniles Be Tried as Adults?

Although most youths charged with crimes should be adjudicated and sanctioned in the juvenile system, some juveniles appropriately are eligible for transfer to criminal court for adjudication and punishment as adults. On our view, teenagers age fifteen or older who have been previously been convicted of serious violent crimes and face charges for (another) violent felony fall in this eligibility category. These criteria make sense for several reasons. These youths have far less compelling claims to mitigation than do most juveniles. Their relative maturity and the severity of the harm that they have caused, together with the current charge, may support the conclusion that they are simply too much like their adult counterparts to justify more lenient treatment in the juvenile system. Moreover, violent recidivists represent a serious threat to public safety and to other youths housed in juvenile facilities. A history of violent offending is the best predictor of future violence, and, as we explain in Chapter 9, public opinion polls show clearly that society is unlikely to tolerate leniency toward very high-risk offenders. Beyond this, older violent recidivists may not benefit from resources in the juvenile system. Indeed, the premise of the developmental model—that most youth crime is driven by developmental influences of adolescence that will decline with maturity—may not apply to older juveniles with a record of serious offending that has not waned with age. The possibility of transfer to criminal court has *always* functioned as a safety valve for the juvenile system. This mechanism acknowledges that a more lenient, rehabilitative approach may be ineffective for some youths and that society can legitimately insist that they be incapacitated so that they are unable to inflict more harm.

Many youths who qualify for transfer will be "life-course persistent" offenders. These are juveniles who differ from normative adolescent offenders, both in the pattern of offending and in their trajectories into adulthood. But the classification of any group of same-aged individuals as presumptively unsuitable for the juvenile system is highly problematic. As we have emphasized in earlier chapters, the "diagnosis" of psychopathy in adolescence is an uncertain, error-prone business and not one that responsible social scientists or policy-makers endorse.[26]

Our task at this point is to propose guidelines for decisions about the transfer of *individual* juveniles, age fifteen to seventeen, to the adult system, a determination that should be made on a case-by-case basis in a judicial proceeding and not as a result of legislative waiver. The categorical waiver of youths on the basis of age and the seriousness of the presenting criminal charges alone is undesirable on social welfare grounds because almost surely it will lead to adult prosecution and punishment not only of life-course persistent offenders but also of many normative adolescents who would likely mature out of their inclinations to get involved in criminal conduct. Prosecutorial direct-file authority is also problematic, as prosecutors may be motivated to charge youths as adults on the basis of short-term public outrage or their own long-term political ambitions.

To avoid sweeping many youths who are not incipient criminals into the adult system, transfer should be precluded for any juvenile with no previous record of serious violent offending. As we have noted throughout this book, under the right (or wrong) social conditions, normative adolescents may get involved in very serious criminal activity. On the street, in the company of other youths, normal teenagers can make bad choices that reflect the immature judgment of adolescence. In some high-crime neighborhoods, only unusual teenagers are successful at staying out of criminal gangs or avoiding involvement in crime. Retaining all youths facing their first felony charges in the juvenile system will greatly reduce the number of normative adolescents who are dealt with as adults by the justice system. At the same time, extended jurisdiction assures that those first offenders who commit serious crimes can receive proportionate punishment—but in an environment that is more likely to preserve their future options. Under the developmental model, only a youth who has been previously convicted of a serious violent felony (murder, attempted murder, armed robbery, rape, aggravated assault, or kidnapping) would be eligible for transfer to criminal court.

Transfer should further be limited to youths whose *current* charges are also violent felonies. Property crimes and drug offenses cause social harm, to be sure, but punishment in the juvenile system is a sufficient response on both fairness and social welfare grounds. A youth who commits multiple serious nonviolent crimes may deserve incarceration, sometimes extending into adulthood, but she can be sanctioned adequately in the juvenile system and with a greater prospect of correction than in the adult system. Youths charged with drug offenses make up a substantial part of the group of juveniles who are tried as adults today. In many cases, however, they are not hardened drug dealers, but subordinates working for adult drug sellers or teens selling drugs to support their own addictions.[27] The juvenile system is far better positioned to respond to these latter youths effectively through age-appropriate substance abuse programs.

The combination of jurisdictional restrictions (that is, only youths ages fifteen to seventeen) and eligibility requirements (that is, only juveniles with a violent felony charge *and* a violent felony record) sharply limits the category of youths potentially subject to transfer to those who can fairly be dealt with as adults on the basis of age and severity of the crime with which they are charged. Thus, under our model, the exercise of judicial and prosecutorial discretion would be restricted in ways that substantially ameliorate the concerns about bias that are often raised about the contemporary legal regime, in which many young defendants are eligible for adult prosecution for a broad range of felonies.[28] Further, as compared with current law, the regulation of transfer under the developmental model greatly reduces the likelihood that normative youths whose crimes represent immature adolescent judgment will be tried and punished as adults.

On what basis should judges decide whether to transfer eligible youths or to retain them in the juvenile system? In our view, within the proposed eligibility constraints, courts can apply the standard transfer criteria, making decisions on the basis of a careful evaluation of the youth's criminal record and the circumstances of the offense with which he is charged, as well as his likely amenability to treatment and his response to past treatment efforts.[29] The treatment-related factors introduce a modest, albeit imperfect, predictive dimension to a regime otherwise committed to basing sanctions of fairness considerations but without unduly compromising proportionality.

Finally, the transfer evaluation should include an evaluation of the youth's competence to stand trial and generally to participate as a defendant in a criminal proceeding. To be sure, the likelihood that incompetent youths will be tried as adults is reduced substantially under the developmental model by the categorical exclusion of teenagers younger than fifteen. Research, including our study of age differences in competence to stand trial, has found no differences between the performance of older adolescents and adults on measures of competence.[30] Nonetheless, some fifteen-year-olds or mentally impaired youths may not be competent. Routine evaluation of youths who face adult prosecution signals a commitment to procedural fairness in a legal proceeding of critical importance to the affected youth. This requirement poses no substantial burden to the justice system, given that the category of youths subject to transfer is small under our proposal.[31]

Should Juveniles in Prison Get Special Treatment?

Under the developmental model, youths who are subject to criminal punishment will be a small number of older recidivists who have committed serious violent crimes. They can fairly be described as the worst juvenile offenders, some of whom are clearly different from normative adolescents. So, the question arises, should any special conditions apply to the punishment of transferred juveniles because of their youth? Under current law in some states, young offenders are processed and sentenced in criminal court under Youthful Offender Statutes; they receive shorter sentences and are confined separately.[32] In many jurisdictions, however, juveniles tried as adults are not given any special treatment; their sentences are similar to those of their adult counterparts, and they are offered no special services or status by virtue of their youth.

This approach seems shortsighted. The reality is that virtually all young offenders in prison will complete their sentences and return to society. Some will resume lives of crime, but this path is not inevitable. Even under our restrictive criteria, normative adolescents may be transferred, and their experiences in the justice system may affect whether they choose criminal careers. Thus, preparing young prisoners for the transition to life in the community by providing them with educational and skill-building services both serves their interests and also promotes social welfare.[33] In many states today, juveniles in adult prisons receive minimal, if any, educational services. Courts have held that states can restrict services available to youths in prison, even in jurisdictions in which the state constitution provides a right to education.[34] According to one study, only 12 percent of formerly incarcerated adolescents received their high school diploma or General Equivalency Degree (GED) as young adults, compared with 86 percent for the population as a whole.[35] Because educational attainment is so strongly linked to both employment and earnings, the failure to provide educational services in the justice system may have lasting adverse effects on the legal earnings of imprisoned youths.[36] This failure also increases the likelihood that they will continue in their criminal activities for want of any skills to undertake noncriminal employment.

Proportionality supports imposing statutory limits on the maximum duration of adult sentences impose on juveniles—a "youth discount," to use Feld's term. Even these most culpable of young offenders can be distinguished from adults on the ground of youthful immaturity. Under the logic of the Supreme Court's opinion in *Roper v. Simmons,* prohibiting the imposition of the death penalty on juvenile offenders, youths also should be excluded from the criminal sentence of Life Without Parole (LWOP). We are skeptical about whether the *constitutional* prohibition of cruel and unusual punishment under the Eighth Amendment extends to LWOP;[37] nonetheless, this punishment is excessive on proportionality grounds. According to *Roper*, diminished decision-making capacity, susceptibility to peer influence, and unformed character are developmental attributes that make juveniles ineligible for capital punishment on the basis of reduced culpability. These same traits also should make them ineligible for LWOP.[38]

LWOP and other long sentences that do not have parole as an option are problematic on social welfare grounds as well. First, incarceration is expensive: in some states, it can exceed $45,000 per prisoner per year.[39] Remember the case of Tim Kane discussed in Chapter 7; by a conservative estimate, his life sentence for felony murder (for hiding under a table while his friends killed two people) will likely cost Florida taxpayers close to a million dollars. Second, because offenders who continue to commit violent crimes beyond age forty are extremely rare,[40] sentences that mandate confinement beyond this age cannot be justified on grounds of public safety. In general, the enthusiasm for extremely long sentences in this country uniquely distinguishes us from other developed countries and makes little sense on social welfare grounds. In the case of juveniles, at least, LWOP cannot be justified on the basis of *either* social welfare or proportionality.

In this section, we have suggested guidelines for translating key scientific lessons about adolescent development into prescriptions for a satisfactory system of juvenile crime regulation. These lessons include the recognition that adolescent immaturity reduces culpability; that normal adolescents in high-crime neighborhoods may get involved in criminal activity, but most are likely to desist with maturity; and that social context (including the correctional context) plays a key role in adolescent development and is likely to affect whether delinquent youths make a successful transition to adulthood. The hallmarks of our science-based regime are proportionate but more lenient punishment in the juvenile system; correctional settings and programs in this system that reduce recidivism and facilitate the acquisition of skills and capacities necessary for the successful transition to adulthood; and policies that narrowly restrict the transfer of juveniles to criminal court. The extension of the dispositional jurisdiction of the juvenile system allows these goals to be realized with serious young offenders, who might well be punished as adults today. The model recognizes and accommodates the key goals of fairness and social welfare. Fairness objectives dictate the severity of a proportionate sentence and the extent to which it constitutes a deprivation of liberty (on the basis of harm and culpability), while social welfare goals determine the context of the punishment and the content of programs that will facilitate healthy development and promote desistence.

How is the developmental model different from earlier approaches to juvenile crime regulation? Differences from the contemporary regime are quite apparent, in the model's commitment to mitigation and reinforcement of the boundary between the juvenile and criminal systems and in the emphasis on the importance of correctional settings. Differences between our model and the traditional approach are a bit more subtle, and some may view our proposal as simply an effort to revive the rehabilitative model. Indeed, some similarities exist. Like the rehabilitative model, our approach emphasizes that young offenders are not responsible adults and that correctional interventions and settings can make a difference in the future lives and prospects of youths in the justice system. (A difference is that, today, solid scientific evidence supports both of these propositions, whereas the Progressive Era reformers were excessively optimistic about the tools of nineteenth-century science.) But there are also important conceptual and practical differences between our approach and the traditional model. The developmental model views young offenders as adolescents who are accountable for their crimes and deserving of punishment, if less so than adults, and not as children solely in need of rehabilitation. The most important *practical* distinction is in our commitment to proportionate punishment and to restricting judicial discretion. This translates into a regime in which sanctions are fairer, more predictable, and less vulnerable to charges of bias and arbitrariness than under the traditional juvenile system.

Dealing with the Hard Cases

The scientific lessons about the role of criminal involvement in adolescence that are the foundation of our model do not apply to all young offenders. Some youths have a history of antisocial behavior and a "prognosis" that is quite different from that of typical teenagers whose criminal activity is largely confined to adolescence and driven by developmental influences. For these individuals, a pattern of antisocial behavior may begin in early childhood and continue through adolescence and into adulthood. They may come into the justice system and face serious charges before they are in high school, and have a substantial criminal record by mid-adolescence. Although these youths represent only a small percentage of young offenders, they pose a substantial threat to public safety, and public and political concern about this threat has had a pernicious effect on policies that affect all young offenders. Thus, in this last part of a chapter in which we offer prescriptions for youth crime policy, we focus directly on youths who do not fit well within our developmental model. Dealing fairly with youths in this group, at whatever age they enter the justice system, and at the same time protecting the public from the harms they cause is a daunting challenge. They are indeed "hard cases."

The Case of Yummy Sandifer

Yummy Sandifer, whose nickname evidenced his love of cookies and Snickers bars, was born in 1983 in Chicago to a teenage mother addicted to crack cocaine and a drug dealer father who was in and out of prison.[41] Yummy was an angry, antisocial child from an early age. Maltreated and neglected from the time he was an infant, he was removed from his mother's custody at age four, along with four brothers and sisters. He lived with his grandmother over the next several years but also spent time in detention homes and foster care—and on the streets. Yummy was very small for his age; nonetheless, he gained a reputation as a neighborhood bully, who would challenge bigger kids to fights and extort money from neighbors, who feared him despite his diminutive size. Local merchants refused to allow him in their stores because he stole so often, and by age ten Yummy had also stolen and burned several cars. A psychiatric examination conducted about this time found him to be impulsive, unpredictable, and illiterate, but also filled with self-hatred and loneliness. In responding to a request to complete the sentence "I am very . . . ," Yummy answered "sick."

Yummy's involvement in serious criminal activity escalated when, at about age ten, he became involved with the Black Disciples, a powerful Chicago street gang. Gang leaders and older members often gave younger kids criminal assignments, which the youngsters eagerly performed to demonstrate their toughness and dedication. Yummy was a devoted acolyte and, according to police records, had been involved in at least twenty-three felonies by the time he was eleven years old. The police arrested him many times, but because of his age, probation was the only sanction permitted under existing Illinois law.

One day in late August 1994, Yummy went to a park near his home and started shooting with a 9 millimeter automatic rifle at a crowd of boys playing football. Although his motivation was never clearly established, experts in gang behavior speculated that he was on a mission of revenge, sent out by Black Disciple leaders to find and shoot a member of a rival gang. Instead, in the rain of bullets, Yummy shot in the head and killed fourteen-year-old Shavon Dean, who was walking by the park on her way to visit a friend. As the police began a massive search for the shooter, gang members moved Yummy from one hiding place to another. Perhaps sensing that he had become a liability to the gang, he appeared three days after the shooting on a neighbor's porch and said he wanted to turn himself in to the police. When the neighbor returned from calling the police, Yummy had disappeared. The next day, he was found shot to death under a railroad underpass, apparently killed by members of his gang. Parents brought their children to see the boy, lying in his coffin with his stuffed animals at his side, hoping that the sight of Yummy would help their children to avoid his fate.

The actual case of Yummy Sandifer was never adjudicated, of course. Nonetheless, it is easy to see how cases like this present a challenge to the developmental model of juvenile justice that we propose. Yummy engaged in criminal activity at a very young age, committing serious property crimes when he was eight or nine years old and violent felonies at age ten. He was clearly developmentally immature. Applying standard criminal law principles, Yummy was less culpable than even a teenage counterpart would be, to say nothing of an adult. Almost certainly, given his age and mental capacity, he also lacked competence to stand trial in a criminal proceeding. Illinois law at the time implicitly recognized his immaturity by limiting the state's options for punishing, or even restraining, him. But Yummy was also extremely dangerous, ready to steal, rob, and even kill, seemingly without compunctions. Moreover, his crimes could not be described as the product of transient developmental influences characteristic of adolescence; his antisocial conduct began early in childhood and seemed far more pathological than that of normative delinquents. Moreover, it is difficult to be optimistic that Yummy would have matured out of his antisocial inclinations, had his life not been cut short. The dilemma for the justice system (and for the developmental model) is clear: while the principle of proportionality points toward a lenient sanction, public protection might be better served by incarcerating Yummy for a long time. What is the law's appropriate response when fairness to immature young offenders and protection of public safety conflict with one another?

Severely Antisocial Youths: The Scientific Evidence

To answer the question of how to deal with these hard cases, it may be useful to look more closely at what we know about the small group of young offenders like Yummy, whose pattern of criminal activity is quite different from that of typical teenagers. The criminal involvement of these youths is typically both persistent over time and extreme in its severity and frequency. Their arrest records tell only a part of the story of the number and frequency of their offending; self-report studies indicate that most serious offenders are arrested for only a fraction of their crimes.[42] During adolescence, their criminal activity may sometimes be similar to that of other teenagers, but over time their history of offending is very different.

Studies over the past few decades have found consistently that a very small group of young offenders is responsible for a large proportion of juvenile crime. In David Farrington's longitudinal study of London youths, 5 percent to 6 percent of young offenders committed 50 percent of the crimes.[43] Similarly, Marvin Wolfgang and his colleagues followed a cohort of youths born in Philadelphia in 1945 (and, in a later study, a cohort of youths born in 1958) over many years and found that 6 percent of the youths committed four or more serious crimes and were responsible for 50 percent of the total crime.[44] The pattern continues in more recent studies. In our group's ongoing study of serious juvenile offenders in Phoenix and Philadelphia, between 5 percent and 10 percent of the sample (*all* of whom were enrolled in the study after being convicted of a felony) chronically re-offended.

A distinguishing feature of this group is that most begin to engage in problem behaviors early in childhood and show a stable pattern of antisocial conduct that continues and escalates in its seriousness as they get older.[45] As early as age three, many are identified as angry and "difficult to manage" by parents and other adults, and as aggressive in their relationships with other children.[46] They may be diagnosed with attention deficit/hyperactivity disorder (ADHD), and their academic performance is often poor. In elementary school, discipline problems escalate to criminal conduct, including stealing, setting fires, and assaulting other children and adults. Yummy's childhood history of antisocial behavior and criminal activity is typical of this pattern. By the age of twelve or thirteen, most have been arrested for a serious violent crime, and they continue to offend thereafter.

A note of caution is in order. Although most individuals who are chronic offenders in adolescence have long histories of problem behaviors, the reverse is not true: not all children who have behavior problems are headed for a life of crime. Many children are aggressive and hard to manage in preschool, throwing tantrums and getting into fights; moreover, the diagnosis of ADHD is ubiquitous among elementary school children today. Serious problem behaviors in childhood may signal even more severe problems in the future and clearly warrant attention, but they should not be taken as compelling evidence that the child is an incipient criminal. Some "difficult" children desist from antisocial behavior later in childhood, through maturation, parental efforts, and appropriate interventions.[47]

Terrie Moffitt, the psychologist whose famous longitudinal study is the basis of her distinction between "adolescent-limited" and "life-course-persistent" offenders, also found a group of children who engaged in antisocial behavior but desisted in late childhood or early adolescence; by late adolescence, they showed few conduct problems.[48] The pattern that characterizes the small group of offenders we are concerned with is persistent and stable antisocial behavior over an extended period of time as a precursor to a pattern of serious violent offending in adolescence.[49]

A strong correlation exists between the age at which an individual first engages in criminal conduct and the likelihood that his offending will persist beyond adolescence. Indeed, the age of first arrest is a key indicator of whether criminal involvement is adolescent experimentation or is likely to be more intractable. Studies show that the average age of first arrest for a violent crime ranges from 15.6 to 16.1.[50] A youth like Yummy, who commits a violent felony at age eleven or twelve, is very different from the typical delinquent—including the typical youth charged with a serious offense—who first offends in mid-adolescence. At one level, this conclusion is simply a logical recognition that when youths get involved in serious criminal activity in the pre-adolescent years, their behavior is not likely to be driven by developmental forces associated with adolescence but by something else, such as individual pathology or pernicious environmental influences. Arrest at an early age often marks a continuation and escalation of an antisocial course of behavior. Again, caution is in order; the crimes of some very young offenders may be aberrant acts that will not be repeated or the late antisocial acts of a youth whose problem behavior is "childhood-limited." Nonetheless, a strong consensus among researchers holds that youths who are first arrested for a serious crime at age thirteen or younger are at significantly elevated risk for becoming career criminals.[51]

Why Do Some Children Become Persistently Antisocial?

What causes some children to behave antisocially at an early age and then to persist in an escalating pattern that may eventually lead them to become career criminals? At this point, knowledge on these matters is somewhat speculative, but developmental psychologists and criminologists point to several factors that distinguish these youths from normative adolescents whose criminal involvement is likely to be transitory.[52] Physiological or neuropsychological deficits may be a source of persistent antisocial tendencies. Studies have linked antisocial conduct to some brain anomalies and also to certain types of fetal brain injuries.[53] Neuropsychological assessments have correlated aggressive and antisocial tendencies with verbal deficits and impairments in the brain's executive functions, particularly impulse control.[54]

Parents may also contribute to antisocial and aggressive conduct through the way they rear their children. Not surprisingly, parental abuse and neglect are linked to antisocial behavior in children.[55] Beyond this, children who are difficult to manage (due to neuropsychological deficits or other sources) may be born into families that are not well suited to deal with the challenges they present. Their parents may lack the necessary psychological or physical resources, either because they share some of their child's deficits or because they are simply unable to provide a healthy developmental environment for a child with compelling needs.[56] The interaction between a difficult child and parents who lack the necessary skills, inclination, temperament, or resources to deal with him can generate a dynamic that contributes to antisocial conduct. In short, a child's aggressive tendencies may be exacerbated if parents are abusive, withdraw from their parental role, or respond inappropriately to a child who frustrates their efforts to assert parental authority.[57]

As the child moves beyond the family into other social contexts, a reciprocal pattern of individual behavior and environmental response often reinforces the tendency toward antisocial conduct. In some children, problems in self-regulation or anger management will continue to manifest themselves behaviorally in different contexts as they move through life. The specific manifestations will change; the four-year-old may have violent tantrums while the fifteen-year-old may hold up a convenience store, but the underlying antisocial inclinations are linked. Other factors maintain this trajectory. Teachers and other adults may respond to the difficult child in ways that encourage, rather than deter, his antisocial conduct. Beyond this, the consequences of antisocial conduct typically are cumulative and tend to restrict opportunities for experiences that might alter the course of the child's life in a positive direction. Thus, very aggressive children fail to develop bonds with normative children that might lead them away from antisocial conduct. They may acquire reputations in school and in their communities that reinforce their identities as "bad kids" and discourage adult authority figures from offering support. These children also tend to have limited educational attainments that eventually limit their abilities to succeed in conventional adult roles.[58] If they are convicted of crimes, they become enmeshed in the criminal justice system, which can reinforce their deviant lifestyle. Thus antisocial youths may be driven to continue on their wayward paths by internal forces that contribute to their inclinations to act aggressively, by the responses of others to their conduct, and by consequences of their conduct that become "external" constraints on their abilities to alter the course of their lives.

The Justice System's Response to Severely Antisocial Youths

Against this backdrop, we return to our earlier question: How can a justice system committed to both fairness and social welfare respond to violent young offenders who present a high risk of re-offending and of becoming career criminals? These youths present quite different challenges from normative young offenders around whom the developmental model is built. They also present different challenges from one another, depending on their age. Although a sixteen-year-old with a long history of serious offending may simply appear to be an older version of Yummy, for *policy* purposes, he is quite different. Differences in age, maturity, and criminal experience distinguish severely antisocial pre-adolescents from older teenagers and dictate a different legal response to their crimes.

PRE-TEENAGE OFFENDERS: TAKING YOUTHFUL VIOLENCE SERI-OUSLY. Pre-teenagers and young adolescent offenders are among the most dangerous of young criminals, presenting a higher risk of reoffending and of becoming career criminals, than youths whose first offenses are at age fifteen or sixteen. However, because of their psychological immaturity, these youths are also less culpable than are older teenagers, and their claims for mitigation are more compelling. Thus, even a youth like Yummy Sandifer, who by any account was a serious threat to the community, could not fairly be punished for his crime to the extent that would be appropriate for an adult or even an older youth. In the traditional juvenile court, leniency was the standard response to even serious crimes by very young offenders. The sanction Yummy received for multiple felonies at age ten and eleven, a brief rehabilitative intervention, was typical. Even today, because of a natural reluctance to crack down on very young offenders, many courts let pre-teenagers off with mild sanctions for serious felonies, hoping these youths will grow out of their antisocial ways. A few years and many crimes later when it becomes clear that this was wishful thinking, the juvenile is punished severely.

On our view, this minimalist response is off the mark. A sanction of probation will have little effect on the child's inclination to get involved in criminal activity, and brief rehabilitative interventions are unlikely to change patterns of antisocial conduct that are already entrenched by late childhood. Waiting until these youths are identified as chronic violent offenders misses the opportunity for remediation at a point when the possibility for rehabilitation is more promising than it will be later.

The best hope for an effective response to very young violent offenders is a policy of rehabilitation that is far more comprehensive than traditional juvenile court "treatment," one that includes interventions that address the complex individual, family, social, and educational deficits of these high-risk youths. Intensive treatment will require substantial supervision of the young offender and his environment, and sometimes that will mean a period of closely supervised residential placement. However, the most effective programs (Functional Family Therapy, for example) focus on instructing parents to competently perform their role under challenging conditions; thus, the involvement of parents or parental authority figures will be a key component of treatment. Further, as the success of Multi-Systemic Therapy (MST) has shown, multi-disciplinary interventions that address the youth's problems in the various contexts in which he lives are most promising.[59]

A legitimate question is whether intensive interventions are warranted for younger adolescents convicted of serious crimes, simply on the basis of their age and the seriousness of the offense. Not all very young offenders will grow up to be career criminals. As we have suggested, some may naturally desist, and their antisocial behavior might more accurately be classified as "childhood-limited." In early adolescence, however, it is very difficult to distinguish these youths from those who are likely to persist in their criminal ways,[60] and the two criteria we have described are sufficiently powerful risk factors to justify the kind of comprehensive interventions that we propose. A youth with both a childhood history of antisocial behavior *and* a serious offense in late childhood or early adolescence (when most conduct-disordered children will have shown signs of desistence) is at high risk for future offending and should receive comprehensive rehabilitative interventions. Directing the system's resources toward these youths would likely have greater pay-off in the prevention of crime than continuing to spend large amounts of money incarcerating youths whose profiles are more consistent with that of normative offenders.

But can dispositions of intensive rehabilitative interventions directed at pre-adolescents be reconciled with the developmental model's commitment to proportionality? We think that the answer is "yes," if one more condition is added to the two described above. This condition is that interventions and programs that extend over a period of years through adolescence must be of types that are available not only to delinquents, but also to children outside the justice system on the basis of need and family circumstances. Thus, remedial services, including parental training, family supervision, and foster care placement; residential and outpatient mental health services; and educational services, including special education plans—all can be part of a coordinated comprehensive rehabilitation package that also includes programs in the juvenile justice system, without imposing disproportionate punishment on offenders whose immaturity limits their culpability.[61]

What should be done with children under the age of ten (the minimum jurisdictional age under our proposal) or with pre-teenagers who, because of their extreme cognitive immaturity, lack minimal competence to participate in a delinquency proceeding? The state should respond to the criminal activity of these children under the juvenile court's dependency jurisdiction, which gives the government the authority to intervene when children engage in problem behaviors that are beyond their parents' capacities to control. Comprehensive social service, mental health, and educational interventions can be employed to control the child's antisocial behavior and begin remediation of his multiple problems.

It would be naive to claim that we currently have the tools to re-habilitate all or even most young adolescent criminals, but the time is ripe to undertake this commitment. Over the past generation, promising rehabilitative programs have been developed in the juve-nile system that have been shown to be cost-effective when directed at delinquent youths, including early adolescents.[62] Also promising as a means of reducing antisocial behavior in high-risk children are early intervention programs, such as nurse home visitation and early childhood education programs.[63] The effectiveness of these programs supports a serious long-term investment of societal re-sources directed at developing and implementing interventions that predictably can influence the trajectories of these young offenders' lives in a positive direction.

This investment will be expensive; in general, a policy of inten-sive intervention will be more costly than probation or conven-tional dispositions for very young offenders. Moreover, there is no guarantee of success; the criminal activity of some youths will con-tinue unabated, as even the most effective program will fail with many young offenders. But the social cost of not making the invest-ment likely will be even greater. If, over time, intensive interven-tions are effective at substantially reducing recidivism among these intractable youths, the cost will be readily justified.

DEALING WITH OLDER SERIOUS OFFENDERS. Older adoles-cents with a history of severely antisocial conduct also represent a major challenge to social welfare. Under the developmental model, whether these youths are adjudicated and punished in the juvenile or adult system will depend largely on whether they meet the crite-ria for transfer that we have described. For the fifteen- or sixteen-year-old charged with a violent felony, whose record includes serious violent crimes, transfer may be appropriate. By mid-adolescence, some antisocial youths already have caused a lot of social harm, and they may seem unlikely to desist in the foreseeable future. Their pattern of antisocial behavior, beginning in childhood, differs substantially from that of normative adolescents who get in serious trouble. In our view, if comprehensive rehabilitative efforts of the kind that are appropriate for younger offenders like Yummy fail, at some point society's interest in public protection must prevail in determining the legal response. That point under our model is not reached until age fifteen and only when a youth has a prior record that includes at least one serious violent felony.

Under the developmental model, the population of older youths who are transferred is likely to be mostly juveniles whose pattern of antisocial conduct and offending identifies them as life-course-persistent offenders and distinguishes them from normative adolescents. However, as we have emphasized, youths in this group should not categorically be excluded from juvenile court jurisdiction on the basis of an error-prone "diagnosis." The determination of whether they will be tried and punished in the juvenile or adult system should be based on neutral rules that apply generally to individuals charged with designated offenses who qualify for transfer on the basis of age and past criminal record.

Applying the Developmental Model

It is instructive to ask how the developmental model we propose might play out in some actual cases. Within our framework, the justice system responses to Lionel Tate, Timothy Kane, and Yummy Sandifer, whose cases are familiar to the reader at this point, would be quite different from their actual treatment—and different from one another.

Lionel Tate, whose case is described in Chapter 1, was twelve when he killed young Tiffany, but he evidently had no prior record of antisocial behavior or emotional disturbance. Under our model, his case would be adjudicated in juvenile court and, presuming that he was found responsible for the crime, he would likely be sent to a secure facility under the auspices of the juvenile justice system, where he would be held in a developmentally appropriate setting for several years. (In fact, these were the terms of the plea agreement that Lionel's mother turned down on his behalf.) His adjudication would be in juvenile court, where it is unlikely that his competence to stand trial would be an issue, under the relaxed competence standard applied in delinquency proceedings under the developmental model.

Timothy Kane was the fourteen-year-old who was convicted of felony murder and sentenced to life in a Florida prison (see Chapter 7). Under the developmental model, Tim would not be eligible for criminal court adjudication for his offense, which involved a burglary accompanying two older teenagers who then killed two people; Tim did not participate in the killing. He had no previous criminal record or even contact with the justice system, and his behavior was likely the result of vulnerability to peer pressure, a normal dimension of developmental immaturity. Timothy would likely be adjudicated delinquent and referred to a community agency for treatment in an evidence-based program aimed at adjusting his social context and giving him the tools to resist antisocial peer pressure.

Yummy Sandifer, whose trouble with the law began at a very early age, would be targeted for thorough and sustained intervention at the point of his first serious contact with the law, which predated his tenth birthday. In view of the great risk for continued antisocial behavior such a young offender poses, Yummy would receive intensive treatment and ongoing supervision administered under the aegis of the child welfare system first, and then, if he continued to offend beyond age ten, under the combined jurisdiction of the child welfare and juvenile justice systems. Given his history of early abuse and neglect, and the absence of competent parents or guardians, he would likely be placed in a group home or with a foster family. In either case, Yummy would receive intensive therapy aimed at treating his obvious mental illness.

We have argued in this book that regulating juvenile crime on the basis of scientific knowledge about adolescent development will result in a regime that is more satisfactory than either the traditional rehabilitative model or the contemporary approach. In this chapter, we have offered some guidelines for translating the developmental model into policy. These guidelines include proportionate sentences in juvenile court, programs that invest in the human capital of young offenders, extended dispositional jurisdiction in the juvenile system, restrictive rules for the transfer of older violent offenders, and intensive interventions with very young serious offenders. Our proposals are designed with the ultimate goal of promoting social welfare without sacrificing essential fairness to young people who have violated the law.

We anticipate that our proposals will not be met with universal approval. Some conservatives who discount the differences between adolescents and adults will claim that our proposals are too lenient and that the transfer rules are too restrictive to provide for public safety. Some liberals will challenge proportionate sentencing and transferring fifteen-year-olds (at all); they also may argue that our proposals for intensive interventions with young teenagers may result in excessive punishment rather than helpful treatment. We are quick to acknowledge that the developmental model is not a panacea that will "solve" the problem of youth crime. Juveniles will always get in trouble, sometimes very serious trouble, and some will continue to offend, despite the state's best efforts to respond to their crimes in ways that promote healthy development. At the same time, the future prospects of some youths will be harmed by a system that holds them to adult levels of accountability for their crimes under our transfer rules. No regime will yield good outcomes for all young offenders, but the developmental model provides a solid framework for policies that will be both stable and satisfactory.

These reforms are possible, of course, only if policy-makers and the public accept the premises and policy implications of the developmental model and endorse the legal changes we advance. The political climate surrounding juvenile crime over the past few decades might suggest that this response is unlikely. However, this climate seems to be changing in important ways, offering some basis for optimism that both the public and policy-makers may be receptive to the important legal changes that we advocate.

CHAPTER 9

Is Society Ready for
Juvenile Justice Reform?

This is a good time to reflect on youth crime policy. After a decade of declining juvenile crime rates, the moral panic that fueled the punitive reforms of the 1990s and early 2000s has subsided and there are signs that the political climate is changing. The tone of the debate has moderated somewhat, as even supporters of tough policies have had second thoughts. John DiIulio, who coined the term "superpredators" in the mid-1990s, has expressed regret about this characterization of young offenders and acknowledged that his predictions about the threat of juvenile crime have not been realized.[1] There is also evidence of more concrete changes, as legislatures across the country are reconsidering punitive statutes enacted with such enthusiasm not so many years ago. What we may be seeing now is a pendulum that has reached its apex and is slowly beginning to swing back toward more moderate policies—as politicians and the public come to regret the high economic costs of the recent reforms and to be troubled (at least sometimes) by the harshness of the sanctions. Even the prosecutor and Florida's Governor Jeb Bush came to see the life sentence imposed on Lionel Tate, whose story we told in Chapter 1, as excessive punishment for a twelve-year-old.[2]

Although describing the recent legal changes as a new wave of reforms would exaggerate their significance, several initiatives are

265

noteworthy. First, in the wake of the Supreme Court's 2005 opinion in *Roper v. Simmons* abolishing the juvenile death penalty, several state legislatures have repealed statutes imposing Life Without Parole (LWOP) on juvenile murderers.[3] Other states have scaled back automatic transfer laws, often in response to the mounting economic costs of categorical criminal prosecution and punishment of young offenders. In 2005, for example, Illinois repealed a statute mandating adult prosecution of anyone over age fourteen charged with selling drugs near a school.[4] That same year, Delaware passed legislation limiting the conditions under which juveniles were automatically tried as adults for burglary or robbery, after it was found that approximately 80 percent of the youths who were transferred were eventually sent back to Juvenile Court, but only after having spent many months in adult detention.[5] States such as Hawaii, Maryland, and Missouri have increased funding for community-based treatment programs as alternatives to institutional placement; in Maryland, for example, the legislature mandated that the Governor appropriate $10 million annually to prevention and diversion programs.[6] In a few states in which the general age of criminal court jurisdiction is sixteen or seventeen, promising efforts to raise the age to eighteen are under way.[7] The Rhode Island legislature repealed a statute *lowering* the jurisdictional age from eighteen to seventeen only a few months after its passage, upon realizing its error in thinking that sending teenagers to prison would cut costs.[8] Finally, a few states have expanded procedural protection for juveniles in criminal court by enacting statutory provisions authorizing findings of incompetence to stand trial on the basis of developmental immaturity.[9]

A brief inspection suggests that a combination of influences have contributed to what at a minimum is a change of direction in youth crime policy. Some of these factors are not surprising. Certainly among the most important is the steady decline in juvenile crime, a trend that began in 1994. As we have described in earlier chapters, for many years, politicians and the public seemed to be unaware of the trend, but slowly, the political climate responded to the reduced threat and become more hospitable to proposals for reform. In the same way that the upward trend in juvenile violence set the stage for the development of punitive legislation in the 1990s, the downward trend has opened the door to discussions about returning to more moderate policies. This, together with legislative concern about the high cost of punitive policies, goes a long way toward policy makers' second thoughts.

More surprisingly, the media, a key influence in arousing public sentiment against young offenders and in generating support for tough laws, has recently played an important role in generating sympathy for juveniles in the justice system. Newspapers and other media outlets have undertaken exposés of the systemic unfairness of punitive laws and of the harsh reality of the conditions faced by youths in prison. For example in Colorado, reform legislation enacted in 2006 that prohibited sentencing juveniles to LWOP was fueled by articles published in the *Rocky Mountain News* and *The Denver Post* about youths serving this sentence in Colorado prisons.[10] The stories emphasized that many of these juveniles had been found guilty of felony murder, a crime that would have resulted in a maximum five-year sentence had the offenses been adjudicated in juvenile court rather than criminal court.[11] In Connecticut, where the state legislature raised the minimum age of criminal court jurisdiction from sixteen to eighteen in 2007, media reports of the suicide of a seventeen-year-old inmate who had been tried and incarcerated as an adult helped rally support for the cause.[12]

In many states, the disproportionately harsh treatment of ethnic minority youths has been publicized, thus framing the punitive policies as racially, as well as developmentally, unjust.[13] In a highly publicized 2004 Georgia case, a seventeen-year-old African American youth, Genarlow Wilson, was sentenced to a ten-year prison term for aggravated child molestation on the basis of consensual oral sex with a fifteen-year-old girl at a New Year's Eve party. The conviction, described as "southern justice" by many outraged observers, led the Georgia legislature to amend the law to make the crime a misdemeanor, but it declined to apply the new statute retroactively to Genarlow's case. In October 2007, however, the Georgia Supreme Court held that Genarlow's sentence was cruel and unusual punishment and ordered him released from prison.[14]

Well-organized coalitions of local and national youth advocacy organizations have also been important catalysts of juvenile justice reform. Far more sophisticated than the child savers of an earlier era, these advocates have drawn on social science research to argue that adolescents are fundamentally different from adults. They have cited well-publicized stories, including some featured on the covers of national newsmagazines, of new discoveries about adolescent brain development. These stories confirm with brain scans what most people already know from personal experience—that adolescents are inherently less mature than are adults. In general, the recent brain research has played an important role in state legislative reform efforts and has captured the attention of journalists, politicians, and the public.[15]

Advocates also have been successful in focusing media and political attention on a broad range of social science evidence about adolescence and youth crime. Editorials and op-eds in local and national newspapers have pointed to this evidence in arguing that adolescents lacked the emotional and mental maturity of adults, that juvenile offenders should be given a second chance, that the public supported rehabilitative efforts, and, perhaps most important, that trying juveniles as adults is simply not cost-effective.[16] Evidence of the economic cost to the government of substantial use of adult incarceration with juveniles—together with descriptions of studies finding that adolescents released from adult correctional facilities were more likely to re-offend than those sentenced to juvenile facilities—have influenced the public debate.[17] These arguments have received special attention in states like Connecticut, Illinois, and North Carolina, where legislation has been introduced to raise the age of criminal court jurisdiction, shifting thousands of juveniles out of adult prisons and into juvenile facilities. The economic evidence was especially critical in responding to concerns that shifting the jurisdictional boundary upward was likely to be costly in the short term.[18]

Those who applaud the trend toward justice policies that recognize the differences between adolescents and adults may be heartened by these developments but should not naively assume that it will proceed unabated. Juvenile crime rates will rise again. Indeed, although rates continue to be low, they have crept up recently; in the past year or two, violent crime by juveniles has increased from the 2004 rates—the lowest in nearly two decades.[19] Some legislatures may be persuaded by arguments that criminal punishment can save taxpayers money, as happened (at least briefly) in Rhode Island, which lowered and then quickly raised its jurisdictional age.[20] Moreover, high-profile crimes by juveniles will surely stir public outrage from time to time, creating political pressure on public officials to "do something," a mandate that in the past has usually generated prompt responses by politicians eager to win public favor. This has been the story of the punitive reforms over the past generation. Is there any reason to be hopeful that it will not be replayed in the future or that substantial legal reforms based on developmental knowledge can be undertaken and maintained?

Our hope, of course, is that policy-makers will embrace our developmental model of juvenile justice and that, once in place, the model will serve as a stable foundation for a system of legal regulation solidly grounded in scientific knowledge. We think there is reason to be optimistic that this framework, balancing public protection and youth welfare, will be acceptable to the public and to policy-makers. Although politicians have tended to respond reflexively to public outrage at violent youth crime by enacting punitive laws, public anger is often transitory, and as we will show in the pages that follow, attitudes are complex and far more supportive of differential treatment of juveniles than is commonly assumed.

Public Opinion and the Accuracy of Surveys

During the 1990s juvenile crime was a hot political issue, and getting "tough on crime" was part of the election platform of politicians across the political spectrum. Governors and legislators claimed that their constituents demanded protection against the threat of young criminals. Indeed, some opinion polls have found support for this claim—and for punishing youths as harshly as their adult counterparts.[21] Polls also indicate public dissatisfaction with the juvenile court, which has been viewed as responding too leniently to young offenders.[22] This survey evidence has reinforced the conventional wisdom that the punitive reforms have been driven by the public's demand for tougher laws and more effective protection from juvenile crime.

This account of public opinion and its impact on punitive policies has been widely accepted, but there is reason to believe that it is incomplete, at best. The public *was* alarmed about juvenile crime in the 1990s—and politicians reacted to these fears by initiating sweeping legislative changes. However, considerable evidence indicates that attitudes about youth crime are more nuanced than policy-makers seem to recognize and that the polls on which they rely do not accurately measure public opinion.

Mass polls that ask a few simplistic questions are not reliable sources of information. As experts on survey research attest, responses to opinion surveys fluctuate as a function of variations— even slight variations—in the ways in which questions are worded or in background events (such as horrendous crimes in the news) that may have a transitory impact on attitudes. Moreover, in probing attitudes about complex issues through simple questions, opinion polls often do not reveal how changing one or more conditions may change respondents' views. An important theme in the analysis of survey research is that opinions change as respondents are asked to consider more complex facts and circumstances. In research on juvenile crime, reflexive punitive attitudes tend to soften when a range of sanctioning options are offered.[23] For example, poll respondents are much more likely to endorse harsh punishment when simply asked whether some designated punitive sentence is appropriate than when also presented with a more lenient alternative sanction. In general, unqualified statements about whether the public endorses lenient or punitive policies are frequently unreliable and uninterpretable.[24]

Moreover, when citizens *do* express punitive attitudes toward young offenders, it is often on the basis of distorted information. For example, years after juvenile crime rates began to steadily decline in the 1990s, numerous opinion polls confirmed that the public mistakenly thought that crime was *increasing*. Surveys also suggest that the public exaggerates the portion of serious crime committed by juveniles.[25] The sources of these misperceptions are unclear, but sensational media coverage of violent youth crime and particularly of high-profile murders plays a likely role.[26] Studies also have shown that individuals' misperceptions about the threat of youth crimes are linked to negative attitudes about the juvenile justice system and support for harsh punishment.[27]

Moral panics represent extreme cases of this kind of distortion (see Chapter 4). A lesson of the research on these phenomena is that public reactions to high-profile juvenile crimes are intense but transitory. Emotional outrage and alarm at horrific murders are understandable, particularly when the lives of children are lost (in lethal school shootings, for example). Moreover, at a cognitive level, individuals exaggerate the importance and probability of events that have the kind of vivid salience of a school shooting, particularly when the horror is described repeatedly by the media and politicians. Predictably, however, the outrage cools with the passage of time and more realistic assessments of the threat replace the distorted perceptions that are fueled by the hysteria surrounding the crime.

The transitory nature of public responses to horrendous crimes is illustrated by the aftermath of the 1996 school shootings in Jonesboro, Arkansas, in which four students and a teacher were killed by two middle school youths. The legislature was not in session during the year that the shootings took place, and thus no immediate legislative action was possible in response to public outrage that the perpetrators could not be tried as adults. By the next year, lawmakers had time to deliberate and study the issue—and some of the public's anger had dissipated. Although the statutory provisions that were eventually enacted were tough measures lowering the age of adult prosecution, it is generally agreed that they were less harsh than any legislation that might have been enacted in the wake of the killings.[28]

This preliminary inspection suggests that the evidence of harsh public attitudes toward young offenders is not as solid as lawmakers assume. Simplistic polling techniques may produce misleading results; thus, evaluating survey findings must include an examination of their methodology. Further, to the extent that opinion about juvenile crime is based on misinformation, education seems like the more appropriate response than the implementation of costly policies to deal with threats that are exaggerated. Finally, attitudes gauged in the midst of moral panics cannot be viewed as accurate reflections of the public's considered preferences about the regulation of youth crime. What is needed is a more careful analysis of the evidence on public attitudes toward juvenile crime policies—a task to which we now turn.

Public Protection Is a Priority

The fact that evidence about public opinion is flawed does not mean that the public is unconcerned about safety or that people generally favor leniency toward violent criminals. General surveys of attitudes about crime and punishment (not focused particularly on juveniles) make clear that the public cares a great deal about safety and draws a sharp distinction between violent and nonviolent crimes. Thus, there is broad support for the incarceration of violent criminals, but far less enthusiasm for the imprisonment of property or drug offenders.[29] Moreover, despite general support for the incapacitation of violent criminals, survey respondents are open to other sanctions, even for these offenders, if public protection can be achieved.[30] The public also distinguishes between first offenders and recidivists in making judgments about deserved punishment.[31] Surveys find a readiness to give all but the most vicious first offenders a second chance, but little patience when it comes to violent recidivists; polls show strong support for the incarceration of these offenders.[32] Opinion is more varied about nonviolent recidivists. For example, support is mixed for three-strikes laws that count nonviolent crimes as "strikes" that can lead to a life sentence.[33]

These generalizations are quite consistent across surveys over time and suggest, at least indirectly, that several of our reform proposals are more compatible with public preferences than is the current regime. Under our developmental model (but not under contemporary law), transfer to criminal court is reserved for violent recidivists, the group who are the target of the most punitive attitudes. First offenders and property offenders are generally deemed less culpable and under our proposal would be retained in juvenile court. Most important, surveys suggest that the public ultimately is pragmatic. Thus, juvenile programs that work to reduce recidivism more effectively than incarceration are likely to be well received.

Public Attitudes toward Juvenile Offenders

What do we know about public attitudes toward juvenile offenders, beyond the polls described above? A review of the research literature indicates that public opinion about differential treatment of juveniles and adults is complicated and not completely consistent; and different polls have found varying degrees of support for lenient treatment of young offenders. Some things are clear; polls show strong support for a separate juvenile justice system but also for the prosecution and punishment of some juveniles as adults. Not surprisingly, both the offender's age and the nature of the crime with which she is charged are deemed important to the judgment of whether criminal processing is appropriate. A number of studies have found that, for purposes of punishment (especially for violent crimes), the public draws a chronological boundary between juveniles and adults at about age fifteen, and the further an individual is in either direction from this age, the more he is likely to be viewed as a juvenile (if younger) or as an adult (if older). But this is hardly a fixed boundary; some surveys show variations about the appropriate jurisdictional line. Moreover, the severity and nature of the crime is important. Youth and immaturity are seen as mitigating factors for nonviolent crimes to a greater extent than for violent offenses, such that most people hold that a fifteen-year-old burglar should be punished more leniently than his adult counterpart, but many are ready to impose criminal punishment on a fifteen-year-old rapist or murderer.

Attitudes about Age, Transfer, and Culpability

In a study by our research group, eight hundred adults were asked what they thought should be the minimum age of transfer for various crimes, including violent crimes such as murder, rape, and armed robbery, as well as nonviolent offenses such as car theft, destruction of property, and drug possession and sale.[34] Our respondents selected age fifteen as the mean minimum age of transfer for violent offenses and age sixteen for nonviolent crimes. This study also found evidence that the public favors more lenient sanctions for young offenders than for adults (even for violent crimes) and views youths as less responsible for their crimes. Study participants were shown a brief video of an actual convenience store armed robbery captured on a surveillance camera, in which the robber's face was covered in a ski mask. Participants were also presented with a photo and told that it was the robber in the video. The robber was described as being a first offender, and the age was given variously as twelve, fifteen, or twenty. The photo had been electronically altered ("morphed") to have the individual's appearance fit the described age. Participants were asked a series of questions about the perpetrator's responsibility for the crime, psychosocial maturity, potential for rehabilitation, and suitability for transfer to the adult system (if the perpetrator was said to be twelve or fifteen). Because all participants had the same crime in mind when evaluating the perpetrator, we were able to compare how responses differed on the basis of the age of the offender.[35]

We found that the age of the perpetrator had a significant influence on attitudes about his responsibility for the crime and the punishment he deserved. Overall, younger offenders were viewed as less responsible, less mature, and less deserving of transfer to adult court. Although the twelve- and fifteen-year-olds were rated as being of comparable psychosocial maturity, mid-adolescents were judged more responsible for the crime and more deserving of transfer to adult court. However, it is notable that a majority of participants favored retention in the juvenile system even of the fifteen-year-old, whose gun-waving participation in the robbery was vividly captured on video. This response may reflect leniency toward a first offender, or it may suggest that when considering cases of individual youths involved in crime rather than abstract propositions, adult citizens respond more leniently.

In general, our study and other surveys support the distinction that we draw in our proposals between offenders who are age fourteen and younger (whom we think should never be eligible for transfer) and those who are age fifteen and older, who, under our guidelines, are eligible for transfer when charged with serious violent crimes but not for first offenses. Moreover, our proposal also acknowledges the need to balance concern for public safety with the recognition of immaturity as a mitigating factor, a trade-off that probably is reflected in the public's greater willingness to impose adult punishment on fifteen-year-old rapists than on burglars.[36] Although some participants in our survey endorsed the transfer of fourteen-year-olds for violent felonies, only a distinct minority approved of this practice, which is allowed under the law in most states today.

Attitudes about Incarceration and Rehabilitation

Public opinion supports the imprisonment of serious violent offenders as a means of public protection. But this does not necessarily indicate naïveté about the impact of prison on juvenile (or adult) offenders. Many people—nearly or more than a majority, depending on the survey—do not think that prison sentences reduce reoffending; indeed, substantial numbers think time in prison makes offenders more dangerous. Thus, support for imposing adult sanctions on older violent teenagers appears to be based on the perception that the incapacitation of dangerous youths carries an immediate public safety benefit—not on any faith in the prison system's success at reforming criminals.

In general, public attitudes toward the rehabilitation of juveniles are complex. Many surveys find far greater support for rehabilitation as an important goal of the justice system in dealing with juvenile offenders than with adults. According to a comprehensive review of this literature, "most Americans believe that it is 'never too late' for wayward youngsters to change and that the correctional system should be involved in redirecting the lives of these offenders."[37] However, the public distinguishes "wayward" youths from those who have offended so often or so heinously that they either have forfeited their chance at rehabilitation on moral grounds or appear to be beyond treatment. Moreover, despite general support for rehabilitation of juveniles, studies show some skepticism about its effectiveness, at least for violent youth. Surveys indicate that many people think that correctional programs for young offenders are largely ineffective. In one study conducted in the mid-1990s, for example, programs that emphasized rehabilitating juvenile offenders were described, and respondents were asked, "How successful would you say these programs have been at controlling juvenile crime?" Almost three-quarters of the public (72 percent) believed that the programs had been "not at all" or "not very" successful.[38]

One explanation for this skepticism is that questions about program effectiveness have often been asked in a context in which study participants know (or believe) that juvenile crime rates are high. Thus, it is not surprising that researchers found little support for the proposition that juvenile justice programs were effective at reducing crime in the early and mid-1990s, with youth crime often in the news—especially given that the public, for years, mistakenly thought that juvenile crime was increasing even when it was declining. Moreover, for many years, the mantra, "Nothing works," accurately described the views even of experts; it may take some time for the recent optimism about juvenile correctional programs among researchers to seep into public consciousness.

Interestingly, this skepticism is far less evident in surveys that describe juvenile correctional programs as effective before eliciting respondents' opinions. Under these conditions, many studies have found broad public support for juvenile programs, both in institutional settings and in the community; such programs are often favored over incarceration alone.[39] Although surveys suggest little support for ordinary probation as a sanction, structured community programs that offer crime-reduction benefits are generally endorsed. An important policy implication is that public support for investing in rehabilitative programs generally, and particularly for violent youths, will depend on the extent to which proponents of such programs can provide evidence of their effectiveness.

Our own research on this issue is informative. In a study published in 2006, we, with colleagues, used a contingent valuation, or "willingness to pay" (WTP), methodology—an approach that survey experts maintain is likely to estimate public opinion more accurately than conventional polling.[40] In our survey, 1,500 respondents were randomly assigned to hear one of two alternative policy scenarios and then were asked how much in additional taxes, if any, they would be willing to pay to implement the reform.[41] Our survey probed respondents' willingness to pay additional tax dollars for either additional incarceration or for a rehabilitation program (with no additional incarceration) for juveniles in a correctional facility for committing robbery.[42] The alternatives were described— accurately, according to other research—as offering a similar prospect of crime reduction. More than 60 percent of the respondents who received the rehabilitation-added scenario were willing to pay at least $100 for the program, while only about 50 percent who received the incarceration-added scenario were willing to pay that much. Also interesting was the finding that 40 percent of the respondents were unwilling to pay for *any* additional incarceration, a significantly higher percentage than the 25 percent unwilling to pay for additional rehabilitation. Of course, in contrast to an actual referendum, our respondents' willingness to pay tax dollars was hypothetical. Nonetheless, the results, and particularly the comparison between rehabilitation and incarceration, are instructive.

These survey results challenge the view held by many politicians that the public endorses the incarceration of young offenders over rehabilitation. In recent years, lawmakers have favored the investment of government revenues in building prisons and secure juvenile facilities, rather than putting resources into programs in the juvenile system that may reduce crime and promote public welfare more effectively. To the extent that these political choices are based on an assumption that the public demands tougher juvenile justice policies, our study indicates that this view may simply be mistaken. Our survey suggests that Americans are concerned about youth crime and want to reduce its incidence but are ready to support effective rehabilitative programs as a means of accomplishing that end—and indeed favor this response over imposing more punishment through longer sentences.[43] Moreover, the greater willingness of our survey respondents to pay for rehabilitation than for incarceration should be interesting to policy-makers, in light of facts about the two options that we did *not* disclose to our participants—that an additional year of juvenile incarceration actually costs *five times* as much as a year-long, community-based rehabilitation program.[44]

The willingness of the public to spend tax dollars to prevent crime through investments in human capital is also clearly evidenced in broad support for programs that focus on childhood interventions, ranging from early childhood education to after-school programs. In our WTP survey, all respondents also were presented with a scenario designed to gauge their interest in spending additional tax dollars for an early intervention prevention program modeled after a highly successful nurse home visitation program that has been proven to reduce juvenile offending.[45] Nearly two-thirds of our respondents were willing to pay at least $75 for the prevention program, and more than 55 percent were willing to pay $150 or more for it. Thus, the average amount respondents were willing to pay for the nurse visitation program was substantially higher than for either the addition of rehabilitative services or additional years of incarceration.

Early intervention programs have substantial public appeal, perhaps because the benefits go to innocent children and not to teenage lawbreakers. Moreover, in contrast to public skepticism about the effectiveness of rehabilitation programs, a large majority of individuals—nearly 80 percent in a 1998 survey of California respondents—believe that prevention programs are effective.[46] In reality, outcome studies show that these programs, by investing in the human capital of at-risk children at an early age offer many benefits, including some crime prevention effects. However, *purely* in terms of crime reduction, the best juvenile correctional programs are more effective than early intervention programs.[47]

On the whole, the survey research on public attitudes about rehabilitation indicates strong support for rehabilitation as a general goal in dealing with juvenile offenders, coupled with some skepticism about the effectiveness of existing programs. Tempering this skepticism, however, are a general willingness to support programs that *would be* effective at reducing crime and a readiness to believe that such programs are possible. The public's favorable view of rehabilitation should not be seen as an endorsement of the philosophy embodied in the traditional model of juvenile justice but rather as evidence of a readiness to invest in the human capital of young people if the investment will change the trajectory of their lives in positive ways. Thus, for example, we find no evidence that the public supports informal procedures for dealing with juvenile offending or indeterminate dispositions, neither of which is likely to facilitate a young person's healthy transition into adulthood. In general, public opinion on juvenile crime tends to be pragmatic rather than punitive. Adult punishment and long incarceration are approved, for the most part, only as a means to protect the public from violent young criminals; however, if other more lenient sanctions are effective, they are favored over incarceration.

Our analysis of opinion polls and survey research on juvenile crime leads us to be cautiously optimistic that the regulatory scheme that we propose will elicit public support. The public's general support for rehabilitation of juvenile offenders and willingness to invest in effective crime reduction programs suggest that a system in which most youths are retained in the juvenile justice system will receive public support—if juvenile correctional programs in fact are effective at reducing recidivism. The research indicates that this is the case, and that investment in juvenile correctional programs is money well spent if crime reduction is a key goal of the justice system.[48] Moreover, our analysis leads us to conclude that the jurisdictional boundaries between the juvenile and the adult system that we propose are compatible with public preferences. The mechanisms for excluding recidivist older youths from the juvenile system and for punishing offenders who commit serious crimes through extended dispositional jurisdiction accommodate the legitimate public concern for protection from violent juveniles.

To be sure, under a legal regime grounded in the developmental model, the public may express outrage occasionally that a younger adolescent or first offender involved in a highly publicized crime cannot be tried and punished as an adult. However, experience shows that this response, like moral panics generally, is likely to be transitory and will subside over time. Moral panics are unfortunate under any circumstances, because, while they last, they inevitably have the flavor of a witch hunt against a hated enemy whose danger to the community is greatly exaggerated. The social cost is dramatically increased, however, if the panic is institutionalized through legislation or policy innovations directed at the perceived threat. The evidence suggests that, in calmer times, public opinion toward juvenile offenders is far less punitive. Thus, the political risk that policy-makers face in responding cautiously to public pressure to "do something" when such incidents arise may not be as great or long lasting as they might surmise. Over time, the public is likely to accept policies grounded in the developmental model and to recognize that policy-makers who support this regulatory scheme act in the public interest.

The developmental model we have advanced can provide stability to an area of regulation that has lacked any firm theoretical grounding since the collapse of the rehabilitative model of juvenile justice policy in the 1970s. For a generation, there has been no clearly articulated rationale for maintaining a separate justice system for juvenile offenders or for dealing with them more leniently than adults. It is reasonable to assume that this conceptual void contributed to the seeming ease with which punitive reforms transformed the juvenile justice system in a relatively short period of time. The developmental model provides this rationale and thus may bolster policies grounded in scientific knowledge during times when political pressures to deal punitively with young offenders are intense. To be sure, over the past generation, critics have assailed the wholesale reclassification as adults of youths charged with serious crimes.

But the challenges often have been ad hoc critiques or simply regretful laments about the demise of the traditional court. What has been needed, and what this book begins to provide, is a new justification for policies that treat juveniles differently from adults and in so doing, protect the community and promote societal welfare.

Notes

1. Introduction

1. Michael Browning, John Pacenti & Jim Ash, "Boy, 14, Gets Life in T.V. Wrestling Death; Killing of 6-Yr.-Old Playmate Wasn't Just Horseplay, Florida Judge Says," *Chicago Sun-Times,* Mar. 10, 2001, 1.
2. Dana Caneady, "As Florida Boy Serves Term, Even Prosecutor Wonders Why," *New York Times,* Jan. 5, 2003; Tamara Lush, "Once Again, Trouble Finds Lionel Tate," *St. Petersburg State Times,* May 25, 2005, 1B.
3. William Claiborne, "13-Year-Old Convicted in Shooting: Decision to Try Youth as Adult Sparked Juvenile Justice Debate," *Washington Post,* Nov. 17, 2001.
4. State v. Tate, 854 So.2d. 44 (Fla. Dist. Ct. App. 2003).
5. See Terry Aguayo, "Youth Who Killed at 12 Gets 30 Years for Violating Probation," *New York Times,* May 19, 2006, A21; Hannah Sampson, "Lionel Tate Pleads No Contest in Pizza Holdup," *Miami Herald,* February 19, 2008.
6. For example, Nevada law provides that the juvenile court does not have jurisdiction over persons charged with murder, regardless of age. Nev. Rev. Stat. Ann. §62.040 (2004). See also Wisc. Stat. Ann. §938.183. (Adult court has jurisdiction over anyone aged ten or over charged with murder). Chapter 4 describes the recent legal trend toward reducing the age of transfer to adult court for serious crimes.
7. Charles Puzzanchera, Anne Stahl, Terrence Finnegan, Nancy Tierney, Howard Snyder, "Juvenile Court Statistics 2000," *Office of Juvenile Justice and Delinquency Prevention* (Washington, DC, 2004).

8. Ill. Comp. Stats. Ann. Ch. 705 Sect. 405/5-130 (1)(a) (2003).

9. A Toledo court intake officer estimated that only 2 of the 1,700 school-related delinquency cases involved serious incidents. See Sara Rimer, "Unruly Students Face Arrest, Not Detention," *New York Times,* Jan. 4, 2004, 11. Bob Herbert, "School to Prison Pipeline," *New York Times*, June 9, 2007, at http://select.nytimes.com/2007/06/09/opinion/09herbert.html?_r=1&oref=slogin, accessed on Feb. 23, 2008.

10. Zero-tolerance policies mandate expulsion from school and often referral to law enforcement agencies for any violation of rules involving violent behavior by students, possession of drugs or weapons, or other misbehavior deemed dangerous. Under these policies, school officials have little if any discretion to exercise judgment or consider mitigating circumstances. This has resulted in a flood of juvenile court cases that in an earlier time would have been dealt with by school officials. It has also resulted in many unfair or absurd expulsions, such as that of a five-year-old kindergarten student in Florida who was expelled for telling a classmate he was going to shoot him during a recess game of cops and robbers. In Virginia, a thirteen-year-old boy was suspended for the remainder of the term for taking a knife from a classmate who had made previous suicide attempts and who told him she was suicidal. The decision was upheld in Ratner v. Loudoun Co. Public Schools, 16 Fed. Appx. 140 (4th Cir. 2001). The American Bar Association issued a report highly critical of zero-tolerance policies. "ABA Juvenile Justice Policies," at www.abanet.org. See also Joan Wasser, "Zeroing in on Zero Tolerance," *Journal of Law & Politics* 15 (1999): 747–779.

11. Carefully tailored curfew ordinances are generally upheld against First Amendment challenges. Schliefer v. City of Charlottesville, 159 F.3d 843 (4th Cir. 1998). A Connecticut ordinance was struck down as a violation of equal protection because it prohibited youths from being on the street with parental consent. Ramos v. Town of Vernon, 353 F.3d 171 (2nd Cir. 2004).

12. This term was coined by University of Pennsylvania criminologist John DiIulio, who in 1995 predicted that the new century would bring a juvenile crime wave far worse than the 1990s. John DiIulio, Jr., "The Coming of the Super-predators," *Weekly Standard,* Nov. 27, 1995. DiIulio later expressed regret for the hyperbole and acknowledged that the prediction had not come to pass. Elizabeth Becker, "As Ex-

Theorist on Young 'Superpredators,' Bush Aide Has Regrets," *New York Times*, Feb. 9, 2001, A19.

13. Franklin Zimring, *American Youth Violence* (New York, 1998), 35–38.

14. Ibid.

15. See William Bennett, John DiIulio, Jr., & John Walters, *Body Count: Moral Poverty and How to Win America's War against Crime and Drugs* (New York, 1995), 32.

16. In the mid-1990s, a number of experts predicted a juvenile crime wave in the next decade or so far worse than that of the 1990s—based primarily on population statistics. See John DiIulio, note 12 above; James A. Fox, "Trends in Juvenile Violence: A Report to the United States Attorney General on Current and Future Rates of Juvenile Offending," *Bureau of Justice Statistics* (Washington, DC, 1995); James A. Fox, "Trends in Juvenile Violence: An Update," *Bureau of Justice Statistics* (Washington, DC, 1997). Many explanations have been offered for the failure of this crime wave to materialize, including the availability of abortion, beginning in the early 1970s. Steven Levitt & John Donahue, "The Impact of Legalized Abortion on Crime," *Quarterly Journal of Economics* 116 (2001): 379–420.

17. Jane Sprott, "Understanding Public Opposition to a Separate Juvenile System," *Crime and Delinquency* 44 (2001): 399–411.

18. Francis Allen, *The Borderland of Criminal Justice: Essays in Law and Criminology* (Chicago, 1964); Monrad Paulsen, "Fairness to the Juvenile Offender," *Minnesota Law Review* 41 (1957): 547–567; Joel Handler, "The Juvenile Court and the Adversary System: Problems of Function and Form," *Wisconsin Law Review* (1965): 7–51.

19. In re Gault, 387 U.S. 1 (1967).

20. Some reformers during this period proposed a model of juvenile justice based on a more realistic view of adolescence and including the procedural protections dictated by due process, but these proposals did not take hold and were swept aside by the upsurge in violent juvenile crime in the late 1980s and early 1990s. Franklin Zimring, *Confronting Youth Crime* (New York, 1979); Robert E. Shepherd, Jr., *IJA-ABA Juvenile Justice Standards, Annotated* (Chicago, 1996).

21. Brian Doherty, "When Kids Kill, Blame Those Who Pull the Trigger," *Milwaukee Journal & Sentinel*, May 31, 1998, 1.

22. Alfred Regnery, "Getting Away with Murder: Why the Juvenile Justice System Needs an Overhaul," *Policy Review* 34 (1985): 65–68.

23. For an example of advocates' rhetoric characterizing young offenders as children, see Equal Justice Initiative, *Cruel and Unusual: Sentencing 13- and 14-Year-Old Children to Die in Prison* (Montgomery, 2007). Our colleague, Robert Schwartz, a leading youth advocate, has recognized that public safety is an important consideration in juvenile crime policy.

24. Laura Stepp, "The Crackdown on Juvenile Crime: Do Stricter Laws Deter Youths?" *Washington Post,* Oct. 15, 1994, A1.

25. Erich Goode & Nachman Ben-Yehuda, *Moral Panics: The Social Construction of Deviance* (Malden, MA, 1994), 1.

26. See note 10 above for examples of such policies.

27. See discussion of California referendum in Chapter 4.

28. A good example is the California reform under Proposition 21, discussed in Chapter 4.

29. Julian Roberts, "Public Opinion and Youth Justice," in *Youth Crime and Youth Justice: Comparative and Cross-National Perspectives,* Michael Tonry & Anthony Doob, eds. (Chicago, 2005), 495; Elizabeth Scott, N. D. Reppucci, Jill Antonishak, & Jennifer DeGennaro, "Public Attitudes about the Culpability and Punishment of Young Offenders," *Behavioral Science & Law* 24 (2006): 815.

30. See note 12 above.

31. Elizabeth Scott, "The Legal Construction of Adolescence," *Hofstra Law Review* 29 (2000): 547–582.

32. National Juvenile Defender Center, "State Juvenile Justice Legislation," November 2005, at http://njdc.org/info/publications.php.

33. Roper v. Simmons, 541 U.S. 1040 (2005).

34. Zimring, *American Youth Violence.*

35. Key advances during adolescence include gains in deductive reasoning, the ability to think about hypothetical situations and to think simultaneously in multiple dimensions, and the ability to think abstractly. John Flavell Patricia Miller & Scott Miller, *Cognitive Development* (Upper Saddle River, NJ, 3rd ed. 1993); Barbel Inhelder & Jean Piaget, *The Growth of Logical Thinking from Childhood to Adolescence* (New York, 1958); R. Siegler, *Children's Thinking* (Upper Saddle River, NJ, 2nd ed. 1991).

36. Laurence Steinberg, *Adolescence* (New York, 5th ed. 1999), 263–265.

37. Typical models of decision-making focus exclusively on the cognitive processes of reasoning and judgment. In earlier work, we developed a model of adolescent decision-making that incorporates both reasoning

and judgment by including psychosocial influences on decision-making. Elizabeth Scott, "Judgment and Reasoning in Adolescent Decision-Making," *Villanova Law Review* 37 (1992): 1607–1669; Elizabeth Scott, N.D. Reppucci, & Jennifer Woolard, "Evaluating Adolescent Decision-Making in Legal Contexts," *Law & Human Behavior* 19 (1995): 221–244; Laurence Steinberg & Elizabeth Cauffman, "Maturity of Judgment in Adolescence: Psychosocial Factors in Adolescent Decision-Making," *Law & Human Behavior* 20 (1996): 249–272.

38. Patricia Spear, "The Adolescent Brain and Age-Related Behavioral Manifestations," *Neuroscience and Bio-Behavioral Reviews* 24 (2000): 417–463.

39. Elizabeth Scott & Thomas Grisso, "Developmental Incompetence, Due Process, and Juvenile Justice Policy," *North Carolina Law Review* 83 (2005): 793–845.

40. Steinberg, *Adolescence;* He Len Chung, Michelle Little, & Laurence Steinberg, "The Transition to Adulthood of Adolescents in the Juvenile Justice System: A Developmental Perspective," in *On Your Own Without a Net: The Transition to Adulthood for Vulnerable Populations*, D. Wayne Osgood, Michael Foster, & Constance Flanagan, eds. (Chicago, 2005).

41. Terrie Moffitt, "Adolescence-Limited and Life-Course-Persistent Antisocial Behavior: A Developmental Taxonomy," *Psychological Review* 100 (1993): 674–701.

42. Ibid.

43. When children reach age eighteen, in most states, parental authority and responsibility end and individuals can execute binding contracts, purchase property, make wills, consent to medical treatment, and vote in state and federal elections. However, adult status is set at age sixteen for driving in most states, while age twenty-one is the minimum age for purchasing alcohol. This classification regime and its rationale are dealt with in Chapter 3.

44. Scott, "The Legal Construction of Adolescence," 550–557.

45. Elizabeth Scott & Thomas Grisso, "Developmental Incompetence"; R. J. Bonnie & Thomas Grisso, "Adjudicative Competence and Youthful Offenders," in *Youth on Trial*, Thomas Grisso & Robert Schwartz, eds. (Chicago, 2000), 73–103.

46. National Center for Juvenile Justice, "State Juvenile Justice Profiles" at www.ncjj.org/stateprofiles; Howard Snyder & Melissa Sickmund,

"Juvenile Offenders and Victims: 1999 National Report," National Center for Juvenile Justice (1999): 51–84.

47. Chapter 7 reviews the research evidence on the impact of increasing sanctions on deterrence and on recidivism of juveniles in the adult and the juvenile systems.

48. The mantra "Nothing works" captured the dominant view at that time about the effectiveness of treatment programs. Douglas Lipton, Robert Martinson & Judith Wilks, *The Effectiveness of Correctional Treatment: A Survey of Treatment Evaluation Studies* (New York, 1975); Robert Martinson, "What Works? Questions and Answers about Prison Reform," *Public Interest* 35 (1975): 22–54; Susan Martin & Robin Redner, eds., *Panel on Research on Rehabilitative Techniques, National Research Council, New Directions in the Rehabilitation of Criminal Offenders* (Washington, DC, 1981).

49. As we will discuss in Chapter 7, some of this research focuses on promising new programs that have been developed in the past twenty years, such as multisystemic therapy. See Scott Henggeler, Sonja Schoenwald, Charles Borduin, Melisa Rowland & Phillippe Cunningham et al., *Multisystemic Treatment of Antisocial Behavior in Children and Adolescents* (New York, 1998); Scott Henggeler, Phillippe Cunningham, S. G. Pickrel, Sonja Schoenwald, & M.J. Brondino, "Multisystemic Therapy: An Effective Violence Prevention Approach for Serious Juvenile Offenders," *Journal of Adolescence* 19 (1996): 47–61. Also, sophisticated meta-analyses of large numbers of outcome studies indicate program dimensions that help reduce recidivism. See Mark Lipsey, "Juvenile Delinquency Treatment: A Meta-analytic Inquiry into the Variability of Effects," in *Meta-Analysis for Explanation: A Casebook* Thomas Cook & Harris Cooper, eds. (New York, 1992); Mark Lipsey, "Can Rehabilitative Programs Reduce the Recidivism of Juvenile Offenders? An Inquiry into the Effectiveness of Practical Programs," *Virginia Journal of Social Policy & Law* 6 (1999): 611–641.

50. The Court drew on a 2003 *American Psychologist* article by the authors as the basis of its proportionality analysis in *Simmons*; Laurence Steinberg & Elizabeth Scott, "Less Guilty by Reason of Adolescence," *American Psychologist* 47 (2003): 723–729.

51. Thomas Grisso et al., "Juveniles' Competence to Stand Trial: A Comparison of Adolescents' and Adults' Capacities as Trial Defendants," *Law & Human Behavior* 27 (2003): 333–363.

52. Julian Roberts, "Public Opinion and Youth Justice"; Scott et al., "Public Attitudes About the Culpability and Punishment of Young Offenders.

2. The Science of Adolescent Development and Teenagers' Involvement in Crime

1. This classic characterization of the field of psychology comes from Edward Boring, *A History of Experimental Psychology* (New York, 1929). Boring attributed it to the pioneer of memory research, Hermann Ebbinghaus.

2. G. Stanley Hall, *Adolescence: Its Psychology and Its Relations to Physiology, Anthropology, Sociology, Sex, Crime, Religion, and Education,* vols. 1 & 2 (New York, 1904).

3. Anna Freud, "Adolescence," in *Psychoanalytic Study of the Child,* vol. 13 (New York, 1958), 255–278; Erik Erikson, *Identity and the Life Cycle* (New York, 1980), 50–100.

4. Richard Lerner & Laurence Steinberg, eds., *Handbook of Adolescent Psychology* (New York, 2nd ed. 2004).

5. Anita Greene, "Future-time Perspective in Adolescence: The Present of Things Future Revisted," *Journal of Youth and Adolescence* 15 (1986): 99–113; Jari Nurmi, "How do Adolescents See Their Future? A Review of the Development of Future Orientation and Planning," *Developmental Review* 11 (1991): 1–59.

6. Laurence Steinberg, "Is Decision-Making the Right Framework for the Study of Adolescent Risk-Taking?" in *Reducing Adolescent Risk: Toward an Integrated Approach,* D. Romer, ed. (Thousand Oaks, CA, 2003), 18–24.

7. Elizabeth Scott & Laurence Steinberg, "Blaming Youth," *Texas Law Review* 81 (2003): 799–840.

8. Ibid.

9. W. Andrew Collins & Laurence Steinberg, "Adolescent Development in Interpersonal Context," in *Social, Emotional, and Personality Development,* vol. 3, N. Eisenberg, ed., *Handbook of Child Psychology,* William Damon & Richard Lerner, eds. (New York, 2006), 1003–1067.

10. Laurence Steinberg, *Adolescence* (New York, 8th ed., 2008).

11. Laurence Steinberg et al., "Psychopathology in Adolescence: Integrating Affective Neuroscience with the Study of Context," in *Developmental Psychopathology, vol 2.,* Dante Cicchetti & Donald Cohen, eds., (New York, 2nd ed., 2006), 710–741.

12. Richard Settersten, Frank Furstenberg, Jr., & Ruben Rumbaut, eds., *On the Frontier of Adulthood* (Chicago, 2005).

13. This is especially true for young people from the social backgrounds that are disproportionately over-represented in the justice system, for whom adolescence has not been significantly lengthened. He Len Chung, Michelle Little, & Laurence Steinberg, "The Transition to Adulthood for Adolescence in the Juvenile Justice System: A Developmental Perspective," in *On Your Own Without a Net: The Transition to Adulthood for Vulnerable Populations*, Wayne Osgood, Michael Foster, Constance Flanagan, & Gretchen Ruth, eds. (Chicago, 2005), 68–91.

14. Collins & Steinberg, "Adolescent Development."

15. B. J. Casey, Nim Tottenham, Conor Liston, & Sarah Durston, "Imaging the Developing Brain: What Have We Learned About Cognitive Development," *Trends in Cognitive Science* 9 (2005): 104–110.

16. Richard Lerner & Laurence Steinberg, "The Scientific Study of Adolescence: Past, Present, and Future," in *Handbook of Adolescent Psychology*, Richard Lerner & Laurence Steinberg, eds. (New York, 2nd ed., 2004), 1–12.

17. Daniel Keating, "Cognitive and Brain Development," in *Handbook of Adolescent Psychology*, R. Lerner & L. Steinberg, eds. (New York, 2nd ed., 2004).

18. Elizabeth Scott, N. Dickon Reppucci, & Jennifer Woolard, "Evaluating Adolescent Decision-Making in Legal Contexts," *Law and Human Behavior* 19 (1995): 221–244; Laurence Steinberg & Elizabeth Cauffman, "Maturity of Judgment in Adolescence: Psychosocial Factors in Adolescent Decision-Making," *Law and Human Behavior* 20 (1996): 249–272.

19. Laurence Steinberg, "Risk-Taking in Adolescence: What Changes, and Why?" *Annals of the New York Academy of Sciences* 1021 (2004): 51–58; Steinberg et al., "Psychopathology in Adolescence."

20. Laurence Steinberg, "Risk-Taking in Adolescence: New Perspectives from Brain and Behavioral Science," *Current Directions in Psychological Science* 16 (2007): 55–59.

21. Collins & Steinberg, "Adolescent Development."

22. Judith Smetana, "Adolescent-Parent Conflict: Resistance and Subversion as Developmental Process," in *Conflict, Contradiction, and Contrarian Elements in Moral Development and Education*, Larry Nucci, ed. (Mahwah, NJ, 2005), 69–91.

23. Laurence Steinberg & Elizabeth Scott, "Less Guilty by Reason of Adolescence: Diminished Immaturity, Diminished Responsibility, and

the Juvenile Death Penalty," *American Psychologist* 58 (2003): 1009–1018.

24. Keating, "Cognitive and Brain Development."

25. Steinberg, "The Study of Adolescent Risk-Taking."

26. Keating, "Cognitive and Brain Development."

27. Scott, Reppucci, & Woolard, "Evaluating Adolescent Decision-Making"; Steinberg & Cauffman, "Maturity of Judgment in Adolescence."

28. Steinberg, "Risk-Taking in Adolescence: New Perspectives."

29. Scott, Reppucci, & Woolard, "Evaluating Adolescent Decision-Making"; Steinberg & Cauffman, "Maturity of Judgment in Adolescence."

30. B. Bradford Brown, "Adolescents' Relationships with Peers," in *Handbook of Adolescent Psychology*, Richard Lerner & Laurence Steinberg, eds. (New York, 2004).

31. Thomas Berndt, "Developmental Changes in Conformity to Peers and Parents," *Developmental Psychology* 15 (1979): 608–616; Laurence Steinberg & Susan Silverberg, "The Vicissitudes of Autonomy in Early Adolescence," *Child Development* 57 (1986): 841–851.

32. Franklin Zimring, *American Youth Violence* (New York, 1998).

33. Anne Bowker, William Bukowski, Shelley Hymel, & Lorrie Sippola, "Coping with Daily Hassles in the Peer Group: Variations as a Function of Peer Experience," *Journal of Research on Adolescence* 10 (2000): 211–243; William Bukowski, Lorrie Sippola, & Andrew Newcomb, "Variations in Patterns of Attraction of Same- and Other-Sex Peers during Early Adolescence," *Developmental Psychology* 36 (2000): 147–154; Phillip Rodkin, Thomas Farmer, Ruth Pearl, & Richard Van Acker, "Heterogeneity of Popular Boys: Antisocial and Prosocial Configurations," *Developmental Psychology* 36 (2000): 14–24.

34. Greene, "Future-Time Perspective in Adolescence"; Nurmi, "How do Adolescents see their Future?"

35. William Gardner & Janna Herman, "Adolescents' AIDS Risk-Taking: A Rational Choice Perspective," in *Adolescents in the AIDS Epidemic*, William Gardner, Susan Millstein, & Brian Wilcox, eds. (San Francisco, 1990), 17–34; Leonard Green, Joel Myerson, & Pawel Ostaszewski, "Discounting of Delayed Rewards Across the Life Span: Age Differences in Individual Discounting Functions," *Behavioural Processes* 46 (1999): 89–96; Bonnie Halpern-Felsher & Elizabeth Cauffman, "Costs and Benefits of a Decision: Decision-Making

Competence in Adolescents and Adults," *Journal of Applied Developmental Psychology* 22 (2001): 257–273.

36. William Gardner, "A Life Span Theory of Risk-Taking," in *Adolescent and Adult Risk Taking: The Eighth Texas Tech Symposium on Interfaces in Psychology*, N. Bell, ed. (Newbury Park, 1992).

37. Elizabeth Cauffman, Laurence Steinberg, & Alex Piquero, "Psychological, Neuropsychological, and Psychophysiological Correlates of Serious Antisocial Behavior in Adolescence: The Role of Self-Control," *Criminology* 43 (2005): 133–176.

38. Steinberg, "The Study of Adolescent Risk-Taking" and "Risk-Taking in Adolescence: What Changes?" There is some evidence that very young adolescents may perceive potentially dangerous activities (e.g., driving while drinking) as even more risky than do adults, perhaps because their parents and teachers explicitly and repeatedly emphasize the dangers of such activities.

39. Margo Gardner & Laurence Steinberg, "Peer Influence on Risk-Taking, Risk Preference, and Risky Decision-Making in Adolescence and Adulthood: An Experimental Study," *Developmental Psychology* 41 (2005): 625–635.

40. Susan Millstein & Bonnie Halpern-Felsher, "Perceptions of Risk and Vulnerability," *Journal of Adolescent Health* 31S (2002): 10–27; Valerie Reyna & Frank Farley, "Risk and Rationality in Adolescent Decision-Making: Implications for Theory and Public Policy," *Psychological Science in the Public Interest* 7 (2006): 1–44.

41. Steinberg, "Risk-Taking in Adolescence: What Changes?"

42. Laurence Steinberg, "A Social Neuroscience Perspective on Adolescent Risk-Taking," *Developmental Review* 28(2008): 78–106.

43. Linda P. Spear, "The Adolescent Brain and Age-related Behavioral Manifestations," *Neuroscience and Biobehavioral Reviews* 24 (2000): 417–463.

44. Baruch Fischhoff, "Risk-Taking: A Developmental Perspective," in *Risk-Taking Behavior,* J. Frank Yates, ed. (New York, 1992), 133–162.

45. Ellen Greenberger, "Education and the Acquisition of Psychosocial Maturity," in *The Development of Social Maturity,* David McClelland, ed. (New York, 1982): 155–189.

46. Steinberg & Cauffman, "Maturity of Judgment in Adolescence."

47. Reed Larson, Mihaly Csikszentmihalyi, & Ronald Graef, "Mood Variability and the Psychosocial Adjustment of Adolescents," *Journal of Youth and Adolescence* 9 (1980): 469–490.

48. Jay N. Giedd et al., "Brain Development during Childhood and Adolescence: A Longitudinal MRI Study," *Nature Neuroscience* 2 (1999): 861–863; Tomáš Paus et al., "Structural Maturation of Neural Pathways in Children and Adolescents: In Vivo Study," *Science* 283 (1999) 1908–1911; Elizabeth Sowell, Dirk Trauner, A. Gamst, & T. L. Jernigan, "Development of Cortical and Subcortical Brain Structures in Childhood and Adolescence: A Structural MRI Study," *Developmental Medicine and Child Neurology* 44 (2002): 4–16.

49. Casey et al., "Imaging the Developing Brain."

50. Giedd et al., "Structural Maturation of Neural Pathways."

51. Eric Nelson, Ellen Leibenluft, Erin McClure, & Daniel Pine, "The Social Re-Orientation of Adolescence: A Neuroscience Perspective on the Process in Its Relation to Psychopathology," *Psychological Medicine* 35 (2005): 163–174; Keating, "Cognitive and Brain Development."

52. Beatriz Luna et al., "Maturation of Widely Distributed Brain Function Subserves Cognitive Development," *Neuroimage* 13 (2001): 786–793.

53. Giedd et al., "Structural Maturation of Neural Pathways."

54. Scientists can often determine that a task activates a particular part of the brain by looking at the performance of individuals who have injuries or lesions in that region. Patients with lesions to the dorsolateral prefrontal cortex perform very poorly on the Tower of London. W. Keith Berg, & Dana L. Byrd, "The Tower of London Spatial Problem Solving Task: Enhancing Clinical and Research Implementation," *Journal of Experimental and Clinical Neuropsychology* 25(5) (2002): 586–604.

55. Steinberg, "A Social Neuroscience Perspective."

56. Individuals with injury or damage to this region of the brain do poorly on the Iowa Gambling Task. Antoine Bechara, Antonio R. Damasio, Hanna Damasio, & Steven W. Anderson, "Insensitivity to Future Consequences Following Damage to Human Prefrontal Cortex," *Cognition* 50 (1994): 7–15.

57. Antoine Bechara, Antonio R. Damasio, & Hanna Damasio, "Emotion, Decision-Making and the Orbitofrontal Cortex," *Cerebral Cortex* 10 (2000): 295–307.

58. Eveline Crone, Ilse Vendel, & Maurits van der Molen, "Decision-Making in Disinhibited Adolescents and Adults: Insensitivity to Future Consequences or Driven by Immediate Reward?" *Personality and Individual Differences* 34 (2003): 1–17; Monica Luciana, "The Neural and Functional Development of Human Prefrontal Cortex," in *The*

Cognitive Neuroscience of Development, M. de Haan & M. H. Johnson, eds.(Brighton, NY, 2003): 157–179; Monica Luciana & Charles Nelson, "Assessment of Neuropsychological Function through Use of the Cambridge Neuropsychological Testing Automated Battery: Performance in 4- to 12-Year-Old Children," *Developmental Neuropsychology* 22 (2002): 595–624.

59. Samuel M. McClure, David I. Laibson, George Loewenstein, & Jonathan D. Cohen, "Separate Neural Systems Value Immediate and Delayed Monetary Rewards," *Science* 306 (2004): 503–507.

60. If the participant indicates that she would prefer the $1,000, the amount associated with the shorter time period is raised to the mid-point between it and $1,000 ($750 in one week) and the question is asked again. If the participant then indicates that she would prefer the smaller reward, we drop the value of the more immediate reward to the mid-point between the last amount and the previous one (i.e., $625) and ask again. This is done until we reach the point at which the subjective value of the smaller, immediate reward is the same as the subjective value of the larger, delayed one. The lower the subjective value of the preferred immediate reward is, the more oriented a person is toward short-term gratification. That is, someone who would trade $100 today for $1,000 in a year is much less future-oriented than someone who would not give up the $1,000 reward unless the immediate reward was $500.

61. Laurence Steinberg, Sandra Graham, Lia O'Brien, Jennifer Woolard, Elizabeth Cauffman, & Marie Banich. "Age Differences in Future Orientation and Delay Discounting." *Child Development* (in press).

62. Steinberg et al., "Psychopathology in Adolescence."

63. Nelson et al., "The Social Re-Orientation of Adolescence."; Steinberg, "A Social Neuroscience Perspective."

64. Ronald E. Dahl, "Affect Regulation, Brain Development, and Behavioral/Emotional Health in Adolescence," *CNS Spectrums* 6(1) (2001): 1–12.

65. Michael Gottfredson & Travis Hirschi, *A General Theory of Crime* (Stanford, 1990).

66. Travis Hirschi & Michael Gottfredson, "Rethinking the Juvenile Justice System." *Crime & Delinquency* (39) 1993: 262–271.

67. Collins & Steinberg, "Adolescent Development."

68. Ibid.

69. Erik Erikson, *Identity: Youth and Crisis* (New York, 1968).

70. Terrie Moffitt, "Adolescence-Limited and Life-Course-Persistent Antisocial Behavior: A Developmental Taxonomy," *Psychological Review* 100 (1993): 674–701; Steinberg, "Adolescence."

71. Alex Piquero, David Farrington, & Alfred Blumstein, "The Criminal Career Paradigm: Background and Recent Developments," *Crime and Justice: A Review of Research* 30 (2003): 359–506.

72. John Laub & Robert Sampson, *Crime in the Making: Pathways and Turning Points Through Life* (Cambridge, 1993).

73. Terrie Moffitt, "Life-Course Persistent Versus Adolescence-Limited Antisocial Behavior," in *Developmental Psychopathology*, vol. 3, Dante Cicchetti & Donald Cohen, eds. (New York, 2nd ed., 2006).

74. Laurence Steinberg, Hen Len Chung, & Michelle Little, "Reentry of Young Offenders from the Justice System: A Developmental Perspective," *Youth Violence and Juvenile Justice* 1 (2004): 21–38.

75. Laurence Steinberg, "We know Some Things: Adolescent-Parent Relationships in Retrospect and Prospect," *Journal of Research on Adolescence* 11 (2001): 1–20.

76. Ibid.

77. Brown, "Adolescents' Relationships with Peers."

78. Collins & Steinberg, "Adolescent Development"; Joseph Mahoney, Reed Larson, Jacquelynne Eccles, & Heather Lord, "Organized Activities as Developmental Contexts for Children and Adolescents," in *Organized Activities as Contexts of Development*, Joseph Mahoney, Reed Larson, & Jacquelynne Eccles, eds. (Hillsdale, NJ, 2005), 3–22; Steinberg, *Adolescence*.

79. Urie Bronfenbrenner & Pamela Morris, "The Ecology of Environmental Process," in *Handbook of Child Psychology* (New York, 1998); Steinberg, Chung, & Little, "Reentry of Young Offenders."

3. Regulating Children in American Law

1. Many historians have written about the Progressive Era as a reform period that focused on children's welfare. Murray Levine & Adeline Levine, *A Social History of the Helping Services: Clinic, Court, School, and Community* (New York, 1970); Joseph F. Kett, *Rites of Passage: Adolescence in America 1790 to the Present* (New York, 1977), 221–227; Susan Tiffan, *In Whose Best Interest? Child Welfare Reform in the Progressive Era* (Westport, 1982).

2. Barbara Woodhouse, "Who Owns the Child? *Meyer* and *Pierce* and the Child as Property" *Willliam and Mary Law Review* 33 (1992): 995–1094. Woodhouse describes the property-like relationship of children to their parents in the eighteenth and nineteenth centuries and argues that the famous Supreme Court opinions from the 1920s *Meyer v. Nebraska* and *Pierce v. Society of Sisters,* which established that parental rights are protected under the Fourteenth Amendment of the U.S. Constitution, reflect vestiges of this conception of children as their parents' property.

3. Anthony Platt, *The Child Savers: The Invention of Delinquency* (Chicago, 1969). Platt argues that the middle-class social reformers who led the child welfare movement were motivated by a desire to establish control and influence over the lives of poor urban youths, substituting the guidance of wholesome (in their view) American social workers and probation officers for immigrant parents.

4. Robert H. Bremner, ed., *Children and Youth in America,* vol. 2 (Cambridge, 1971), 601–717; Bremner, ed., *Children and Youth in America,* vol. 3 (Cambridge, 1974), 299–518.

5. David Tanenhaus, *Juvenile Justice in the Making* (Oxford, 2004); Ellen Ryerson, *The Best Laid Plans: America's Juvenile Court Experiment* (New York, 1978). There are several "insider" accounts of the juvenile court during its early days by judges and reformers. See Ben Lindsey & Harvey O'Higgins, *The Beast* (Seattle, 1970); Miriam Van Waters, *Youth in Conflict* (New York, 1925). Judge Lindsey wrote an enthusiastic and rosy account of the Denver Juvenile Court during the Progressive Era.

6. G. Stanley Hall, *Adolescence* (New York, 1904). Hall first identified adolescence as a developmental stage at the turn of the twentieth century. He described adolescence as "torn by dualisms which disrupted the harmony of childhood; hyperactivity and inertia, social sensibility and self-absorption, lofty intuitions and childish folly." See also Kett, *Rites of Passage,* 217.

7. Lindsey, *Beast.* Judge Ben Lindsey's account of his experience as judge in the Denver Juvenile Court is full of tales of misguided youths who went astray because of the failings of adults.

8. Ginzberg v. New York, 390 U.S. 629 (1968).

9. Schliefer v. City of Charlottesville, 159 F.3d 843 (4th Cir. 1998). Curfew ordinances have generally been upheld if they are not excessively broad and if they include reasonable exceptions and allow the exercise of constitutional rights. For example, many ordinances include excep-

tions to allow youths to respond to an emergency, engage in employment or school activities, engage in interstate travel, or exercise First Amendment rights.

10. Kiefer v. Fred Howe Motors, 158 N.W.2d 288, 290 (Wis. 1968).

11. Janet Currie, *The Invisible Safety Net: Protecting The Nation's Poor Children and Families* (Princeton, 2006).

12. Samuel Davis, Elizabeth Scott, Walter Wadlington, & Charles Whitebread, *Children in the Legal System* (New York, 3rd ed. 2004), 507–684.

13. Child abuse reporting statutes mandate that certain designated professionals, such as teachers, physicians, nurses, social workers, probation officers, and day care providers, must report suspected child abuse to child protective service agencies. Other individuals may but are not required to comply. The statutes also prescribe the procedure by which complaints are handled. See Va. Code Ann. §63.2-1509 et seq. (Lexis 2003 Supp.).

14. Bellotti v. Baird, 442 U.S. 622 (1979).

15. H. L. v. Matheson, 450 U.S. 398, 441 (1981), Marshall, J., dissenting. In fact, despite the rhetoric, abortion jurisprudence is one area in which adolescents are treated as a separate category, not like children and not like adults. See note 32 below and accompanying text.

16. Douglas Rendleman, "Parens Patriae: From Chancery to the Juvenile Court," *South Carolina Law Review* 23 (1971): 205.

17. The police power is the power of the state to promote the general welfare. Art. I, Sect. 8 of the U.S. Constitution gives Congress the power to tax to provide for the general welfare.

18. U.S. Const., Art. I, Sect. 2. sets the minimum age for service in the House of Representatives at twenty-five. For the Senate, it is thirty. Id. at Sect. 3.

19. Virginia Grace Cook, *The Age of Majority,* vol. 6 (Lexington: Council of State Governments, 1972). Whether this account of the original basis of setting the age of majority is accurate or apocryphal is unclear, but it is mentioned repeatedly, including in the report of the Senate Committee recommending that the minimum voting age be lowered from twenty-one to eighteen. U.S. Senate Committee on the Judiciary, "Lowering the Voting Age to 18," S. Rep. No. 92–26 at 5 (1971).

20. F. Furstenberg, "Keynote Address: Vulnerable Youth and the Transition to Adulthood," *Temple Law Review* 79 (2006): 325–335. Furstenberg discusses the harm that can come to children in foster care when support is cut off and they must fend for themselves at age eighteen.

21. Gary B. Melton, "Toward Personhood for Adolescents: Autonomy and Privacy in Public Policy," *American Psychologist* 38 (1983): 99–103; Lois Weithorn & Susan Campbell, "The Competency of Children and Adolescents to Make Informed Treatment Decisions," *Child Development* 53 (1983): 1589–1599.

22. See for example Cal. Fam. Code §1601 (West 2004).

23. Sen. Rep. No. 92–96 at 7.

24. 23 U.S.C. §158 (1982).

25. Franklin Zimring, *The Changing Legal World of Adolescence* (New York, 1982). Zimring discusses the logic and policy justification of separating the minimum age of driving and drinking and notes that regardless of what the minimum age is for drinking, youths a year or two below that age will have access to alcohol.

26. See Cariseo v. Cariseo, 459 A.2d 523 (CT 1983); Jones v. Jones, 257 S.E. 2d 537 (GA 1979). Other courts have found that noncustodial parents cannot be required to pay for college because parents in intact families do not have this obligation. See Dowling v. Dowling, 679 P2d 480 (AK 1984); In Re Marriage of Plummer, 735 P2d 165 (CO 1987). The Pennsylvania Supreme Court on this basis found a state statute authorizing this kind of support to violate the noncustodial parent's right of Equal Protection under the Fourteenth Amendment of the U.S. Constitution. Curtis v. Kline, 542 Pa. 249 (1995). For a discussion of this issue, see Charles Wilson, "But Daddy, Why Can't I Go to College? The Frightening De-Kline of Support for Children's Post-Secondary Education," *Boston College Law Review* 37 (1996): 1099–1132.

27. Many states authorize post-majority support by statue. See Colo. Rev. Stat. Ann. §14-10-115 (1.5(b1)(2002 Supp.); Ill. Rev. Stat., Ch. 750 §5/513 (2003).

28. See Walter Wadlington "Minors and Health Care: The Age of Medical Consent," *Osgoode Hall Law Journal* 11 (1973): 115; Weithorn & Campbell, "Competency of Children and Adolescents."

29. Younts v. St. Francis Hospital and School of Nursing, Inc., 469 P2d 330, 336 (KS 1970). A surgical (or medical) procedure is a battery unless there is informed consent by someone competent to provide it.

30. Wadlington, "Minors and Health Care: The Age of Consent."

31. The Supreme Court has reviewed state statutes regulating adolescents' access to abortion in several cases. See the discussion of this issue and description of the cases in S. Davis et al., *Children in the Legal System,*

195–214. See also Robert Mnookin, "Bellotti v. Baird: A Hard Case," in *In the Interest of Children: Advocacy, Law Reform, and Public Policy,* Mnookin (New York, 1985).

32. Bellotti v. Baird, 443 U.S. 622 (1979). The Supreme Court proposed the use of by-pass hearings and the questions that should be addressed in such proceedings.

33. Examples include Va. Code. Ann. §54.1-2979 (West 2004); 22 Me. Rev. Stat. Ann. Sect. 1502; 1823 (West 2004).

34. Studies indicate that minors exaggerate the likelihood that their parents will react negatively to their sexual activity. Susan Newcomer & Richard Udry, "Parent-Child Communication and Adolescent Sexual Behavior," *Family Planning Perspectives* 17 (1985): 169–174. Another study has shown that requiring parental consent before issuing contraceptives to teens would lead many to abandon contraception. Aida Torres, Jacqueline Darroch Forrest & Susan Eisman, "Telling Parents: Clinic Policies and Adolescents' Use of Family Planning and Abortion Services," *Family Planning Perspectives* 12 (1980): 284–292, 291.

35. Many statutes explicitly provide that courts give substantial weight to older children's preferences. One study found that courts weigh older children's preferences heavily even without statutory direction. See Elizabeth Scott, N.D. Reppucci, & Mark Aber, "Children's Preferences in Adjudicated Custody Decisions," *Georgia Law Review* 22 (1988): 1035–1078.

36. In California, Maryland, and a few other states, minors cannot drive after midnight unless supervised by an adult. Cal. Veh. Code §12814.6 (West 2000); Md. Code Ann. Transp. §16-113 (West 1999). In some states, they can only drive during daylight hours. S.C. Code Ann. §56-1-175 (West 2005).

4. Why Crime Is Different

1. Ben Lindsey & Rube Borough, *The Dangerous Life* (New York, 1931), 102–104.

2. Ibid., 130–138.

3. Ben Lindsey & Harvey O'Higgins, *The Beast* (Seattle, 1970), 144, 149.

4. At common law, the infancy defense excused children under age seven from criminal responsibility. The defense could be rebutted by the state for youths age seven to fourteen and was not available for youths age fourteen and over, who were conclusively presumed to have the

moral capacity of adults. See Andrew Walkover, "The Infancy Defense in the New Juvenile Court," *UCLA Law Review* 31 (1984): 503–562.

5. Miriam Van Waters, *Youth in Conflict* (New York, 1925).

6. Lindsey noted, "How can we expect Jimmie to stay out of court and in his home unless he had a home to stay in? And what is a home with a stricken father and a distracted mother?" Lindsey & Borough, *The Dangerous Life*, 146.

7. Van Waters, *Youth*, 3.

8. Julian Mack, "The Juvenile Court," *Harvard Law Review* 23 (1909): 104, 107.

9. See Lindsey & O'Higgins, *The Beast*.

10. Ibid., 133.

11. Anthony Platt, *The Child Savers: The Invention of Delinquency* (Chicago, 1977), 139.

12. Richard J. Bonnie, ed., *Psychiatrists and the Legal Process: Diagnosis and Debate* (New York, 1977).

13. Because the state under the rehabilitative model was essentially stepping in as a substitute for parents with the goal of providing for the child's welfare, most believed that there was no need for the full protection of criminal due process given to adults, and thus judges needed no legal training. W. Vaughan Stapleton & Lee E. Teitelbaum, *In Defense of Youth: A Study of the Role of Counsel in American Juvenile Courts* (New York, 1972), 15–21, 25–26.

14. Mack, "The Juvenile Court," 115–122. Murray Levine & Adeline Levine, *A Social History of the Helping Services: Clinic, Court, School and Community* (New York, 1970), 11–21.

15. Platt, *Child Savers*, 141–142. Many have written critiques of the traditional juvenile justice system, targeting judicial discretion, the lack of procedural protections, and the failure of rehabilitation. See Shelden Glueck, "Some 'Unfinished Business' in the Management of Juvenile Delinquency," *Syracuse Law Review* 15 (1964): 628–659, 629; Francis Allen, *The Borderland of Criminal Justice: Essays in Law and Criminology* (Chicago, 1964); Monrad Paulsen, "Fairness to the Juvenile Offender," *Minnesota Law Review* 41 (1957): 547–576.

16. Robert Dawson, "The Future of Juvenile Justice: Is it Time to Abolish the System?" *The Journal of Law and Criminology* 81 (1990): 136–155.

17. Allen, *The Borderland of Criminal Justice*; Paulsen, "Fairness to the Juvenile Offender"; Joel Handler, "The Juvenile Court and the Adver-

sary System: Problems of Function and Form," *Wisconsin Law Review* (1965): 7–51.

18. See In re Gault, 387 U.S. 1, 18 n. 23 (1967).

19. Ibid., 387 U.S. at 1.

20. Ibid., 387 U.S. at 4.

21. Ibid., 387 U.S. at 28 (1967).

22. The most ambitious reform effort was the Juvenile Justice Standards Project, launched by the American Bar Association and the Institute for Judicial Administration in the mid-1970s. Volumes included Transfer between Courts, Adjudication, Dispositions, Delinquency, Sanctions, etc. See also Franklin Zimring, *Twentieth-Century Fund Taskforce on Sentencing Policy toward Young Offenders: Confronting Youth Crime* (New York, 1978).

23. In re Gault, 387 U.S. at 22. The Court reported that the survey was conducted by the Stanford Research Institute and described in a report of the President's Commission on Crime in the District of Columbia.

24. In re Gault, 387 U.S. at 6.

25. This tension led Barry Feld, a liberal advocate, to argue for abolition of the juvenile court. Barry Feld, *Bad Kids: Race and the Transformation of the Juvenile Court* (New York, 1999).

26. This term was coined by John DiIulio, a University of Pennsylvania criminologist, who predicted a wave of juvenile crime perpetrated by urban youth in the first decade of the twenty-first century far worse than the crime wave of the 1990s. John DiIulio, "The Coming of the Super-Predators," *Weekly Standard,* Nov. 27, 1995, p. 23. [On June 28, 2007, the term "superpredator" generated 30,300 Google hits, suggesting its salience.]

27. In one 1989 study, 70 percent of those questioned believed leniency in the juvenile system was a contributing factor to violent youth crime. Timothy Flanagan & Kathleen Maguire, eds., *Sourcebook of Criminal Justice Statistics* (Washington, DC, 1990), p. 157. Other studies indicate that the public believes the system is too lenient and supports prison terms for youth offenders. J. Sprott, "Understanding the Public Opposition to a Separate Youth Justice System," *Crime and Delinquency* 44 (1998): 399–411.

28. Franklin Zimring, "The Punitive Necessity of Waiver," in *The Changing Borders of Juvenile Justice: The Transfer of Adolescents to the Criminal Court,* Jeffrey Fagan & Frank Zimring, eds. (Chicago, 2000).

29. See Barry Feld, "The Juvenile Court Meets the Principle of the Offense: Punishment, Treatment, and the Difference It Makes," *Boston University Law Review* 68 (1988): 821–915, 837.

30. Pennsylvania was a leader in the Balanced and Restorative Justice movement. Its new Juvenile Act in 1995 states that its purpose is "to provide for children committing delinquent acts programs of supervision, care, and rehabilitation which provide balanced attention to the protection of the community, the imposition of accountability for offenses committed, and the development of competencies to enable children to become responsible and productive members of the community." Pennsylvania Commission on Crime and Delinquency at http://www.pccd.state.pa.us/pccd/cwp (visited on Oct. 29, 2007).

31. Justine Wise Polier, "Dissenting View," *Juvenile Justice Standards: Standards Relating to Noncriminal Misbehavior* (Cambridge, MA, 1982). For a contemporary example of youth advocates' sympathetic characterization of young offenders, see Equal Justice Initiative, *Cruel and Unusual: Sentencing 13- and 14-Year-Old Children to Die in Prison* (Montgomery, 2007).

32. Homicide rates doubled during this period. Frank Zimring, *American Youth Violence* (New York, 1998), 35–38.

33. During the three-year period between 1992 and 1995, eleven states lowered the age for transfer, and ten states added crimes to judicial waiver statutes. See Patricia Torbet et al., *State Responses to Serious and Violent Juvenile Crime,* vol. 6 (Washington, DC, 1996). For example, North Carolina added all Class A felonies to its list of crimes that trigger transfer hearings, and Missouri lowered its minimum transfer age from fourteen to twelve for all felonies.

34. Ibid., 25.

35. Matthew Wagman, "Innocence Lost in the Wake of Green: The Trend is Clear—If You Are Old Enough to Do the Crime, You Are Old Enough to Do the Time," 49 *Catholic University Law Review* 49 (2000): 643–677, 643.

36. In twenty-seven states a ten-year-old charged with murder can be charged as an adult. See Office of Juvenile Justice and Delinquency Prevention, *Juvenile Offenders and Victims: A National Report* (Washington, DC, 1995), 86–87. See generally National Center for Juvenile Justice, "National Overviews," at http://www.ncjj.org/stateprofiles (accessed June 29, 2007).

37. See generally National Center for Juvenile Justice, "National Overviews," at http://www.ncjj.org/stateprofiles (accessed June 29, 2007). See also Barry Feld, "The Juvenile Court Meets the Principle of the Offense.

38. Cal. Welf. and Inst. Code §707 (West 2000).

39. Between 1992 and 1995, twenty-four states either created or expanded (by adding crimes) automatic/legislative waiver statutes. See Torbet et al., *State Responses*. See also National Center for Juvenile Justice,"National Overviews," at http://www.ncjj.org/stateprofiles (accessed June 29, 2007).

40. Cal. Welf. and Inst. Code §602.

41. N.Y. Fam. Ct. Act §301.2 (McKinney 2007); N.C. Gen. Stat. §7B-1604 (West 2007).

42. See generally Office of Juvenile Justice and Delinquency Prevention, *Juvenile Justice Reform Initiatives in the States: 1994–1996* (Washington, DC, 1997), 81. See also Torbet et al., *State Responses*, 4.

43. See, e.g., Neb. Rev. Stat. §43-276 (West 2006). In Wisconsin, youths may be prosecuted, at the prosecutor's discretion, in criminal court proceedings for any state crime after their fifteenth birthday. See Wisc. Stat. Ann. §928.18 (West 2006).

44. See Torbet et al., *State Responses*, 4–6; Barry Feld, "Juvenile and Criminal Justice Systems' Responses to Juvenile Justice," *Crime and Justice* 24 (1998): 189–250, 202; Donna Bishop, "Juvenile Offenders in the Adult Criminal Justice System," *Crime and Justice* 27 (2000): 81–167, 93. See, e.g., Wis. Stat. Ann. §938.18 (West 2006); Mo. Stat. Ann. §211.031, 211.071 (West 2006).

45. Cal. Welf. and Inst. Code §602, 707.01 (West 2006).

46. Office of Juvenile Justice and Delinquency Prevention, *Juvenile Justice Reform Initiatives*, 86.

47. Office of Juvenile Justice and Delinquency Prevention, *Juvenile Offenders and Victims: A National Report* (Washington, DC, 1999), 115.

48. Steve Aos, *The Juvenile Justice System in Washington State: Recommendations to Improve Cost-Effectiveness* (Olympia, WA, 2002), 3.

49. Tex. Fam. Code Ann. §52.04, 53.045 (West 2006). See also Paul Duggan, "George W. Bush: The Texas Record: Youth Feel the Force of a Vow Kept; Juvenile Justice Overhaul Reflects Tougher Approach," *Washington Post*, Nov. 9, 2000, A1.

50. In Colorado, until 2006, youths as young as age fourteen could be sentenced to life without parole. A new law signed by the governor in

May 2006, however, provided for parole hearings after forty years, re-placing the prior life without parole sentencing option. See National Center for Juvenile Justice, Colorado at http://www.ncjj.org/stateprofiles (accessed on June 29, 2007).

51. This point was made by advocates challenging the death penalty in the Supreme Court in *Roper v. Simmons*. For an amicus curiae brief that emphasized the age of majority for different purposes, see http://www .jlc.org/files/briefs/simmons-brief.pdf.

52. Pete Wilson, "The Governor vs. the Gangs," *San Francisco Examiner,* Aug. 2 1998, D7; Evelyn Nieves, "The 2000 Campaign: California; Those Opposed to Initiatives Had Little Chance from Start," *New York Times,* Mar. 9, 2000, A27.

53. "Prop. 21: No Youth Crime Remedy," *Los Angeles Times,* Feb. 22, 2000, B4.

54. Cal. Welf. and Inst. Code §707 (Lexis 2004).

55. Studies conducted by the Office of Juvenile Justice and Delinquency Prevention and the National Criminal Justice Reference Service show that in Los Angeles, the number of gang homicides peaked in 1995 and then decreased. "Youth Gangs and Violence" at www.ojjdp.ncjrs.gov (accessed on June 27, 2007); "Adolescent Homicides in Los Angeles: Are They Different from Other Homicides?" at www.ncjrs.gov (accessed on June 27, 2007).

56. Robert Conot, "L.A. Gangs: Our City, Their Turf," *Los Angeles Times,* Mar. 22, 1987, 1.

57. Jeffrey Mayer, "Individual Moral Responsibility and the Criminaliza-tion of Youth Gangs," *Wake Forest Law Review* 28 (1993): 943–985, 945.

58. Gang members faced up to three years in prison for their gang-related activities separate from the underlying substantive offense. Cal. Penal Code Ann. §186.22 (Lexis 1999).

59. Under the three-strikes statute, a felon can be sent to prison for life upon conviction of a third offense. The felony of "active participation in a criminal gang" counts under this statute. Cal. Penal Code Ann. §1170.12 (West 2006).

60. Rick Bragg, "Judge Punishes Arkansas Boys Who Kill 5," *New York Times,* Aug. 12, 1998, A1. After the incident, Arkansas passed the Extended Juvenile Jurisdiction Act, which enabled prosecutors to charge any child with murder, as long as he appeared to possess the requisite mental state and understood the criminal consequences of

his conduct. The act allowed a prosecutor to charge a child under the age of thirteen with murder if "the state has overcome presumptions about the lack of fitness to proceed and lack of capacity." Ark. Code. Ann. §9-27-501 (Lexis 1999). This statute, by most accounts, would have been even harsher except that the legislature was not in session until the next year, by which time public outrage had cooled and a legislative committee had studied the issue. See discussion in Chapter 9.

61. According to the Administrative Office of the Courts, there was a 30 percent drop in juvenile arrests throughout the 1990s. Anna Gorman, "State Juvenile Court Still Struggles to Find Balance; Participants in the System Gather in L.A. for Its 100th Anniversary and Discuss How Best to Blend Punishment and Rehabilitation," *Los Angeles Times,* Dec. 26, 2003, B2. Between 1994 and 2002, juvenile homicide rates fell by 65 percent nationwide to the lowest level since 1984. OJJDP [Office of Juvenile Justice and Delinquency Prevention] Statistical Briefing Book, "Homicide" at http://www.ojjdp.njcrs.gov (accessed on June 29, 2007). Aggravated assaults by juveniles declined by 33 percent between 1994 and 1995, while by 1997 the rate of robberies by juveniles had declined to its lowest levels since the 1970s. OJJDP Statistic Briefing Book, "Other Violent Crime" at http://www.ojjdp.ncjrs .gov/ (accessed on June 29, 2007).

62. Lori Dorfman & Vincent Schiraldi, *Off Balance: Youth, Race, and Crime in the News* (Washington, DC, 2001), 4. While youth homicides decreased by 68 percent between 1993 and 1999, and are at their lowest rate in a generation, polls demonstrated that 62 percent of the public believed youth crime was on the rise. Violence in schools had also decreased by 72 percent since 1992, yet 71 percent of those polled by the Wall Street Journal believed a school shooting may occur at their children's school. Sixty percent of those polled by the California Wellness Foundation believed that youth commit most crimes today despite the fact that in California, juvenile crimes amounted to less than 15 percent of all arrests. Ibid.

63. Richard Zoglin, "Now For the Bad News: A Teenage Time Bomb," *Time,* Jan. 15, 1996, 52, quoting James Alan Fox. See also John DiIulio, "Super-Predators."

64. California provided its citizens with arguments for and against Proposition 21, available at http://primary2000.ss.ca.gov/Voter-Guide (accessed on May 31, 2006). The super-predator prediction

and the deterrence argument were included as arguments for the initiative.

65. Samuel R. Gross & Phoebe C. Ellsworth, Americans' Views on the Death Penalty at the Turn of the Century, in *Capital Punishment and the American Future*, Stephen P. Garvey, ed.(Durham, 2001), downloaded at http://papers.ssrn.com/paper.taf?abstract_id=264018.

66. Dorfman & Schiraldi, *Off Balance*, 10.

67. See Franklin Gilliam & Shanto Iyengar, "Prime Suspects: The Influence of Local Television News on the Viewing Public," *American Journal of Political Science* 44 (2000): 560–573.

68. Dorfman & Schiraldi, *Off Balance*.

69. Michael Bradbury, "Debate on Proposition 21; More Tools Are Needed to Curb Juvenile Crime," *Los Angeles Times,* Feb. 9, 2000, B2.

70. Mark DiCamillo & Mervin Field, "Release #1956: Prop. 21 Running Ahead in Counties with Long Ballot Label Wording," *The Field Poll,* Feb. 29, 2000, 5.

71. In January 2000, ministers and youths gathered on Martin Luther King Day and displayed signs urging the defeat of Proposition 21. Henry Weinstein, "Calls Made to Carry on King's Work: Spirit of Civil Rights Leader Is Celebrated at Events in Inglewood, South Central Oxnard, and Elsewhere. "We Have not Overcome, a Leader Says," *Los Angeles Times,* Jan. 18, 2000, B1. In the 2000 race for District Attorney of Los Angeles, only one candidate, Barry Groveman, a man with little prosecuting experience, supported Proposition 21. "Cooley for District Attorney," *Los Angeles Times,* Feb. 27, 2000, M4. The chief probation officer of San Luis Obispo also spoke out against the initiative, stating that it would do nothing to make the streets safer; he described the prison systems and boot camps the proposition supported as "a dumping ground for young Latinos." James Rainey, "Probation Chief's Views Clash with Trend towards Tough Juvenile Justice Policy," *Los Angeles Times,* Nov. 20, 2000, A1.

72. The California Legislative Analyst's office estimated the costs of building new prisons and hiring additional law enforcement personnel could reach $750 million, with additional operational costs of as much as $350 million annually. C. Parenti, "No Mercy: California's Juvenile Justice System Could Become One of the Nation's Toughest," *In These Times,* Mar. 20, 2000, 8. In Ventura County alone, for example, it was predicted that officials would have trouble funding the new attorneys, staff, etc. T. Wilson, "Probation Officer Warns of

Costs of New Juvenile Crime Measure," *Los Angeles Times,* Mar, 26, 2000, B1.

73. Erich Goode & Nachman Ben-Yehuda, *Moral Panics: The Social Construction of Deviance* (Oxford, 1994).

74. Amos Tversky & Daniel Kahneman, "Judgment Under Uncertainty: Heuristics and Biases," in *Judgment Under Uncertainty: Heuristics and Biases,* Daniel Kahneman, Paul Slovic & Amos Tversky, eds. (Cambridge, 1982), 11. Other scholars have analyzed how the availability hueristic can contribute to exaggerated public fears about particular threats. See note 72 above.

75. Public opinion based on distorted perceptions continues to gain momentum, contributing to increased pressure on politicians and policymakers to enact legislation to respond to the perceived threat. Those who are skeptical remain silent rather than voicing unpopular opinions. Timur Kuran & Cass Sunstein, "Availability Cascades and Risk Regulation," *Stanford Law Review* 51 (1999): 683–768, 720–723.

76. Comment, "When The Punishment Cannot Fit the Crime: The Case for Reforming the Juvenile Justice System," *Arkansas Law Review* 52 (1999): 563–590, 569; "Arkansas Law to Permit Life Sentence for Youths," *New York Times,* Apr. 8, 1999, A25; Rick Bragg, "Judge Punishes Arkansas Boys Who Killed 5," *New York Times,* Aug. 12, 1998, A1.

77. Evelyn Nieves, "California's Governor Plays Tough on Crime," *The New York Times,* May 23, 2000, A16.

78. George Allen, "Juvenile Justice Reform Will Make Virginia Safer," *Richmond Times Dispatch,* Apr. 9, 1996, A-7.

79. One study showed that minorities are 8.3 times more likely than white youths to be sentenced in an adult court, and 2.7 times more likely to be arrested for a violent felony in California. In Los Angeles, police officers estimated that 47 percent of African American youths were involved in gangs. Nicholas Espiritu, "(E)racing Youth: The Racialized Construction of California's Proposition 21 and the Development of Alternate Contestations," *Cleveland State Law Review* 52 (2005): 189–209, 200. See also Michael Tonry, *Malign Neglect: Race, Crime, and Punishment in America* (New York, 1998), 134–148. In the mid-1990s reports showed that African American youths made up 12.5 percent of the population but accounted for nearly 29 percent of juvenile arrests and more than half of the arrests for violent crime, including 59 percent of juvenile homicide arrests. Office of Juvenile Justice and

Delinquency Prevention, *Juvenile Justice Reform Initiatives*, 4. See also D. Tanenhaus & S. Drizin, "'Owing to the Extreme Youth of the Accused:' The Changing Legal Response to Juvenile Homicide," *Journal of Criminal Law and Criminology* 92 (2003): 641–706, 666–667.

80. See Espiritu, "(E)racing Youth." See also Donna Bishop & Charles Frazier, "The Influence of Race in Juvenile Processing," *Journal of Research in Crime and Delinquency* 25 (1998): 242–263; Darlene Conley, "Adding Color to a Black and White Picture: Using Qualitative Data to Explain Racial Disproportionality in the Juvenile System," *Journal of Research in Crime and Delinquency* 31 (1994): 135–148; David Huizinga & Delbert Elliott, "Juvenile Offenders: Prevalence, Offender Incidence, and Arrests by Race," *Crime and Delinquency* 33 (1987): 206–233, 218; David Tanenhaus & Steven Drizin, "Owing to the Extreme Youth of the Accused," 666–667.

81. Elizabeth Scott, N. Dickon Reppucci, Jill Antonishak, and Jennifer De-Gennaro, "Public Attitudes about the Culpability and Punishment of Young Offenders," *Behavioral Science and Law* 24 (2006): 815–832. Participants were each presented with a photo of either a Caucasian or an African American young offender who was described as holding up a convenience store. In response to questions about the youth's maturity and deserved punishment, participants responded similarly to the white and black youths.

82. George Bridges & Sara Steen, "Racial Disparities in Official Assessments of Juvenile Offenders: Attributional Stereotypes as Mediating Mechanisms," *American Sociological Review* 63 (1998): 554–570, 561.

83. Sandra Graham & Brian Lowery, "Priming Unconscious Racial Stereotypes about Adolescent Offenders," *Law and Human Behavior* 28 (2004): 483–504, 487–501.

84. Scott et al., "Public Attitudes."

5. Immaturity and Mitigation

1. Tate v. State, 864 So. 2d 44, 48 (Fla. Dist. Ct. App. 2003); see also Michael Dale, "Making Sense of the Lionel Tate Case," *Villanova Law Review* 28 (2004): 468.

2. Maire Cocco, "Ashcroft Uses Virginia for Its Death Penalty," *Newsday*, Nov. 21, 2002, A39; J. Goodman, "Overturning Stanford v. Kentucky: Lee Boyd Malvo and the Execution of Juvenile Offenders," *The Law*

Review of Michigan State University—Detroit College of Law 2 (2003): 408.

3. Libby Copeland, "The Fatherless Son; For Lee Boyd Malvo, a Twisted Version of a Classic Literary Quest," *Washington Post,* Dec. 19, 2003, C1; Serge Koveleski & Mary Beth Sheridan, "A Boy of Bright Promise and No Roots; After Transient Childhood, Sniper Suspect Latched onto Strong Father Figure," *Washington Post,* Jan. 12, 2003, C1.

4. For a discussion of proportionality see Richard Bonnie, Anne Coughlin, John Jeffries & Peter Low, *Criminal Law* (New York, 2004), 901–958. The Supreme Court has addressed proportionality in the context of the death penalty, including the application of the death penalty to juveniles. Id. Roper v. Simmons, 543 U.S. 551 (2005).

5. Remember the statement of Albert Regnery, quoted in Chapter 4, describing juvenile offenders as "criminals who happen to be young, not children who happen to be criminal."

6. Several versions of the insanity defense have been offered over the past 150 years, and courts have explored the extent to which mental illness can mitigate blameworthiness under doctrines such as diminished capacity. See generally Bonnie, et. al., *Criminal Law,* 445–56, 477–502 (discussing the ways the law has defined the relationship between mental abnormality and criminal responsibility). Mental disorder as an excuse from criminal responsibility has also been a topic of great interest to criminal law scholars. See generally Joel Feinberg, *Doing and Deserving: Essays on the Theory of Responsibility* (Princeton, NJ, 1970), 272–292; Michael S. Moore, *Law and Psychiatry: Rethinking the Relationship* (Cambridge, 1984), 217–224 (discussing madness as an excuse for criminal activity); Norval Morris, *Madness and the Criminal Law* (Chicago, 1982). Criminal law theorists assume without inquiry that the immaturity of youth functions to mitigate or excuse young actors from responsibility for their crimes, but they also appear to assume that this conclusion has little contemporary importance in criminal law, perhaps because they believe that youths continue to be dealt with in a separate justice system in which their reduced blameworthiness is recognized (as was historically true). See R. A. Duff, "Choice, Character, and Criminal Liability," *Law and Philosophy* 12 (1993): 345–383, 367–68; Michael S. Moore, "Choice, Character, and Excuse," *Social Philosophy and Policy* 7 (1990): 29–58, 49–58 (mentioning infancy as a status excuse).

7. The views of Judge Ben Lindsey, discussed in Chapter 4, are representative of the paternalistic attitudes of the Progressive Era reformers of the early court. According to Judge Lindsey, "Our criminal laws are as inapplicable to children as they would be to idiots." Ben Lindsey & Harvey O'Higgins, *The Beast* (1910).

8. This classification scheme is discussed in Chapters 3 and 4.

9. Many believe that the laxness of the traditional juvenile justice system contributed to juvenile crime. In a 1989 study, for example, 70 percent of those questioned stated that the leniency of the system was a cause of violent youth crime. T. Flanagan & K. Maguire, eds., "Bureau of Justice Statistics," *U.S. Department of Justice, Sourcebook of Criminal Justice Statistics* (1990), 157. Other studies demonstrate that the public supports prison systems for juveniles because the juvenile system is too lenient. Jane Sprott, "Understanding Public Opposition to a Separate Youth Justice System," *Crime and Delinquency* 44 (1998): 399–411.

10. The insanity defense is representative of the first type of excuse, based on incapacity, and the defense of duress is an example of a situational excuse based on coercive circumstances. See Duff, "Choice, Character, and Criminal Liability," 345. Under the prevailing formulation of the insanity defense, a defendant is excused from liability if, because of "mental disease or defect," he does not understand the nature and quality of his criminal act or that it was wrong. See Bonnie, *Criminal Law*, 445–456. The classic case of duress is the defendant who robs a bank because someone is pointing a gun at his head. For a discussion of duress, see Bonnie, *Criminal Law*, 399–409.

11. Bonnie, et. al., *Criminal Law*, 9–10; See Stephen Morse, "Justice, Mercy, and Craziness," *Stanford Law Review* 36 (1984): 1485–1515.

12. Coker v. Georgia, 433 U.S. 584, 585 (1977). See Katherine K. Baker, "Once a Rapist? Motivational Evidence and Relevancy in Rape Law," *Harvard Law Review* 110 (1997): 594–595. Baker discusses the disparate treatment of black rapists and notes that the overwhelming majority of men executed for rape between 1930 and 1967 were black, citing Michael Meltsner, *Cruel and Unusual: The Supreme Court and Capital Punishment* (New York, 1973), 75.

13. Paul Robinson & John Darley, "The Utility of Desert," *Northwestern Law Review* 91 (1997): 457–458.

14. For a general description of various theories see Duff, "Choice, Character, and Criminal Liability," 367–368. Jeremy Horder, "Criminal Culpability: The Possibility of a General Theory," *Law*

and Philosophy 12 (1993): 193–215. Other scholars, such as Jean Hampton, offer alternatives to the choice- and character-based theories. See Jean Hampton, "Mens Rea," *Social Philosophy and Policy* 7 (1990): 1–28.

15. The intellectual architect of choice theory was H.L.A. Hart, a British legal philosopher; for his overview of choice theory see Hart, *Punishment and Responsibility: Essays in the Philosophy of Law* (Oxford, 1968), 152. See also Sanford Kadish, "The Decline of Innocence," *Blame and Punishment: Essays in the Criminal Law* (New York, 1987), 65; Joshua Dressler, "Reflections on Excusing Wrongdoers: Moral Theory, New Excuses, and the Model Penal Code," *Rutgers Law Journal* 19 (1988): 701–702; Moore, "Choice, Character, and Excuse," 31–58; Stephen Morse, "Culpability and Control," *Pennsylvania Law Review* 142 (1994): 1587–1660; Stephen Morse, "Rationality and Responsibility," *Southern California Law Review* 74 (2000): 251–268.

16. For an overview of character theory see R. B. Brandt, "A Motivational Theory of Excuses in the Criminal Law," in J. Roland Pennock & John Chapman, *Criminal Justice: Nomos* (eds.) (New York & London 1985) 27: 165–198; Nicola Lacey, *State Punishment: Political Principles and Community Values* (London, 1988), 65–68; Michael Bayles, "Character, Purpose, and Criminal Responsibility," *Law and Philosophy* 1 (1982): 5–20, 8–11; George Vuoso, "Background, Responsibility, and Excuse," *Yale Law Journal* 96 (1986): 1662. See also George Fletcher, *Rethinking Criminal Law* (Oxford, 1978), 802.

17. As R. A. Duff aptly put it, choice theory is too arid and character theory is too rich. Choice theorists deny the relevance of the link between the act and the actor's underlying personal identity, while (many) character theorists discount the importance of the criminal act itself. See Duff, "Choice, Character, and Criminal Liability," 367–368.

18. Reasonable provocation reduces murder to manslaughter. Jerome Michael and Herbert Wechsler describe the reasonableness requirement as a measure of character: "Provocation . . . cannot be measured by the intensity of the passions aroused in the actor by the provocative circumstances. It must be estimated by the probability that such circumstances would affect most men in like fashion. . . . [T]he greater the provocation, measured in that way, the more ground there is for attributing the intensity of the actor's passions and his lack of self-control . . . to the extraordinary character of the situation . . . rather than to any extraordinary deficiency in his own character. . . .

[T]he more difficulty [most men] would experience in resisting the impulse to which he yielded, the less does his succumbing serve to differentiate his character from theirs." Jerome Michael & Herbert Wechsler, "A Rationale of the Law of Homicide II," *Columbia Law Review* 37 (1937): 1281.

19. As we will discuss shortly, character formation (identity development) takes place over a period extending into late adolescence or early adulthood. See discussion, Laurence Steinberg, *Adolescence* (New York, 2002), 263–279.

20. This characterization is based loosely on an observation by Sanford Kadish; see Kadish, "Excusing Crime," 75 *California Law Review* 75 (1987): 265.

21. At common law, children were presumed to lack the capacity to understand the wrongfulness of their conduct. The presumption could be rebutted for youths between the ages of seven and fourteen. After age fourteen, young offenders were conclusively presumed to have the moral capacity as adults. Andrew Walkover, "The Infancy Defense in the New Juvenile Court," *UCLA Law Review* 31 (1984): 510–512 with citations from William Blackstone, *Commentaries on the Laws of England* (Oxford, 1769), 23–24.

22. The excuse of duress, for example, is only available when the actor faces the threat of death or serious bodily harm that a person of "reasonable firmness" would not be able to resist. See, for example, U.S. v. Willis, 38 F.3d 170, 178–179 (5th Cir. 1994).

23. The Federal Sentencing Guidelines were amended to include "aberrant behavior" as a mitigating factor. U.S. Sentencing Guidelines Manual §5K2.20, cmt. n.1(c) (1998). Such behavior must "represen[t] a marked deviation by the defendant from an otherwise law-abiding life." State guidelines also include mitigating factors based on past reputation and character. See, for example, N.C. Gen. Stat. §15A-1340.16(e)(12) (2001), in regard to recognizing good character or good reputation in community as mitigating factors.

24. Some jurisdictions, for example, recognize homicide defenses of diminished capacity or partial responsibility or reduce murder to manslaughter. See Bonnie, *Criminal Law,* 538–540. Under the Model Penal Code, the actor's extreme mental or emotional disturbance reduces the homicide to manslaughter. Model Penal Code §210.3(1)(B). Mental illness is also often a general mitigation factor at sentencing. See U.S. Sentencing Manual §5K.213 (2001); Kan. Stat. Ann. §21-

4637(h) (1995); Neb. Rev. Stat. §29-2523(2)(g)(Supp. 2000). When Andrea Yates was found guilty of killing her five children, the jury rejected her insanity plea but declined to impose the death penalty because of her mental illness. Jim Yardley, "Mother Who Drowned Five Children in Tub Avoids a Death Sentence," *New York Times,* Mar. 16, 2002, A1.

25. All excusing conditions, such as duress, may be mitigating in a less extreme form. See H.L.A. Hart, *Punishment and Responsibility,* 16.

26. Statutory formulations of homicide reveal this grading scheme. See Model Penal Code §210. See generally Jerome Michael & Herbert Wechsler, "A Rationale of the Law of Homicide II," 1274–1290.

27. See note 18 above and accompanying text. See also Dan Kahan & Martha Nussbaum, "Two Conceptions of Emotion in Criminal Law," *Columbia Law Review* 96 (1996): 269–374.

28. Statutory sentencing guidelines almost always include endogenous conditions as mitigating factors. For example, see Fla. Stat. Ann. §921.0026 (West 2001), including impaired cognitive/volitional capacity, mental disorder, and youth; Kan. Stat. Ann. §21-4637(b), (e), (g)–(h), (1995) including extreme mental distress, mental disorder, domination by another, impaired cognitive/volitional capacity, and age; Neb. Rev. Stat. §29-2523(2)(b)–(d), (g) (1995 & Supp. 2001).

29. See N.J. Stat. Ann. §2C:44-1(b)(3), listing provocation as a "mitigating circumstance," and §2C:44-1(b)(13), listing undue influence as by an older person; N.C. Gen. Stat. §15A-1340.16(e)(1)(2001), listing duress, coercion, and threat insufficient to constitute defense, but reducing culpability, and §15A-1340.16(e)(8)(provocation); Tenn. Code Ann. §40-35-113(12), listing duress or domination not sufficient to constitute a defense.

30. See "United States Sentencing Commission," *United States sentencing guidelines manual* (Washington, DC, 1998), Section 5K2.20.

31. During adolescence, youths improve basic developmental processing skills and make gains in deductive reasoning and abstract reasoning. See generally Bärbel Inhelder & Jean Piaget, *The Growth of Logical Thinking from Childhood to Adolescence,* A. Parsons & S. Milgram, trans. (New York, 1958); Robert Siegler and Martha Alibali, *Children's Thinking* (Englewood Cliffs, NJ, 2005), 55–64.

32. See S. Ward & W. Overton, "Semantic Familiarity, Relevance, and the Development of Deductive Reasoning," *Developmental Psychology* 26 (1990): 488–493. Adolescent decision-making under

stress, for example, is often poorer than in hypothetical situations, and research suggests that the effects of stress on decision-making are more marked for adolescents than for adults. L. Mann, "Stress, Affect, and Risk-Taking," in *Risk-Taking Behavior*, J. F. Yates, ed.(West Sussex, England: John Wiley and Son, 1992), 201–230, 214–215; Elizabeth Cauffman & Laurence Steinberg, "Researching Adolescents' Judgment and Culpability," in *Youth on Trial: A Developmental Perspective on Juvenile Justice*, Thomas Grisso & Robert Schwartz, eds. (Chicago, 2000); Laurence Steinberg, "Risk-Taking in Adolescence: What Changes and Why?" *Annals of the New York Academy of Sciences* 1021 (2004): 51–58.

33. See discussion in Chapter 2. Susceptibility to peer pressure peaks at age fourteen and declines throughout the high-school years. See Laurence Steinberg & Susan Silverberg, "The Vicissitudes of Autonomy in Early Adolescence," *Child Development* 57 (1986): 841–851, 848; Elizabeth Scott, N.D. Reppucci, & Jennifer Woolard, "Evaluating Adolescent Decision-Making in Legal Contexts," *Law and Human Behavior* 19 (1995): 221–244, 229–230; Elizabeth Cauffman & Laurence Steinberg, "Researching Adolescents' Judgment and Culpability," 257–259.

Regarding risk preference, adolescents focus less on protection against losses and more on opportunities for gains in making choices, which may explain in part why they are more likely to engage in risky behavior, such as unprotected sex. See William Gardner & Janna Herman, "Adolescents' AIDS Risk-Taking: A Rational Choice Perspective," *New Directions for Child Development* 50 (1991): 17–34, 24; See also Lita Furby & Ruth Beyth-Marom, "Risk-Taking in Adolescence: A Decision-Making Perspective," *Developmental Review* 12 (1992): 1–44, 1–2.

34. See Gardner & Herman, "Adolescents' AIDS Risk Taking," 25–26. Young adolescents are preoccupied with the present; a sense of the extended future has not yet formed. See Thomas J. Cattle, Peter Howard & Joseph Pleck, "Adolescent Perception of Time: The Effect of Age, Sex, and Social Class," *Journal of Personality* 37 (1969): 636–650. Changes in temporal perspective continue through late adolescence until age eighteen. Anita Greene, "Future-Time Perspective in Adolescence: The Present of Things Future Revisited," *Journal of Youth and Adolescence* 15 (1986): 99–113, 100; Jari-Erik Nurmi, "How do Adolescents See Their Future? A Review of the Development of Future Orientation and Planning," *Developmental Review* 11 (1991): 1–59, 29 (1991).

Studies also tend to show a gradual increase in self-direction and ability to control impulsivity through the final years of high school. E. Greenberger, "Education and the Acquisition of Psycho-Social Maturity," in *The Development of Social Maturity*, D. McClelland, ed. (New York, 1982), 155–189.

35. See Elkhonon Goldberg, *The Executive Brain: Frontal Lobes and the Civilized Mind* (Oxford, 2001), 35; L. P. Spear, "The Adolescent Brain and Age-Related Behavioral Manifestations," *Neuroscience and Biobehavioral Reviews* 24 (2000): 417–463.

36. This scenario is adapted from an earlier article by one of the authors. Elizabeth Scott & Thomas Grisso, "The Evolution of Adolescence: A Developmental Perspective on Juvenile Justice Reform," *Journal of Criminal Law and Criminology* 88 (1997): 137–189.

37. Albert Reiss, Jr., & David Farrington, "Advancing Knowledge about Co-Offending: Results from a Prospective Longitudinal Survey of London Males," *Journal of Criminal Law and Criminology* 82 (1991): 360–395, 361–62. Even adults, however, can make riskier choices in groups. Think about mob behavior, for example.

38. See Chapter 2. Terrie Moffitt postulates that young adults may cease to commit crimes because they come to understand that the decision to offend carries the risk of lost future opportunities. Terrie Moffitt, "Adolescence-Limited and Life Course Persistent Antisocial Behavior: A Developmental Taxonomy," *Psychological Review* 100 (1993): 674–701, 690.

39. Thompson v. Oklahoma, 487 U.S. 815, 835 (1988).

40. Jeffery Fagan, "Context and Culpability in Adolescent Crime," *Virginia Journal of Social Policy and Law* 6 (1999): 535–538; Jeffery Fagan, "Contexts of Choice by Adolescents in Criminal Events," in *Youth on Trial*, Grisso & Schwartz, eds., 376.

41. Jens Ludwig, Greg Duncan & Paul Hirschfeld, "Urban Poverty and Juvenile Crime," *Quarterly Journal of Economics* 116 (2001): 655–680, 676.

42. The inability to escape and normal psychological immaturity distinguish adolescents from adult offenders who might argue that they are less culpable than other criminal actors because of their "rotten social background." Some commentators have argued that such a defense should be available to adult lawbreakers who grew up in crime-inducing settings without inculcation in pro-social norms or opportunities to succeed in socially acceptable ways, on the ground that these social forces combine to constrain their freedom to avoid crime. Richard Delgado,

" 'Rotten Social Background': Should the Criminal Law Recognize a Defense of Severe Environmental Deprivation?" *Law and Inequalities* 3 (1985): 9–90, 63–65, 64 n.363. This defense generally has been rejected by lawmakers (rightly, we think), in part because of the high social cost incurred if a defense were available to a large open-ended category of adult offenders otherwise indistinguishable from the norm. More importantly, perhaps, the defense threatens to dissolve the important but delicate line between free will and determinism, the boundary of criminal responsibility. Stephen Morse, "The Twilight of Welfare Criminology: A Reply to Judge Bazelon," *Southern California Law Review* 49 (1976): 1251–1253. In contrast, recognition of social context as situational mitigation that is limited to juveniles as a class does not carry the same threat of unraveling the core of criminal responsibility.

43. See Fagan, "Context and Culpability in Adolescent Crime."

44. These courts have evaluated adolescent criminal conduct under the "reasonable person" standard by using the typical *adolescent* as the measure. See, for example, In re William G., 963 P.2d 187, 293 (Ariz. App. Div. 1987).

45. See the discussion in Chapter 2. See Terrie Moffitt, "Adolescence-Limited and Life Course Persistent Antisocial Behavior," 675.

46. As we explain in Chapter 2, it is well documented that most youths desist from criminal activity in late adolescence. See David Farrington, "Age and Crime," in *Crime & Justice: An Annual Review of Research* 7, Michael Tonry and Norval Morris eds. (Chicago, 1986), 189–250; E. P. Mulvey & M. Aber, "Growing Out of Delinquency: Development and Desistance," in *The Abandonment of Delinquent Behavior: Promoting the Turnaround*, R. L. Jenkins & W. K. Brown eds.(New York, 1988), 99–116, 100; Marvin Wolfgang, Robert Figlio & Thorsten Sellin, *Delinquency in a Birth Cohort* (Chicago, 1972), 89; Alfred Blumstein & Jacqueline Cohen, "Characterizing Criminal Careers," *Science* 237 (1987): 985–991, 991; Travis Hirschi & Michael Gottfredson, "Age and the Explanation of Crime," *American Journal of Sociology* 89 (1983): 552–584.

47. *American Psychiatric Association, Diagnostic and Statistical Manual of Mental Disorders* (Washington, D.C., 4th ed. 1994). See also Daniel Seagrave & Thomas Grisso, "Adolescent Development and the Measurement of Juvenile Psychopathy," *Law and Human Behavior* 26 (2000): 219–239, 224.

48. Many researchers have challenged the use of this diagnosis with juveniles and have questioned the validity of using a "psychopathy checklist," an instrument designed to facilitate diagnosis of psychopaths, on this population. See Elizabeth Cauffman & J. L. Skeem, "Views of the Downward Extension: Comparing the Youth Version of the Psychopathy Checklist with the Youth Psychopathic Traits Inventory," *Behavioral Sciences and Law* 21 (2003): 737–770; Daniel Seagrave & Thomas Grisso, "Adolescent Development and the Measurement of Juvenile Psychopathy" and Lisa Ells, "Note, Juvenile Psychopathy, The Hollow Promise of Prediction," 105 *Columbia Law Review* 105 (2005):158–207.

49. *American Psychiatric Association, Diagnostic and Statistical Manual of Mental Disorders* (Washington D.C., 4th ed. 1994).

50. See Lisa Ells, "Note, Juvenile Psychopathy," 194–197.

51. Moffitt labels these offenders "life course persistent offenders." See Terrie Moffitt, "Adolescence-Limited and Life Course Persistent Antisocial Behavior," 682–685.

52. African American youths make up a disproportionate number of youths in the justice system. *Office of Juvenile Justice & Delinquency Prevention, Justice Reform Initiatives in the States: 1994–1996 Program Report* 4 (1997), reporting that black juveniles made up 12.5 percent of the population in 1994 but accounted for nearly 29 percent of juvenile arrests and more than half of the arrests for violent crime, including 59 percent of juvenile homicide arrests. Most analysts believe that the phenomenon reflects both higher offending rates and differential responses to minority and white youths by system participants, including police, prosecutors, judges, and corrections officers. See Donna M. Bishop & Charles E. Frazier, "The Influence of Race in Juvenile Justice Processing," *Journal of Research in Crime and Delinquency* 25 (1998): 242–263; Micheal Tonry, *Malign Neglect: Race, Crime, and Punishment in America* (Oxford, 1995), 134–148.

Several studies, discussed in Chapter 4, show evidence of bias. See George S. Bridges & Sara Steen, "Racial Disparities in Official Assessments of Juvenile Offenders: Attributional Stereotypes as Mediating Mechanisms," *American Sociological Review* 63 (1998): 554–570, 561–564; Sandra Graham & Brian Lowery, "Priming Unconscious Racial Stereotypes about Adolescent Offenders," *Human Behavior* 28(5) (2004): 483–504. For studies examining the role of the media, see Franklin Gilliam & Shanto Iyengar, "Prime Suspects: The Influence of Local Television News on the Viewing Public," *Amercian Journal of Political Science* 44 (2000): 560–573.

53. Graham & Lowery, "Priming Unconscious Racial Stereotypes About Adolescent Offenders."

54. Elizabeth Scott & Laurence Steinberg, "Blaming Youth," *Texas Law Review* 838 81 (2003).

55. Curtis Bradley, "The Juvenile Death Penalty and International Law," *Duke Law Journal* 52 (2003): 485–557.

56. See Robert Shepherd, "Supreme Court Revisits Juvenile Death Penalty," *Criminal Justice* 19 (2004): 51; *Simmons*, 543 U.S., 562 (2005).

57. *Simmons*, 543 U.S., 568.

58. Ibid., 561.

59. *Thompson*, 487 U.S., 835.

60. Stanford v. Kentucky, 492 U.S. 361, 380 (1989).

61. Atkins v. Virginia, 122 S. Ct. 2242, 2252 (2002).

62. *Simmons*, 543 U.S., 552.

63. Ibid., 569. Justice Kennedy points out that juveniles are more immature, irresponsible, and subject to peer pressure than are adults. Drawing on our framework, he described three key attributes of adolescence: immature decision-making skills, vulnerability to peer pressure, and an undeveloped character, citing Elizabeth S. Scott & Laurence Steinberg, "Less Guilty by Reason of Adolescence: Developmental Immaturity, Diminished Responsibility, and the Juvenile Death Penalty," *American Psychologist* 58 (2003): 1009–1018, 1014.

64. *Simmons*, 543 U.S., 570.

65. Ibid., 614–17.

66. Elizabeth Emens, "Aggravating Youth: Roper v. Simmons and Age Discrimination," *Supreme Court Review* (2006): 51–102; James Carlson, "Victim's Sister Tries to Live on," *St. Louis Post-Dispatch,* Mar. 2, 2005, 2.

67. The Court noted: "As legal minors, [juveniles] lack the freedom that adults have to extricate themselves from a criminogenic setting." 543 U.S., 569, citing Steinberg & Scott, "Less Guilty by Reason of Adolescence," 1014.

68. *Simmons* 543 U.S., 567–570.

69. Ibid., 573, citing Steinberg & Scott, "Less Guilty by Reason of Adolescence," 1014–1018); Elizabeth Emens argues that where aggravating aspects, such as youth and immaturity, threaten to overwhelm

the juror's ability to consider mitigation, a categorical rule protecting juveniles is needed. Emens, "Aggravating Youth," 51.

70. Ibid.

71. *Simmons*, 543 U.S., 574.

72. Although the discretionary authority of juvenile court judges has been substantially restricted under the recent reforms, few states have implemented a regime of proportionate determinate sentences. See discussion in Chapter 8. An exception is the state of Washington.

73. See discussion in Chapter 4 of the various reforms since the late 1980s.

74. Barry Feld has argued for this approach. Barry Feld, "Abolish the Juvenile Court: Youthfulness, Criminal Responsibility and Sentencing Policy," *Journal of Criminal Law and Crimonology* 88 (1998): 68–136. In Chapter 8 we address this issue in greater depth.

6. Developmental Competence and the Adjudication of Juveniles

1. State v. Tate, 854 So. 2d., 44, 48 (Fla. Dist. Ct. App. 2003).

2. *Tate*, 854 So. 2d., 44. Lionel's case suggests the complexity of the ways that youthful immaturity can impede competence, as suggested in the text. The attorney thought that Lionel was unable to make an independent decision and was subject to undue influence. Dana Canedy, "Sentence of Life without Parole for Boy, 14, in Murder of Girl, 6," *New York Times*, Mar. 10, 2001, A1.

3. This chapter draws largely on previously published work, specifically, Elizabeth S. Scott & Thomas Grisso, "Developmental Incompetence, Due Process, and Juvenile Policy," *North Carolina Law Review* 83 (2005): 793–845.

4. Pate v. Robinson, 383 U.S.375 (1966).

5. Richard E. Redding & Lynda E. Frost, "Adjudicative Competence in the Modern Juvenile Court," *Virginia Journal of Social Policy and Law* (2001) 9: 353–406, 400–401 (listing statutes and case law that require competency hearings for juveniles).

6. Pate v. Robinson, 383 U.S.375 (1966).

7. Dusky v. United States, 362 U.S. 402 (1960). *Dusky* defined the standard to be applied in federal courts, but state courts have also adopted the *Dusky* standard. For a discussion of the competence requirement, see Gerald Bennett, "A Guided Tour through Selected ABA Standards Relating to Incompetence to Stand Trial," *George Washington Law*

Review 53 (1985): 375–413; Richard J. Bonnie, "The Competence of Criminal Defendants with Mental Retardation to Participate in Their Own Defense," *Journal of Criminal Law & Criminology* 81 (1990): 419–446; Bruce Winick, "Restructuring Competency to Stand Trial," *U.C.L.A. Law Review* 32 (1985): 921–985.

8. As we discuss in Chapter 4, Judge Ben Lindsey, of the Denver Juvenile Court, was an outspoken early advocate of informal delinquency proceedings. Ben B. Lindsey & Harvey J. O'Higgins, *The Beast* (Seattle, 1970), 133 (arguing that the privilege against self-incrimination has no place in a juvenile delinquency proceeding because young offenders should confess their wrongdoing).

9. See discussion in Chapter 4. *Gault* extended the right to counsel, the privilege against self-incrimination, the right of confrontation, and the right to notice of the charges to delinquency proceedings. In re Gault , 387 U.S. at 33, 41, 55–56. See also In re Winship, 397 U.S. 358, 368 (1970) (proof beyond a reasonable doubt required); Breed v. Jones, 421 U.S. 519 (1975) (juveniles were protected against double jeopardy). The Court has made clear that not all constitutional protections accorded to criminal defendants are required in juvenile delinquency proceedings. See note 15 below.

10. Almost all courts have held that competence to stand trial is required in juvenile delinquency proceedings. See Golden v. State, 21 S.W.3d 801 (Ark. 2000); State ex rel. Dandoy v. Superior Court, 619 P.2d 12 (Ariz. 1980); James v. Superior Court, 143 Cal. Rptr. 398 (Cal. Ct. App. 1978); In re K.G., 808 N.E.2d 631 (Ind. 2004); State ex rel. Causey, 363 So.2d 472 (La. 1978); In re J.M., 769 A.2d 656 (Vt. 2001). An exception is the Oklahoma Court of Criminal Appeals. G.J.I. v. State, 778 P.2d 485, 487 (Okla. Crim. App. 1989).

11. Golden v. State, 21 S.W.3d 801, 803 (Ark. 2000); In re K.G., 781 N.E.2d 700 (Ind.App. 2002); In re Carey, 615 N.W.2d 742, 746 (Mich.App. 2000); Matter of W.A.F., 573 A.2d 1264, 1267 (D.C.App. 1990).

12. In *McKiever v. Pennsylvania*, for example, the Court held, on this basis, that juveniles in delinquency proceedings have no right to a jury trial. 403 U.S. 528 (1971).

13. Va. Code Ann. §16.1-269.1(3) (2003).

14. In 1985, 6 percent of juveniles waived to a criminal court were under sixteen years old. Jeffrey A. Butts, *Delinquency Cases Waived to Criminal Court, 1985–1994* (Washington, DC, 1997), 1. By 1999, 14 percent

of juveniles waived were under sixteen years old. Charles M. Puzzanchera, *Delinquency Cases Waived to Criminal Court, 1990–1999*
(Washington, DC, 2003), 2.

15. Chapter 4 describes the legal changes under which many youths are
potentially liable to adult prosecution.

16. An exception is the Arkansas statute—enacted after the Jonesboro
shootings (see note 18)—under which a juvenile under the age of thirteen can receive extended juvenile jurisdiction, or blended sentencing,
if she commits capital murder or first-degree murder. The statute presumes that juveniles under the age of thirteen are incompetent to stand
trial and requires the prosecution to overcome this presumption by a
preponderance of the evidence. Ark. Code Ann. §9-27-502(b) (2003).

17. Courts have recognized the functional nature of the competence requirement in barring adjudication in rare instances when defendants
are incompetent due to a medical condition. Bruce J. Winick, "Restructuring Competency to Stand Trial," *UCLA Law Review* 32
(1985); 921, 950.

18. See note 1 above. Another high profile case was the Jonesboro,
Arkansas shooting, in which eleven-year-old Andrew Golden and
thirteen-year-old Mitchell Johnson killed four classmates and a
teacher. Andrew's attorneys unsuccessfully claimed he was incompetent to stand trial in a delinquency proceeding. Rick Bragg, "Judge
Punishes Arkansas Boys Who Killed Five," *New York Times,* Aug. 12,
1998, A1. In a Chicago case, two boys, ages seven and eight were
wrongly accused of the rape and murder of their eleven-year-old
neighbor, Ryan Harris. Carlos Sadovi, "Ryan Harris Slaying Haunts
Mother and City," at www.chicagotribune.com, Oct. 5, 2005.

19. See statutes and bills collected in 2006 State Juvenile Justice Legislation, National Juvenile Defender Center, at www.njdc.org, p. 14.

20. Mass. Gen Laws Ann. 119§58 (West 2004). See discussion in Chapter
4. Chauncey E. Brummer, "Extended Juvenile Jurisdiction: The Best of
Both Worlds?" Arkansas Law Review 54 (2002): 777, 778–79.

21. These factors are based on the *Dusky* test. Dusky v. U.S., 362 U.S. 402,
402 (1960).

22. See generally Thomas Grisso, *Evaluating Competencies: Forensic As-
sessments and Instruments* (New York, 2nd ed. 2003); Ronald Roesch
& Stephen L. Golding, *A System of Analysis of Competency to Stand
Trial* (New York, 1980).

324 · Notes to Pages 159–161

23. Gary B. Melton, John Petrilla, Norman Poythress, & Christopher Slobogin, *Psychological Evaluations for the Courts* (New York, 3rd ed. 2007), 122.

24. Thomas Grisso, *Juveniles' Waiver of Rights: Legal and Psychological Competence* (New York, 1981), 42–53; Thomas Grisso, "What We Know about Youths' Capacities as Trial Defendants," in *Youth on Trial*, Thomas Grisso & Robert G. Schwartz, eds. (New York, 2000), 139–140.

25. Thomas Grisso, *Evaluating Competencies*, 84.

26. Elizabeth Scott, N.D. Reppucci, & Jennifer Woolard, "Evaluating Adolescent Decision-Making in Legal Contexts," *Law & Human Behavior* (1995) 19: 221–244.

27. Thomas Grisso, "Juveniles' Waiver of Rights: Legal and Psychological Competence," 148.

28. Elizabeth Scott & Thomas Grisso, "Developmental Incompetence," 819.

29. Daniel Keating, "Cognitive and Brain Development," in *Handbook of Adolescent Psychology*, Richard Lerner & Laurence Steinberg, eds. (New York, 2nd ed. 2004), 45–84.

30. Although the capacity to make decisions is not explicitly required by *Dusky*, it was described as a component of competence to stand trial by the U.S. Supreme Court in *Godinez v. Moran*, 509 U.S. 389, 397–399 (1993).

31. An example of this kind of immaturity in a related context is the greater tendency of youths than adults to waive Miranda rights. Grisso, *Juveniles' Waiver of Rights*. David Tanenhaus and Steven Drizin have examined the other costly consequences of immaturity in the interrogation setting, where youths are more likely to give false confessions. *See* David S. Tanenhaus & Steven A. Drizin, " 'Owing to the Extreme Youth of the Accused': The Changing Legal Response to Juvenile Homicide," *Journal of Criminal Law & Criminology* 92 (2002): 641–705, 677–678.

32. The study summarized here is described in detail in Thomas Grisso et al., "Juveniles' Competence to Stand Trial: A Comparison of Adolescents' and Adults' Capacities as Trial Defendants," *Law and Human Behavior* 27 (2003): 333–364.

33. Norman Poythress, Richard Bonnie, John Monahan, Randy Otto, & Steven Hoge, *Adjudicative Competence: The MacArthur Studies* (New York, 2002), 112. Items in the assessment instrument are scored 2 (adequate), 1 (questionable), or 0 (inadequate), according to strict

criteria for each item, provided in the manual. The total score for the first set of items ("a" above, 8 items) is called the Understanding score, and the total for the second group ("b" above, 8 items) is called the Reasoning score.

34. Ibid., 117–118.

35. Youths with intellectual impairments are disproportionately represented in juvenile justice facilities. Peter Leone & Sheri Meisel, "Improving Education Services for Students in Detention and Confinement Facilities," *Children's Legal Rights Journal* 17 (1997): 1–12, 2–3. About 13 percent of juvenile offenders are mentally retarded, and about 36 percent have learning disorders. Pamela Casey & Ingo Keilitz, "Estimating the Prevalence of Learning disabled and Mentally Retarded Juvenile Offenders: A Meta-Analysis," in *Understanding Troubled and Troubling Youth*, Peter Leone, ed. (Newbury Park, 1990), 82, 86; Travis Hirschi & Michael J. Hindelang, "Intelligence and Delinquency: A Revisionist Review," *American Sociological Review* 42 (1977): 571–587, 584.

36. The MacJEN instrument was based on an instrument developed by Jennifer Woolard, a member of our research group, as part of her doctoral dissertation. See Jennifer Woolard, Developmental Aspects of Judgment and Competence in Legally Relevant Contexts, Unpublished dissertation (Charlottesville, 1998); Melinda Schmidt, N. D. Reppucci & Jennifer Woolard, "Effectiveness of Participation as a Defendant: The Attorney-juvenile Client Relationship," *Behavioral Sciences and the Law* 21 (2003): 175–198.

37. Grisso, *Juvenile's Waiver of Rights*. The study involved about 400 youths age fourteen and under and two hundred adults.

38. Deborah K. Cooper, "Juveniles' Understanding of Trial-Related Information: Are They Competent Defendants?" *Behavioral Science & Law* 15 (1997): 167–180, 177–178; Vance Cowden & Geoffrey McKee, "Competency to Stand Trial in Juvenile Delinquency Proceedings: Cognitive Maturity and the Attorney-Client Relationship," *Journal of Family Law* 33 (1995): 629–660; Michele Peterson-Badali & Rona Abramovitch, "Children's Knowledge of the Legal System: Are They Competent to Instruct Legal Counsel?" *Canadian Journal of Criminology and Criminal Justice* 34 (1992): 130–160; Michele Peterson-Badali, Roma Abramovitch & Juliane Duda, "Young Children's Legal Knowledge and Reasoning Ability," *Canadian Journal of Criminology and Criminal Justice* 39 (1997): 145–170; Jeffrey C. Savitsky & Deborah

Karras, "Competency to Stand Trial among Adolescents," *Adolescence* 19 (1984): 349–358.

39. Rona Abramovitch et al., "Young People's Understanding and Assertion of Their Rights to Silence and Legal Counsel," *Canadian Journal of Criminology and Criminal Justice* 37 (1995): 1–18; Michele Peterson-Badali & Rona Abramovitch, "Grade Related Changes in Young People's Reasoning about Plea Decisions," *Law and Human Behavior* 17 (1993): 537–552; Peterson-Badali et al., "Young Children's Legal Knowledge and Reasoning Ability," 145–170.

40. Va. Code Ann. §16.1-169.1 (2004); Virginia Commission on Youth, Study of Juvenile Competency Issues in Legal Proceedings, H. Doc. No. 42 (1999).

41. Most incompetent defendants are required to participate in competence training that includes instruction about the trial, the participants, the charges facing the defendant, the meaning of pleas, and the possible consequences. Redding & Frost, "Adjudicative Competence," 367.

42. Jackson v. Indiana, 406 U.S. 715 (1972). Jackson was mentally impaired, deaf, and mute; he had been confined for three and one-half years after the trial court found him incompetent. Ibid., 717. The Supreme Court held that due process requires that a person "committed solely on account of his incapacity to proceed to trial cannot be held more than the reasonable period of time necessary to determine whether there is a substantial probability that he will attain that capacity in the foreseeable future." Ibid., 738.

43. See, for example, Ariz. Rev. Stat. Ann. §13-4510 (2004) (six months); Fla. Stat. Ann. §916.13 (2001) (six months); Ga. Code Ann. §17-7-130 (2004) (nine months); Ind. Code Ann. §35-36-3-3 (1998) (six months). Some states have no statutory limitation. See, for example, Va. Code Ann. §19.2-169.2 & 169.3 and §37.1-67.3 (2004) (providing for reassessments every six months).

44. Va. Code Ann. §16.1-269.1

45. See Godinez v. Moran, 509 U.S. 389, 402 (1993), regarding declining to hold that an independent determination of defendants' competence to make specific decisions (waiving right to counsel and enter a guilty plea) is mandated by due process.

46. State v. Settles, No. 13-97-50, 1998 Ohio App. LEXIS 4973, *9 (Sept. 30. 1998).

47. See People v. Carey, 615 N.W.2d 742, 748 (Mich. Ct. App. 2000). The court stated, "A juvenile need not be found incompetent just because, under adult standards, the juvenile would be found incompetent in a criminal proceeding." Ibid.

48. Moreover, some courts insist that the adult standard be applied in delinquency proceedings, although without analyzing the implications of doing so. See, for example, In re W.A.F., 573 A.2d 1264, 1267 (D.C. App. 1990).

49. In McKeiver v. Pennsylvania, 403 U.S. 528 (1971), the Court emphasized the detrimental impact of a jury trial on delinquency proceedings, in light of the purposes of the juvenile court. See also Schall v. Martin, 467 U.S. 253, 281 (1984) (holding that juveniles can be held in pretrial detention without a bail hearing).

50. *McKiever*, 403 U.S., 540, 550 (faulting the jury trial for bringing "delay, the formality, and the clamor of the adversary system and, possibly, the public trial" which ignores "every aspect of fairness, of concern, of sympathy, and of paternal attention that the juvenile court system contemplates"). *McKiever* emphasized the rehabilitative purposes of the juvenile court and expressed a reluctance to give up on those purposes. See *McKiever*, 403 U.S., 547.

51. Ibid. Under the Court's general approach to due process, the type and extent of procedural protection required depend on contingencies of the legal setting, particularly the stakes for the individual. In the context of civil proceedings, the Court has emphasized the flexibility of the constitutional norm, which "calls for such procedural protections as the particular situation demands." Mathews v. Eldridge, 424 U.S. 319, 334 (1976), with quotes from Morrissey v. Brewer, 408 U.S. 471, 481 (1972).

52. In general, due process analysis focuses on whether particular procedures are necessary to avoid error—and promote accuracy. Mathews v. Eldridge, 424 U.S. 319, 334 (1976). The Court has not been consistent about whether the *Mathews* test applies to criminal proceedings, but it has been applied to many noncriminal procedures in which the deprivation of individual liberty is at stake. See, for example, *Parham*, 442 U.S., 599–600 (involving voluntarily committed children in a state mental hospital); Addington v. Texas, 441 U.S. 418, 425 (involving civil commitment procedures).

53. Addington v. Texas, 441 U.S. 418, found that involuntary civil commitment can be ordered upon proof by clear and convincing evidence;

because of the state's purpose is not punitive, proof beyond a reasonable doubt was not required. Ibid., 428.

54. This standard was proposed by Bonnie & Grisso. "Adjudicative Competence in Juveniles," 76.

55. For model guidelines, see generally Thomas Grisso, *Evaluating Competencies: Forensic Assessments and Instruments* (New York, 2nd ed. 2003).

56. We recommend age ten as the minimum age for delinquency adjudication. See Chapter 8. The state can intervene with youths under the age of ten who engage in criminal activity through its dependency jurisdiction. As the text suggests, such interventions can include out-of-home placement or mandated parental involvement.

57. Under a 2006 Georgia statute, juveniles found to be incompetent to proceed are automatically subject to the juvenile court's dependency jurisdiction.

58. The Individuals with Disabilities Education Act requires that every child in public school eligible for special education services be provided with Individualized Educational Plans, and that government resources be dedicated to implementing the plan. 20 U.S.C. Sect. 1400 et. sec.

59. Under blended sentencing, discussed in Chapter 4, a juvenile serves her sentence in the juvenile system, but it may be extended into an adult sentence if she violates probation or commits another crime. In some states, juveniles can receive sentences extending into adulthood, without condition. Most sex offender statutes require juvenile sex offenders to register.

60. See Chapter 7.

7. Social Welfare and Juvenile Crime Regulation

1. Adam Liptak, "Jailed for Life after Crimes as Teenagers," *New York Times*, Oct. 3, 2005, A1.

2. See Chapter 9. This has become a key issue in adult sentencing as well. As Rachel Barkow has shown, state legislatures have retreated from harsh sentencing reforms in the face of rising costs. See Rachel Barkow, "Federalism and the Politics of Sentencing," *Columbia Law Review* 105 (2005): 1276–1314.

3. Economists find that increasing the rate of incarceration has diminishing marginal returns. See "The Criminal Justice System in Washington State: Incarceration Rates, Taxpayer Costs, Crime Rates, and Prison

Economics," *Washington State Institute of Public Policy* (January 2003), at www.wsipp.wa.gov.

4. As we discuss in Chapter 8, social welfare may well be promoted by imposing tough sanctions on youths who are chronic serious offenders.

5. In the 1990s, Delbert Elliot established the Blueprints program at the University of Colorado, evaluating juvenile justice programs under demanding criteria for effectiveness and designating as "proven" only those programs that meet these criteria. Delbert Elliot, *Blueprints for Violence Prevention* (Boulder, 1997). For an excellent analysis of which programs do and do not work to reduce juvenile crime, see Peter Greenwood, *Changing Lives: Delinquency Prevention as Crime Control Policy,* (Chicago, 2006).

6. Anna Gorman, "Few D.A.s Use New Power to Try Juveniles as Adults," *Los Angeles Times,* Aug. 8, 2004, 1.

7. Rhode Island reverted to a jurisdictional age of eighteen within six months, acknowledging that its assumption that imprisonment of seventeen-year-olds lowered costs was mistaken. Ray Henry, "Rhode Island Lawmakers Repeal Law Imprisoning Teens," Associated Press Oct. 31, 2007. Wisconsin, New Hampshire, and Wyoming have recently lowered the general jurisdictional age. Altogether, fourteen states set the upper boundary of the juvenile court jurisdictional age below age eighteen. Howard Snyder & Melissa Sickmund, "Juvenile Offenders and Victims: 2006 National Report," *Office of Juvenile Justice and Delinquency Prevention,* at http://ojjdp.ncjrs.gov/ojstatbb/nr2006/downloads/NR2006.pdf www.ojjdp.ncjrs.gov. Fifteen states make judicial waiver mandatory for certain offenses, if certain criteria are met. See Patrick Griffin, "National Overviews," *State Juvenile Justice Profiles.* National Center for Juvenile Justice (2006).

8. Snyder & Sickmund, "Juvenile Offenders and Victims: 2006 National Report," 186.

9. Ibid. Transfer for drug offenses has increased substantially since the mid-1980s.

10. Ibid, 186.

11. The absence of age data on youths categorically classified as adults is due to the fact that information about age usually is not included in statistics about criminal charges, convictions, and sentences of adults.

12. See note 7 above. ncjj.org/stateprofiles/overviews. In New York, for example, general juvenile court jurisdiction ends at age sixteen; jurisdiction for murder ends at age thirteen. Twenty-three states have

no minimum age for transfer to criminal court; the rest have minimum ages ranging from ten to fifteen years of age. Ibid., at http://www.ncjj.org/stateprofiles/overviews/transfer5.asp (accessed on Nov. 1, 2007).

13. Ibid.

14. Robert Barnoski, "Changes in Washington State's Jurisdiction of Juvenile Offenders: Examining the Impact," *Washington State Institute for Public Policy* (January 2003): 16–20, at www.wsipp.wa.gov. See also Jeffrey Fagan, "The Comparative Impacts of Juvenile and Criminal Court Sanctions on Adolescent Felony Offenders," *Law & Policy Review* 18 (1996): 77–119 (46 percent of youths convicted of robbery were sentenced to prison or jail for first offenses in New York, whereas, in New Jersey, only 18 percent of those processed as juveniles were incarcerated).

15. This research institute was created by the state legislature to study the cost-effectiveness of the justice system and other social legislation and policies, primarily in Washington, but nationally as well. The institute conducts sophisticated and comprehensive research that is an important source of information in evaluating the costs and benefits of juvenile justice; see http://www.wsipp.wa.gov.

16. Barnoski, "Changes in Washington State's Jurisdiction of Young Offenders," 17–18. The study examined cases over a period of two and a half years before the enactment of the statute and a similar period after enactment. Barnoski found that under Washington's discretionary transfer law, youths who were transferred received an average sentence of almost six years compared with those retained in juvenile court, who received less than a year. The combined average was 1.78 years. After the enactment of the state's automatic transfer law (under which all youths were tried as adults), the average was 2.8 years.

17. Ibid., 17–18.

18. Steven Aos, "The Juvenile Justice System in Washington State: Recommendations to Improve Cost Effectiveness," *Washington State Institute for Public Policy*, (2002): 2, at www.wsipp.wa.gov.

19. In the past few years, legislatures have begun to examine the budgetary burden of harsh sanctions. As we discuss in Chapter 9, legislatures across the country have revised and moderated harsh sentencing regimes in response to evidence that criminal justice system costs doubled in the 1990s. See Barkow, "Federalism and the Politics of Sentencing"; Daniel Wilhelm & Nicholas Turner, "Is the Budget Crisis

Changing the Way We Look at Sentencing and Incarceration?" *Vera Institute* (New York, 2002).

20. Aos, "The Juvenile Justice System in Washington State," 2.

21. In Virginia, a 2005 report by the Department of Juvenile Justice reported that the per capita cost of holding one juvenile for a year was $88,271. *Virginia Department of Juvenile Justice, Data Resource Guide: Fiscal Year 2005*, Appendix. See also Barnoski, "Changes in Washington State's Jurisdiction of Young Offenders" (describing yearly per youth cost of juvenile facility as almost $45,000).

22. Barnoski, "Changes in Washington State's Jurisdiction of Young Offenders." Yearly per-prisoner costs in Washington were estimated at about $36,000.

23. In Washington the average cost of confinement per youth increased from $65,000 under the discretionary transfer regime to $75,000 under the automatic transfer law. See Barnoski, "Changes in Washington State's Jurisdiction of Juvenile Offenders," 20.

24. Steve Peoples, Elizabeth Gudrais, & Amanda Milkovits, "House Budget Final: Much Debate, Few Surprises," *Providence Journal*, June 16, 2007.

25. Snyder & Sickmund, "Juvenile Offenders and Victims: 2006 National Report."

26. George Allen, the Governor of Virginia during the 1990s, cut state health and education funding while substantially increasing the budget of the Department of Corrections. Several prison construction projects were undertaken during Allen's administration. See "Virginia Legislature Rejects Tax Cuts," *New York Times*, Feb. 5, 1995, A21.

27. Youths who persist in criminal activity tend to have poor educational outcomes, unstable relationships in adulthood, and poor employment records; they also tend to be poor parents to their own children, who are more likely to get involved in criminal activity than other children. Terrie Moffitt, Avshalom Caspi, & Michael Rutter, "Measured Gene-Environment Interactions in Psychopathology. Concepts, Research Strategies, and Implications for Research, Intervention, and Public Understanding of Genetics," *Perspectives on Psychological Science* 1 (2006): 5–27.

28. See Richard Bonnie, Anne Coughlin, John Jeffries, Peter Low, *Criminal Law* (Westbury, NY, 2004): 11–30.

29. Jeremy Bentham famously described general deterrence as the primary goal of criminal punishment. Jeremy Bentham, *The Rationale of Punishment* (London, 1830). According to Bentham, "The punishment

suffered by the offender presents to everyone an example of what he himself will have to suffer if he is guilty of the same offense." Ibid., 20.

30. Herbert Packer, *The Limit of the Criminal Sanction* (Stanford, CA, 1968): 180. Thus, although sentencing shoplifters to life in prison might effectively deter this crime, this punishment would be unfair on proportionality grounds. H.L.A. Hart argued that retributive principles are important in a consequentialist system because they will contribute to widespread public acceptance. Hart, *Punishment and Responsibility* (Oxford, 1968), 180.

31. Politicians have often justified tougher laws on the ground that the juvenile system presented no threat to young criminals. Missouri Governor Mel Carnahan praised a new law removing the minimum age for adult prosecution of young drug dealers, suggesting that youths were lured into the drug trade because they saw no possible risks. "Now these teenagers will know there's a risk, and it is real time in prison." Mark Schlinkmann & Kim Bell, "Carnahan Signs Juvenile Crime Bill: Allows Trial as Adults in Serious Cases," *St. Louis Post Dispatch,* June 3, 1995, B1.

32. See Elizabeth Emens, "Aggravating Youth: *Roper v. Simmons* and Age Discrimination," *Supreme Court Review* (2005): 51.

33. John DiIulio, "The Coming of the Superpredators" *Weekly Standard* 21, Nov. 27, 1995. DiIulio described super-predators, as youths who grow up in extreme "moral poverty," without the care and love of responsible parents who teach their children right from wrong. This leads them to be radically present-oriented, such that they perceive no connection between crime and later punishment, and radically self-regarding, with no feeling for their victims. He predicted that tens of thousands of young super-predators would roam the streets in the next decade, committing heinous violent acts for trivial reasons. "They live by the meanest code of the meanest streets, a code that reinforces, rather than restrains, their violent, hair-trigger mentality." Although DiIullio's prescription for dealing with the crisis was to bring religion into these youths' lives, others who adopted the image and repeated the frightening predictions argued for harsh justice policies. See statement by McCollum, 1996 Testimony before House Committee, quoted in Franklin Zimring, *American Youth Violence* (New York, 2000), 4–5.

34. Michael Tonry & Joan Petersilia, "American Prisons at the Beginning of the Twenty-First Century," in *Prisons, Crime and Justice: A Re-*

view of Research, Michael Tonry & Joan Petersilia, eds. (Chicago, 1999), 3–4.

35. James Fox & Alex Piquero, "Deadly Demographics: Population Characteristics and Forecasting Homicide Trends," *Crime & Delinquency* 49 (2003): 339–359.

36. See James Q. Wilson & Richard Herrnstein, *Crime and Human Nature* (New York, 1985). The argument that today's young criminals are "super-predators," in part, is the mirror image of this argument. According to adherents, these youths lack any sense of moral responsibility because their parents did not instill it in them.

37. Zimring, *American Youth Violence.*

38. Daniel Nagin, "Criminal Deterrence Research at the Outset of the Twenty-First Century," in *Crime and Justice,* vol. 23, Michael Tonry, ed. (Chicago, 1998), 12–23; Raymond Paternoster & Alex Piquero, "Reconceptualizing Deterrence. An Empirical Test of Personal and Vicarious Experiences," *Journal of Research in Crime and Delinquency* 32(3) (1995): 251–286. The limitation of this type of research is that the relationship between criminal behavior and responses to questions in a study is uncertain.

39. For example, in the 1990s researchers studied patterns of criminal activity responding to recently enacted "three strikes" laws, which mandate a life sentence on conviction of a third felony. Several types of deterrence research are described by Nagin, "Criminal Deterrence," 2.

40. Nagin, "Criminal Deterrence," 4–7.; Andrew Von Hirsh, *Doing Justice* (1976, Toronto), 37–44.

41. Nagin, "Criminal Deterrence." Nagin describes impediments to evaluating the effectiveness of policies.

42. Anthony Doob & Cheryl Webster, "Sentencing Severity and Crime: Accepting the Null Hypothesis," in *Crime and Justice,* vol. 30, Michael Tonry, ed. (Chicago, 2003), 143–195.

43. H. Laurence Ross, *Deterring the Drinking Driver: Legal Policy and Social Control* (Lexington, MA, 1982).

44. Nagin, "Criminal Deterrence," 12–19.

45. Thus, if criminal arrests and convictions are common in a neighborhood or peer group, the associated stigma may be diluted. Nagin, "Criminal Deterrence."

46. Some criminologists go a step further, arguing that the evidence supports the conclusion that harsh sanctions do not deter crime. See Doob & Webster, "Sentencing Severity and Crime."

47. Wanda Foglia, "Perceptual Deterrence and the Mediating Effect of Internalized Norms Among Inner-City Teenagers," *Journal of Research in Crime and Delinquency* 34 (4) (1997): 414–442.

48. Richard Redding provides an excellent review of the research on the impact of adult punishment on deterrence and on recidivism by juvenile offenders. Richard Redding, "The Effects of Adjudicating and Sentencing Juveniles as Adults," *Youth Violence and Juvenile Justice* 1 (2005): 128–155.

49. The study examined juvenile crime rates four years before and six after the enactment. Simon Singer & David McDowell, "Criminalizing Delinquency: The Deterrent Effects of the New York Juvenile Offender Law," *Law & Society Review* 22 (1988): 521–535.

50. Eric Jensen & Linda Metsger, "A Test of the Deterrent Effect of Legislative Waiver on Violent Juvenile Crime," *Crime & Delinquency* 40 (1994): 96–104.

51. Steve Levitt, "Juvenile Crime and Punishment," *Journal of Political Economy* 106 (6) (1998):1158–1185.

52. Levitt calculated the relative punitiveness of each state's adult and juvenile system and then examined the time path of criminal involvement before and after the age of majority. His measure of the relative punitiveness of a state's adult and juvenile system involved comparing the ratio of adult prisoners to adult violent crime in a state with the ratio of confined juvenile delinquents to juvenile violent crimes. This measure has been criticized by Doob & Webster, in part on the basis that the statistics on which the calculus is based are unreliable and that juvenile and adult crime rates and confinement statistics are not classified as Levitt asserts. Further, the 23 percent jump in violent crime from age seventeen to eighteen in states where the transition is the most lenient is puzzling, given the evidence that the criminal system is universally harsher than the juvenile system.

53. Richard Redding & Elizabeth Fuller, "What Do Juveniles Know about Being Tried as Adults? Implications for Deterrence," *Juvenile & Family Court Journal* (Summer 2004): 35–44. They quote one youth: "Before I thought that since I'm a juvenile I could do just about anything and just get six months." Ibid., 39.

54. Barry Glassner, Margret Ksander, Bruce Berg, & Bruce Johnson, "A Note on the Deterrent Effect of Juvenile v. Adult Jurisdiction," *Social Problems* 31 (1983): 219–221.

55. Anne Schneider & Laurie Ervin, "Specific Deterrence, Rational Choice, and Decision Heuristics: Applications in Juvenile Justice," *Social Science Quarterly* 71 (1990): 585–601.
56. Donna Bishop & Charles Frazier, "Consequences of Transfer," in *The Changing Borders of Juvenile Justice,* Jeffery Fagan & Franklin Zimring, eds. (Chicago, 2000): 227–277, 250. See also Martin Forst, Jeffery Fagan, & T. Scott Vivona, "Youths in Prisons and Training Schools: Perceptions and Consequences of the Treatment-Custody Dichotomy," *Juvenile & Family Court Journal* 40 (1989): 1–14.
57. Lawrence Sherman, "Defiance Deterrence and Irrelevance: A Theory of the Criminal Sanction," *Journal of Research in Crime and Delinquency* 30 (4) (1993): 445–473.
58. See, for example, Marcy Podkapacz & Barry Feld, "The End of the Line: An Empirical Study of Judicial Waiver," *Journal of Criminal Law & Criminology* 86 (1996): 449–492. In this study, the transferred youths were charged with more serious offenses. The researchers found that 58 percent of the youths who were waived to criminal court committed new offenses within two years of incarceration versus 42 percent of the youths who were retained in juvenile court.
59. An example is a study by Robert Barnoski examining the effect on recidivism of adult sentencing under Washington's statute mandating adult processing of youths charged with certain crimes. The study found that adult sanctions had no short-term effect on re-offending. See R. Barnoski, "Changes in Washington State's Jurisdiction of Juvenile Offenders," 21–23. The study is of limited value because, at the time of the study, only 23 percent of the youths sentenced under the automatic transfer statute had been released. Further, because the statutory change was relatively recent (and because many youths in the study were still incarcerated), it was not possible to compare long-term effects on recidivism.
60. Donna Bishop, Charles Frazier, Lonn Lanza-Kaduce, & Lawrence Winner, "The Transfer of Juveniles to Criminal Court: Does It Make a Difference?" *Crime & Delinquency* 42 (1996): 171–191.
61. Jeffery Fagan, Aaron Kupchik, and Akiva Liberman, "Be Careful What You Wish for: The Comparative Impacts of Juvenile versus Criminal Court Sanctions on Recidivism among Adolescent Felony Offenders," *Columbia Law School, Pub. Law Research Paper No. 03-61,* at http://ssrn.com/abstract=491202 (2003).

62. Robbery is classified as a serious violent crime because it involves a threat of the use of force. Burglary does not involve such a threat and, for this reason, is considered a less serious crime.

63. Further, it is difficult to explain why recidivism rates did not differ for burglary offenders in the New York–New Jersey study.

64. Deterrence studies are sometimes critiqued on the ground that they are actually measuring incapacitation. See Doob & Webster, "Sentencing Severity and Crime," critiquing a study by Steven Levitt claiming to find weakened deterrence in response to a federal court mandate that Alabama reduce its prison population to prevent overcrowding. Steven Levitt, "The Effect of Prison Population Size on Crime Rates: Evidence from Prison Overcrowding Litigation," *Quarterly Journal of Economics* 111 (1996): 319–351.

65. This would be compatible with the uncontroversial view among criminologists that having a criminal justice system has a general deterrent effect, compared to a world without criminal sanctions. See Redding & Fuller, "What do Juveniles Know about Being Tried as Adults?" 39.

66. Urie Bronfenbrenner & Pamela Morris, "The Ecology of Environmental Process," in *Handbook of Child Psychology*, William Damon, ed. (New York, 1998); He Len Chung, Michelle Little, & Laurence Steinberg, "The Transition to Adulthood for Adolescents in the Juvenile Justice System: A Developmental Perspective," in *On Your Own without a Net: The Transition to Adulthood for Vulnerable Populations*, D. Wayne Osgood, E. Michael Foster, & Constance Flanagan, eds. (Chicago, 2005), 68–91.

67. John Laub & Robert Sampson, "Understanding Desistance from Crime," in *Crime and Justice*, vol. 28, Tonry, ed. (Chicago, 2001), 1–69; Robert Sampson & John Laub, *Crime in the Making: Pathways and Turning Points through Life* (Cambridge, MA, 1993); John Laub & Robert Sampson, *Shared Beginnings, Divergent Lives* (Cambridge, MA, 2003). Sampson and Laub treat marriage and employment as fortuitous exogenous events that facilitate desistance. It seems more likely that the attainment of psychosocial maturity may assist some youths to succeed in these adult roles that have a stabilizing effect, while others who fail to successfully complete developmental tasks do not make this transition.

68. Laurence Steinberg, He Len Chung, & Michelle Little, "Reentry of Young Offenders from the Justice System: A Developmental Perspective," *Youth Violence and Juvenile Justice* 1 (2004): 21–38.

69. The authors of one national survey summarized their findings by reporting that they found "little evidence of efforts to customize programs for youthful offenders." James Austin, Kelly Johnson, & Maria Gregoriou, "Juveniles in Adult Prisons and Jails: A National Assessment," *U.S. Department of Justice* (Washington, DC, 2000).

70. Donna Bishop and Charles Frazier have provided an excellent comparison of youths' experiences in prison and juvenile facilities, based on their research and other studies. Our discussion of these issues draws on their account. See Bishop & Frazier, "Consequences of Transfer," 251–261. Another useful study, by Forst, Fagan, and Vivona, compared reports by youths after release from prison describing their incarceration experience with reports by youths on release from training schools. See Forst, Fagan, & Vivona, "Youths in Prisons and Training Schools."

71. "Correctional Population in the United States, 1995," U.S. Department of Justice, Bureau of Justice Statistics (Washington, DC, 1997).

72. Dale Parent, "Conditions of Confinement. Juvenile Detention and Correctional Facilities," National Institute of Justice, Office of Juvenile Justice and Delinquency Prevention (Washington, DC, 1994).

73. Kenneth Adams, "Adjusting to Prison Life," in *Crime and Justice*, vol. 16, Michael Tonry, ed. (Chicago, 1992), 275–359.

74. Richard Mendel, "Less Hype, More Help: Reducing Juvenile Crime, What Works—and What Doesn't," *American Youth Policy Forum* (Washington, DC, 2003).

75. See discussion in Chapter 8 of cases finding limited or no duty to provide educational services in prison.

76. Allen Beck et al., "Survey of State Prison Inmates, 1991," Bureau of Justice Statistics, Department of Justice (Washington, DC, 1993).

77. Bishop & Frazier, note 56 above, "Consequences of Transfer," 256. They suggest that the custodial staff tend to view treatment professionals with suspicion and hostility, perhaps because their role is not integral to the operation of the prison.

78. Ibid.

79. Bishop & Frazier, "Consequences of Transfer."

80. Austin, Johnson, & Gregoriou, "Juveniles in Adult Prisons and Jails." States with Youthful Offender statutes, like New York, separate youths in adult prisons from adults. Austin and colleagues found that juvenile and adult prisoners were separated in 13 percent of facilities. For a guide to developmentally based treatment of juveniles in the adult sys-

tem (emphasizing separation from adults), see American Bar Association, *Youths in the Criminal Justice System* (Washington, D.C., 2001).

81. Bishop & Frazier, "Consequences of Transfer," 257.

82. Forst, Fagan, & Vivona, "Youths in Prisons and Training Schools," 9–10.

83. Marilyn McShane & Frank Williams, "The Prison Adjustment of Juvenile Offenders," *Crime & Delinquency* 35 (1989): 254–269.

84. Bishop & Frazier, "Consequences of Transfer," 33. See also Richard McCorkle, "Preventive Precautions to Violence in Prison," *Criminal Justice & Behavior* 19 (1992) 160–174.

85. Bishop & Frazier offer this hypothesis (see Bishop & Frazier, "Consequences of Transfer," 257–258). See also McShane & Williams, "The Prison Adjustment of Juvenile Offenders." These researchers found that serious and violent juvenile offenders in prison engaged in misconduct at a rate twice that of similar offenders age seventeen to twenty-one.

86. Laub & Sampson, *Shared Beginnings, Divergent Lives* (Cambridge, MA, 2003): 41–51.

87. Parent et al., "Conditions of Confinement."

88. Cognitive behavior therapy is the basis for many successful delinquency programs. See note 101 below. J. Platt & M. Prout, "Cognitive-Behavioral Theory and Interventions for Crime and Delinquency," in *Behavioral Approaches to Crime and Delinquency: A Handbook of Application, Research, and Concepts,* Edward Morris and Curtis Braukmann, eds. (New York, 1987), 477–497.

89. Bishop & Frazier, "Consequences of Transfer."

90. Forst, Fagan, & Vivona, "Youths in Prisons and Training Schools"; Bishop & Frazier, "Consequences of Transfer."

91. See Snyder & Sickmund, "Juvenile Offenders and Victims: 2006 National Report." Cites statistics from the Office of Juvenile Justice and Delinquency Prevention that 54 percent of youths receive some form of probation.

92. Laurence Steinberg, Ilana Blatt-Eisengart, & Elizabeth Cauffman, "Patterns of Competence and Adjustment among Adolescents from Authoritative, Authoritarian, Indulgent, and Neglectful Homes: Replication in a Sample of Serious Juvenile Offenders," *Journal of Research on Adolescence* 16 (2006): 47–58

93. One recent study found that about half of the parents of a sample of serious juvenile offenders practiced the sort of harsh and negligent parenting seen among the "worst" parents in a community sample, but

about one-sixth of the offenders' parents practiced parenting that was as warm and involved as that observed among the more highly skilled parents in the community. Thus, familial influences on delinquency are important, but other factors, especially the peer group, may be more powerful influences. Steinberg et al., "Patterns of Competence and Adjustment among Adolescents," 50–51.

94. Edward Mulvey, Maryfrances Porter, & He Len Chung, "Building Pathways out of Crime and Delinquency for Serious and Violent Juvenile Offenders," *Arizona Juvenile Justice Symposium* (2002): 16–20.

95. In Boston, for example, probation officers visit their charges' homes unannounced in the evening hours to check on compliance with curfews. "Operation Night Light—Boston, MA," in *Promising Strategies to Reduce Gun Violence, Office of Juvenile Justice and Delinquency Prevention* (1999): Profile No. 33 at www.ojjdp.ncjrs.org. Some research suggests, however, that closely supervised probation is not associated with lower recidivism rates. Aos, "The Juvenile Justice System in Washington State."

96. Snyder & Sickmund, "Juvenile Offenders and Victims: 2006 National Report." Figures shows increase in formal v. informal processing since mid-1980s.

97. Douglas Lipton, Robert Martinson, & Melanie Wilks, *The Effectiveness of Correctional Treatment: A Survey of Treatment Evaluation Studies* (New York, 1975); Robert Martinson, "What Works? Questions and Answers about Prison Reform," *Public Interest* 35 (1975): 22–54; Susan Martin & Robin Redner, eds., *Panel on Research on Rehabilitative Techniques, National Research Council, New Directions in the Rehabilitation of Criminal Offenders* (Washington, DC, 1981).

98. See Peter Greenwood, *Changing Lives.*

99. See Mark Lipsey, "Can Rehabilitative Programs Reduce the Recidivism of Young Offenders? An Inquiry into the Effectiveness of Practical Programs," *Virginia Journal of Social Policy & Law* 6 (1999): 611–641. Researchers began to use meta-analysis to evaluate the effectiveness of juvenile programs in about 1990, and numerous meta-analyses have been undertaken. Lipsey has undertaken comprehensive analyses of juvenile programs, and he is prominent among researchers using this now widely used approach. See also Steve Aos, Polly Phipps, Robert Barnoski, & Roxanne Lieb, "The Comparative Costs and Benefits of Programs to Reduce Crime," *Washington State Institute for Public Policy* (Olympia, WA, 2001): 1–74, at www.wsipp.wa.gov.

100. Mark Lipsey, "What Do We Learn from 400 Research Studies on the Effectiveness of Treatment with Juvenile Delinquents?" in *What Works? Reducing Reoffending*, James McGuire, ed. (New York, 1995).
101. Cognitive behavioral therapy is employed in many juvenile correctional programs, both in residential facilities and in community settings. It is a problem-focused approach that is designed to help individuals identify beliefs, thoughts, and behaviors that contribute to their problems—in the case of delinquent youths, to alter contributors to criminal conduct. It has been used extensively with youths having substance abuse problems that are linked to their criminal conduct. See Aaron Beck, *Prisoners of Hate: The Cognitive Basis of Anger, Hostility, and Violence* (New York, 1999); Judith Beck, *Cognitive Therapy: Basics and Beyond* (New York, 1995); Mark Lipsey, Gabrielle Chapman, & Nana Landenberger, "Research Findings from Prevention and Intervention Studies: Cognitive-Behavioral Programs for Offenders," *Annals of the American Academy of Political and Social Science* 578 (2001): 144–157.
102. See Peter Greenwood, *Changing Lives;* Robert Barnoski, "Outcome Evaluation of Washington State's Research-Based Programs for Juvenile Offenders," *Washington State Institute for Public Policy* (Olympia, Wash., 2004): 1–20, at www.wsipp.wa.gov.
103. Scott Henggeler, Gary Melton, & Linda Smith, "Family Preservation Using Multisystemic Therapy: An Effective Alternative to Incarcerating Serious Juvenile Offenders," *Journal of Consulting & Clinical Psychology* 60 (1992): 953–961. One role of therapists is to expand natural social support systems for the family (extended family, neighbors, church members, etc.) and to remove impediments to effective functioning (parents' substance abuse, stress). See Multisystemic Therapy, *Office of Juvenile Justice and Delinquency Prevention Model Programs Guide*, at www.dsgonline.com/mpg2.5/.
104. Scott Henggeler, Gary Melton, & Linda Smith, "Family Preservation Using Multisystemic Therapy: An Effective Alternative to Incarcerating Serious Juvenile Offenders."
105. Scott Henggeler, Gary Melton, Linda Smith, Sonja Schoenwald, & Jerome Hanley, "Family Preservation Using Multisystemic Treatment: Long-Term Follow-up to a Clinical Trial with Serious Juvenile Offenders." *Journal of Child and Family Studies* 2 (1993): 283–293. Eighty percent of the control group had re-offended, compared with 60 percent of the group receiving multisystemic therapy.

106. Steve Aos, Polly Phipps, Robert Barnoski, & Roxanne Lieb, "The Comparative Costs and Benefits of Programs to Reduce Crime."

107. Robert Barnoski, "Outcome Evaluation of Washington State's Research-Based Programs for Juvenile Offenders," *Washington State Institute for Public Policy* (Olympia, WA, 2004), 1–20, at www.wsipp.wa.gov.

108. Ibid.

109. Mark Lipsey, Gabrielle Chapman, & Nana Landenberger, "Research Findings From Prevention and Intervention Studies: Cognitive-Behavioral Programs for Offenders," *Annals of the American Academy of Political and Social Science* 578 (2001): 144–157. Multisystemic therapy averages sixty hours of contact over a four-month period, and therapists are always on call. "Multisystemic Therapy," *Office of Juvenile Justice and Delinquency Prevention Model Programs Guide*, at www.dsgonline.com/mpg2.5.

110. Ibid.

111. Steve Aos, Polly Phipps, Robert Barnoski, & Roxanne Lieb, "The Comparative Costs and Benefits of Programs to Reduce Crime," 17–18.

112. Ibid. For FFT, the recidivism effect is somewhat less than for MST. The average cost is $2,161 and value to taxpayers is about $14,000 per participant; $59,000 per participant if benefit to victim is included. Thus the benefit per dollar spent is $29. On the other hand, because "scared straight" programs increase recidivism, taxpayers *lose* an average of $6,500 in increased costs for each participant; $24,500 if costs to crime victims are calculated.

8. The Developmental Model and Juvenile Justice Policy for the Twenty-First Century

1. See, for example, the platform of the America First Party of Mississippi: "It being necessary to restore the protections and rights of parents, while protecting the public from criminal conduct and punishing wrongdoers, the Party demands the State Legislature abolish the juvenile court system, thereby restoring the traditional rights of parents, the common law standards of proof and presumptions of innocence, and requiring juveniles to pay the full consequences for criminal conduct which has up until now been excused and treated as mere delinquency." "Positions and Platform," at www.mississippi.americafirstparty.org (accessed on June 18, 2007).

2. Barry Feld, *Bad Kids: Race and the Transformation of the Juvenile Court* (New York, 1999); Barry Feld, "The Transformation of the Juvenile Court," *Minnesota Law Review* 75 (1991): 691–726; Barry Feld, "Abolish the Juvenile Court: Youthfulness, Criminal Responsibility, and Sentencing Policy," *Journal of Criminal Law and Criminology* 88 (1) (1997): 68–136; Janet E. Ainsworth, "The Court's Effectiveness in Protecting the Rights of Juveniles in Delinquency Cases," *Future of Children* 6 (3) (Winter, 1996): 64–74.

3. See discussion in Chapter 4.

4. See discussion in Chapter 4. A study comparing juveniles tried as adults under Washington's automatic transfer statute and those adjudicated under the earlier judicial transfer law found a higher percentage of minority youths were tried in criminal court under discretionary transfer. Robert Barnoski, *Jurisdiction of Juvenile Offenders: Examining the Impact* (Olympia, WA, 2003), 11. Some studies have found that non-white juveniles receive harsher dispositional outcomes than white juveniles; Donna Bishop & Charles Frazier, "Race Effects in Juvenile Justice Decision-Making: Findings of a Statewide Analysis," *Journal of Criminal Law and Criminology* 86 (1996): 392–414; Charles Frazier, Donna Bishop, & John Henretta, "The Social Context of Race Differentials in Juvenile Justice Dispositions," *The Sociological Quarterly* 33 (1992): 447–458; Robert Sampson & John Laub, "Structural Variations in Juvenile Court Processing: Inequality, the Underclass, and Social Control," *Law and Society Review* 27 (1993): 285–312. However, others indicate that minority and white juveniles receive similar outcomes once legal factors are controlled. John Henretta, Charles Frazier, & Donna Bishop, "The Effect of Prior Case Outcomes on Juvenile Justice Decision-Making," *Social Forces* 65 (1986): 554–562. Some researchers have argued that the relationship between race and disposition decision varies widely by the jurisdiction of the juvenile court. Chester Britt, "Social Context and Racial Disparities in Punishment Decisions," *Justice Quarterly* 17 (2000): 707–732.

5. Feld, *Bad Kids*.

6. In re Gault, 387 U.S. 1 (1967), requiring that juveniles be afforded notice of charges, right to counsel, right to confront witnesses, privilege against self incrimination; In re Winship, 397 U.S. 358 (1970), requiring proof of charges beyond a reasonable doubt; Breed v. Jones, 421 U.S. 519 (1975), prohibiting double jeopardy.

7. Feld recommends such restrictions. Feld, "Bad Kids," 128–130.

8. IJA-ABA Juvenile Justice Standards recommend voluntary participation in programs in the juvenile system, and Feld indicates that the state should provide programs to juveniles in his integrated system on a voluntary basis. Institute of Judicial Administration–American Bar Association Joint Commission on Juvenile Justice Standards, *Juvenile Justice Standards: Dispositions* (Cambridge, MA, 1980); Feld, *Bad Kids*.

9. See Chapter 7.

10. The state of Washington adopted determinate sentencing in 1977. Offenses are graded by severity, with a corresponding standard range of punishment. For example, murder in the first degree is an A+ offense, corresponding to a sanction of 180 weeks; in contrast, driving while under the influence is a class D offense, punishable by a fine up $500. Wash. Rev. Code. Ann. §13.40.0357 (West 2007).

11. John Monahan, "Actuarial Support for the Clinical Assessment of Violence Risk," *International Review of Psychiatry* 9 (1997): 167–170.

12. Mary Ann Campbell & Fred Schmidt, "Comparison of Mental Health and Legal Factors in the Disposition Outcome of Young Offenders," *Criminal Justice and Behavior* 27 (2000): 688–715; Robert Hoge, D. A. Andrews, & Alan Leschied, "Investigation of Variables Associated with Probation and Custody Dispositions in a Sample of Juveniles," *Journal of Clinical Child Psychology* 24 (1995): 279–286; Horwitz & Wasserman, "Formal Rationality."

13. Elizabeth Cauffman, Alex Piquero, Eva Kimonis, Laurence Steinberg, & Laurie Chassin, "Legal, Individual, and Contextual Predictors of Court Disposition," *Law and Human Behavior* 31 (2007): 519–535.

14. This sample was composed of juvenile felons convicted of very serious offenses. Thus, the absence of a race effect is consistent with the notion that racial bias is less likely to affect dispositional decision-making for more serious offenses.

15. Francois Poulin, Thomas Dishion, & Eric Haas, "The Peer Influence Paradox: Friendship Quality and Deviancy Training within Male Adolescent Friendships," *Merill-Palmer Quarterly* 45 (1999): 42–61.

16. Jeffrey Butts & Daniel Mears, "Reviving Juvenile Justice in a Get-Tough Era," *Youth and Society* 33 (2001): 169–198; Peter Greenwood, *Changing Lives: Delinquency Prevention as Crime-Control Policy* (Chicago, 2006).

17. Greenwood, *Changing Lives;* Steve Aos, Robert Barnoski, & Roxanne Lieb, "Watching the Bottom Line: Cost-Effective Interventions for Reducing Crime in Washington," at www.wsipp.wa.gov.

18. Wendy Mager, Richard Milich, Monica Harris, & Anne Howard, "Intervention Groups for Adolescents with Conduct Problems: Is Aggregation Harmful or Hurtful?" *Journal of Abnormal Child Psychology* 33 (2005): 349–362.

19. See "A Testing Case: *People v. Delury,*" in Richard Bonnie et al., *Criminal Law* (New York, 1997). George Delury assisted his wife in ending her life, following her incapacitation and the deterioration of her health from multiple sclerosis. Delury pleaded guilty to second-degree attempted manslaughter, and his case is frequently used to illustrate the tensions among the purposes of criminal punishment.

20. Michael Moore argues that it is appropriate and respectful to hold criminals to high standards of accountability. Michael Moore, "The Moral Worth of Retribution," in *Responsibility, Character, and the Emotions,* Frederick Schoeman, ed. (Cambridge, 1987).

21. See the following study finding public support for a minimum age of fifteen for transfer. Elizabeth Scott, N. Dickon Reppucci, Jill Antonishak, & Jennifer DeGennaro, "Public Attitudes about the Culpability and Punishment of Young Offenders," *Behavioral Sciences and the Law* 24 (2006): 815–832. The IJA-ABA juvenile Justice Standards also propose age fifteen as the minimum age of transfer. Institute of Judicial Administration–American Bar Association, "Standards Relating to Transfer between Courts," *Juvenile Justice Standards* (Cambridge, 1980).

22. The exceptions are states in which jurisdiction ends at age sixteen or seventeen. These are Georgia, Louisiana, Illinois, Massachusetts, Michigan, Missouri, New Hampshire, New York, North Carolina, South Carolina, Texas, and Wisconsin.

23. A majority of states have a form of extended dispositional jurisdiction, most setting their dispositional age at twenty or twenty-one. California extends jurisdiction until age twenty-five. See "Extended Age of Juvenile Court Jurisdiction," at www.ojjdp.ncjrs.org (accessed on July 3, 2007).

24. Tex. Hum. Res. Code §61.079 (Vernon 2005).

25. Feld, *Bad Kids,* 164–165.

26. For critiques of the use of psychopathy checklists with juveniles, see Jennifer Skeem & Elizabeth Cauffman, "Views of the Downward Extension: Comparing the Youth Version of the Psychopathy Checklist

with the Youth Psychopathic Traits Inventory," *Behavioral Sciences and the Law* 21 (2003): 737–770; Daniel Seagrave & Thomas Grisso, "Adolescent Development and the Measurement of Juvenile Psychopathy," *Law and Human Behavior* 26 (2002): 219–239.

27. Michelle Little & Laurence Steinberg, "Psychosocial Correlates of Adolescent Drug Dealing in the Inner-City: Potential Roles of Opportunity, Conventional Commitments, and Maturity," *Journal of Research on Crime and Delinquency* 4 (2006): 1–30.

28. California, for example, lists thirty felonies ranging from murder and arson to carjacking and selling drugs. Ann. Cal. Welf. and Inst. Code §707(b)(1–30)(West 2000).

29. See Va. Code Ann. §16.1-269.1(4)(a–j).

30. Thomas Grisso et al., "Juveniles' Competence to Stand Trial: A Comparison of Adolescents' and Adults' Capacities as Trial Defendants," *Law and Human Behavior* 27 (2003): 333–363.

31. As we discussed in Chapter 6, we recommend that the threshold for competence in juvenile court be lower than it is in criminal court; as a result, very few juveniles would be incompetent to proceed in juvenile court. See Elizabeth Scott & Thomas Grisso, "Developmental Incompetence, Due Process, and Juvenile Justice Policy," *North Carolina Law Review* 83 (2005): 793–846.

32. McKinney's Penal Law §60.02.

33. For a guide to minimizing the developmental harm of imprisonment see American Bar Association, *Youth in the Criminal Justice System* (2001).

34. In Tunstall v. Bergeson, 141 Wash. 2d. 201 (2000), the Washington Supreme Court found that juveniles held in adult facilities had no right to general elementary or secondary educational services at the same level of quality as their non-institutionalized peers. See also Handberry v. Thompson, 436 F.3d 52, 71 (2d. Cir. 2006).

35. Martin Haberman & Lois Quinn, "The High-School Re-Entry Myth: A Follow-up Study of Juveniles Released from Two Correctional High Schools in Wisconsin," *Journal of Correctional Education* 37 (1986): 114–117; "Digest of Education Statistics, 2001," at www.nces.ed.gov (accessed on June 26, 2007).

36. Jeffrey Fagan & Richard Freeman, "Crime and Work," *Crime and Justice* 25 (1999): 225–290; Richard Freeman, "Crime and Economic Status of Disadvantaged Young Men," in *Urban Labor Markets and Job Opportunities,* G. Peterson & W. Vroman, eds.(Washington, DC,

1992), 112–152; Marvin Wolfgang, Terence Thornberry, & Robert Figlio, *From Boy to Man, from Delinquency to Crime* (Chicago, 1987); David Ward & Charles Tittle, "Deterrence of Labeling: The Effects of Informal Sanctions," *Deviant Behavior* 14 (1993): 43–64.

37. Eighth Amendment jurisprudence makes clear that "death is different;" few non-capital penalties, especially those involving imprisonment, are likely to qualify. See Ewing v. California, 538 U.S. Moreover, it is not clear that LWOP violates the "emerging standards of decency" standard that the Supreme Court applies to Eighth Amendment claims. The Court generally looks to evidence that the punishment at issue is an outlier, based on legislation across the country. On the other hand, youths can be sentenced to LWOP in the United States at age thirteen and fourteen in some states, a sentence that no other country imposes. Adam Liptak, "Lifers as Teenagers, Now Seeking a Second Chance," *New York Times,* Oct. 17, 2007, A1.

38. Ibid. Seventy-three youths are currently serving LWOP for crimes committed as thirteen- or fourteen-year-olds. Of these, only twenty-two are white.

39. Public Safety Performance Project of Pew Charitable Trust. "Public Safety, Public Spending: Forecasting America's Prison Population 2007–2011," at http://www.pewpublicsafety.org (accessed on July 3, 2007).

40. Travis Hirschi & Michael Gottfredson, "Age and the Explanation of Crime," *American Journal of Sociology* 89 (1983): 552–584.

41. The report of Yummy Sandifer's life is based on a cover story in *Time,* immediately after his death. See Nancy Gibbs, "Murder in Miniature," *Time,* Sept. 19, 1994, 54.

42. See Rolf Loeber, David Farrington, & Daniel Waschbusch, "Serious and Violent Offenders," in *Serious and Violent Juvenile Offenders,* Rolf Loeber & David Farrington, eds. (Washington, DC, 1998).

43. David Farrington, Lloyd Ohlin, & James Q. Wilson, *Understanding and Controlling Crime* (New York, 1986).

44. Marvin Wolfgang, Robert Figlio, & Thorsten Sellin, *Delinquency in a Birth Cohort* (Chicago, 1972).

45. The stability of severely antisocial conduct is shown in research by Gerald Patterson, who found that of the 5 percent of youths found most aggressive in third grade, 39 percent scored above the 95th per-

centile on measures of aggression ten years later and 100 percent scored above average. Gerald Patterson, *Coercive Family Process* (Eugene, OR, 1982).

46. Terrie Moffitt, "Adolescence-Limited and Life-Course-Persistent Antisocial Behavior: A Developmental Taxonomy," *Psychological Review* 100 (1993): 674–701.

47. Rolf Loeber & Magda Stouthamer-Loeber, "Development of Juvenile Aggression and Violence," *American Psychologist* 53 (1998): 242–259.

48. Candace Odgers et al., "Predicting Prognosis for the Conduct-Problem Boy: Can Family History Help?" *Journal of the American Academy of Child and Adolescent Psychiatry* 46 (2007), 1240–1249.

49. Terrie Moffitt clarifies the importance of the pattern of seriously antisocial behavior extending over a long period of time in her classification of offenders as life-course persistent and adolescence-limited (normative) offenders. She points out it may be hard to distinguish these groups through a "cross-sectional" analysis during adolescence, even on the basis of the seriousness and intensity of their criminal conduct. Some juvenile offenders may engage in a spate of criminal activity over a short period of time, but they are not likely to persist in such activity into adulthood. Assessments of the likely trajectory of criminal involvement, she argues, can only be made by including pre-adolescent history of antisocial conduct. Moffitt, "A Developmental Taxonomy," 677–678.

50. Howard Snydor, "Serious, Violent and Chronic Offenders—An Assessment of the Extent of and Trends in Officially Recognized Serious Criminal Behavior in a Delinquent Population," in *Serious and Violent Juvenile Offenders: Risk Factors and Successful Intervention,* Rolf Loeber & David Farrington, eds. (Washington, DC, 1998).

51. Loeber et al., "Serious and Violent Offenders." Only a very small percentage of violent adult criminals do not have a history of aggressive antisocial conduct. Loeber and Stouthamer-Loeber describe this group as "late-onset" offenders. Loeber & Stouthamer-Loeber, "Development of Juvenile Aggression."

52. Terrie Moffitt, "Life-course Persistent Versus Adolescence-Limited Antisocial Behavior," in *Developmental Psychopathology,* Dante Cicchetti & Donald Cohen, eds. (New York, 2nd ed. 2006).

53. The injuries could be a result of maternal drug use, poor nutrition, or complications of delivery. Moffitt, "A Developmental Taxonomy," 680.

54. Verbal deficits include restricted capacities for reading, problem solving, receptive listening, and expressive speech. Symptoms of executive function deficits include impulsivity and attention problems. Moffitt found that youths who scored high on assessments of antisocial conduct from age three to age fifteen often performed poorly on neuropsychological tests and were diagnosed with attention deficit disorder. Terrie Moffitt, "The Neuropsychology of Delinquency: A Critical Review of Theory and Research," in *Research on Crime and Justice*, vol.12, Norval Morris & Michael Tonry, eds. (Chicago, 1990), 99; Terrie Moffitt, "Juvenile Delinquency and Attention Deficit Disorders: Boys' Developmental Trajectories from Age 3 to Age 15," *Child Development* 61 (1990): 893–910.

55. David Farrington, "Predictors, Causes, and Correlates of Male Youth Violence," *Crime and Justice* 24 (1998): 421–475.

56. Thomas O'Connor, Kirby Deater-Deckard, David Fulker, Michael Rutter, & Robert Plomin, "Genotype-Environment Correlations in Late Childhood and Early Adolescence: Antisocial Behavioral Problems and Coercive Parenting," *Developmental Psychology* 34 (1998): 970–981.

57. Gerald Patterson, John Reid, & Thomas Dishion, *Antisocial Boys* (Eugene, OR, 1992).

58. Moffitt argues that adolescence-limited offenders are able to make the transition to employment and social roles of adulthood because of educational and social groundwork laid before they got involved in criminal activity. Many life-course persistent offenders, she argues, never acquire the skills and abilities needed to accomplish this transition.

59. Greenwood, *Changing Lives*.

60. Odgers et al., "Predicting Prognosis for the Conduct-Problem Boy."

61. In some states, such as Pennsylvania, the juvenile court's dependency jurisdiction carries greater authority to mandate parental involvement in programs than does its delinquency jurisdiction.

62. Aos, "Watching the Bottom-Line"; Youth Transition Funders Group, "A Blueprint for Juvenile Justice Reform"; Greenwood, *Changing Lives;* Mark Lipsey, "Is Delinquency Prevention a Cost-Effective Strategy? A California Perspective" *Journal of Research in Crime and Delinquency* 21 (1984): 279–302.

63. Greenwood, *Changing Lives*.

9. Is Society Ready for Juvenile Justice Reform?

1. Elizabeth Becker, "As Ex-Theorist on Young 'Super-predators,' Bush Aide Has Regrets," *New York Times,* Feb. 9, 2001, A19. During an interview in which he expressed regret for advocating teenage prison sentences and condemning them as super-predators, John Dilulio stated, "If I knew then what I know now, I would have shouted for the prevention of crimes."
2. "United States of America (Florida): Legal Concern, Lionel Tate," at www.web.amnesty.org/library/engindex (accessed on July 10, 2007); "Larry King Live, March 12, 2001," at www.transcripts.cnn.com (accessed on July 10, 2007). Governor Bush commented, "I am not sure it is right to consign such a young child to a life without any hope."
3. Legislation abolishing LWOP for juvenile offenders was approved in Colorado in 2006; it is pending in other states, including California.
4. National Juvenile Defender Center, "2005 State Juvenile Justice Legislation," Nov. 2005, at " http://www.njdc.info/publications.php.
5. S.R. 200, 143rd Gen. Ass., Reg. Sess. (Del. 2005) amended Del. Code. Ann. Tit. 10 §1010 (West 2007). National Juvenile Defender Center, "2006 State Juvenile Justice Legislation," Jan. 1, 2007.
6. National Juvenile Defender Center, "2006 State Juvenile Justice Legislation," Jan. 1, 2007.
7. Connecticut passed legislation raising the jurisdictional age to eighteen in 2007. S.R. 1500, Gen. Ass., June Sp. Sess. (CT 2007) amended Conn. Gen. Stat. Ann. §46b-120 (West 2007). Four other states that currently set their jurisdictional boundary either at sixteen or seventeen, Illinois, Missouri, North Carolina, and Wisconsin, are considering legislation to raise it to eighteen.
8. Ray Henry, Rhode Island Lawmakers Repeal Law Imprisoning Teens, Associated Press Oct. 31, 2007.
9. "2006 State Juvenile Justice Legislation," at http://www.njdc.info/publications.php (accessed on July 10, 2007). Colorado, Connecticut, Georgia, Louisiana, Maryland, and New Hampshire all have considered legislation that addresses the question of juveniles' competence to stand trial, with respect to the grounds for incompetence (e.g., providing for immaturity as a potential source of incompetence in addition to mental illness or disability), the evaluation of juveniles' competence (e.g., establishing professional standards for the

conduct of juvenile competence evaluations), the procedural requirements for juvenile competence, and the responses to a finding of
incompetence.

10. Gwen Florio, Sue Lindsay, & Sarah Langbein, "Life for Death; Should
Teen Murderers Get a Second Chance at Freedom?" *Rocky Mountain
News,* Sept. 17, 2005, 1A; Florio, Lindsay, & Langbein, "Locked up
Forever; Emotions Run High in Debate Over Whether to Allow Parole
for Juveniles Who Murder," *Rocky Mountain News,* Sept. 17, 2005,
21A; Mike Moffeit & Kevin Simpson, "Man Who Killed Mother Says
System Fails Youths," *Denver Post,* Feb. 21, 2006; Mike Moffeit, "De-
mands for Change Echo at Statehouse," *Denver Post Online,* Feb. 22,
2006; Miles Moffeit & Kevin Simpson, "Teen Crime, Adult Time,"
Denver Post, Dec. 28, 2006.

11. Generally, a felony murder requires only participation in a violent
felony (such as robbery) in which someone dies—including nonviolent
participation, such as driving the getaway car.

12. "Don't Give Up on Youths," *Hartford Courant,* Feb. 26, 2006.

13. Illinois Juvenile Justice Commission. "Disproportionate Minority Contact in the Illinois Juvenile Justice System," *Annual Report to the Governor and General Assembly.* 2005.

14. Tammy Joyner, "Genarlow Wilson Rejoices over his Release," *Atlanta
Journal-Constitution* Oct. 26, 2007, reported at ajc.com.

15. Jordan Schraeder, "Trying Juveniles as Adults: What Age?" *Asheville
Citizen-Times,* April 15, 2007; "Don't Give up on Youths," *Hartford
Courant,* Feb. 26, 2006. Sharon Begley, "Getting Inside a Teen Brain,"
Newsweek, Feb. 28, 2000, 58. Claudia Wallis, "What Makes Teens
Tick," *Time,* May 10, 2004, 56.

16. Toni N. Harp & Toni E. Walker, "No Justice for Teens Treated As
Adults." The *Hartford Courant.* Jan. 19, 2007.

17. See Olson Huff, "Imprisoning Teens Doesn't Get the Results That We
Want," *Asheville Citizen-Times,* May 20, 2007.

18. The Connecticut legislature's Juvenile Jurisdiction Planning and Implementation Committee, which was constituted to study the proposed
increase in the minimum age of criminal court jurisdiction from sixteen to eighteen, noted in its final report to the legislature that "Assuming that the recidivism rate of youth on probation after the
jurisdictional change conservatively drops to 32.4 percent, the total
annual savings on contracted services alone is estimated at $819,000.
Should the impact of the services be greater than the conservative pro-

jection, the total annual savings will increase correspondingly." JJPIC, "Final Report," Feb. 12, 2007, 13.

19. "Table 36, Current Year Over Previous Year Arrest Trends," *Uniform Crime Reports,* at www.fbi.gov (accessed on July 11, 2007); Howard Snyder, "OJJDP Bulletin: Juvenile Arrests 2004," at www.ncjrs.gov (accessed on July 11, 2007).

20. Edward Fitzpatrick, "At 17, Robbery Suspect Now Treated as Adult," *Providence Journal,* Jul. 4, 2007, B1. As described in Note 8, the Rhode Island legislature within six months repealed the statute lowering the jurisdictional age to age seventeen and returned it to age eighteen.

21. Bureau of Justice Statistics, *Sourcebook of Criminal Justice Statistics,* 31st ed. (Albany, N.Y., 2003); Mark Soler, *Public Opinion on Youth, Crime and Race: A Guide for Advocates* (Washington, DC, 2001); D. W. Moore, "Majority Advocate Death Penalty for Teenage Killers," *GallupPoll Monthly* (September 1994): 2–3.

22. Jane Sprott, "Understanding Public Opposition to a Separate Youth Justice System," *Crime and Delinquency* 44 (1998): 399–411; T. C. Hart, "Causes and Consequences of Juvenile Crime and Violence: Public Attitudes and Question-Order Effect," *American Journal of Criminal Justice* 23 (1998): 129–143.

23. Melissa M. Moon, Jody L. Sundt, Francis T. Cullen & John Paul Wright, "Is Child Saving Dead? Public Support for Rehabilitation," *Crime and Delinquency* 46 (2000): 38–60. Survey respondents also become less punitive in their responses to offenders when they are provided with personal information. See also Julian Roberts, "Public Opinion and Youth Justice," *Crime and Justice* 31 (2004): 495–542.

24. This problem is compounded by the fact that many polls on public attitudes toward crime and punishment are designed and paid for by advocacy organizations with the goal of generating evidence to support their position; these are referred to as "push polls" because they are designed to shape, rather than measure, public opinion. For example, in early 2007 the Campaign for Youth Justice, an organization "dedicated to ending the practice of trying, sentencing and incarcerating children (under eighteen) in the adult criminal justice system" issued a press release trumpeting that a recent poll commissioned by the National Council on Crime and Delinquency (itself an advocacy organization that favors alternatives to incarceration)

found that "the public overwhelmingly supports rehabilitation and treatment for young people in trouble, not incarceration in adult jails or prisons." One of the findings that informed this conclusion is that two-thirds of respondents agreed that "Persons under age 18 should not be incarcerated in jails and prisons that hold adults." It seems likely additional facts might change responses.

25. Soler, *Public Opinion;* Frank Zimring, *American Youth Violence* (New York, 1998).

26. Timur Kuran & Cass Sunstein, "Availability Cascades and Risk Regulation," *Stanford Law Review* 51 (1999): 683–768. Television coverage of juvenile crime focuses overwhelmingly on violent crime.

27. Loretta Stalans, "Measuring Attitudes to Sentencing," in *Changing Attitudes to Punishment: Findings from Around the Globe,* Julian Roberts & Mike Hough, eds.(Cullompton, UK, 2002); Sprott, "Understanding Public Opposition."

28. David Firestone, "Arkansas Tempers a Law on Violence by Children," *The New York Times,* April 11, 1999. See discussion in Chapter 4.

29. Julian Roberts, "Public Opinion and Youth Justice."

30. Ibid.

31. Paul Robinson & John Darley, *Justice, Liability, and Blame: Community Views and the Criminal Law* (San Francisco, 1995).

32. Francis Cullen, Bonnie Fisher, & Brandon Applegate, "Public Opinion about Punishment and Corrections," *Crime and Justice,* 27 (2000): 1–79.

33. Ibid.

34. Elizabeth Scott, N. Dickon Reppucci, Jill Antonishak, & Jennifer De-Gennaro, "Public Attitudes about the Culpability and Punishment of Young Offenders," *Behavioral Sciences and the Law* 24 (2006): 815–832.

35. Participants were also given other identical information about the crime (e.g., that no one was actually hurt during the robbery) to further ensure that the only factors that varied between participants were the age, race, and physical appearance of the perpetrator.

36. Another explanation is that most adults have either committed minor offenses when they were young (e.g., shoplifted, used an illegal drug, got into fights), have a child who has done so, or at the very least are acquainted with an otherwise "normal" juvenile who has committed this sort of infraction. Few have had direct experience with armed rob-

bery, rape, or homicide (either as a victim, perpetrator, or as the parent or acquaintance of a perpetrator). Minor crimes are therefore seen as youthful indiscretions—part of normative adolescent behavior that virtually everyone engages in; serious violent offenses are seen as a sign of pathology.

37. Cullen et al., "Is Child Saving Dead," 60.

38. Ibid.

39. Ibid.; see also Francis Cullen, "It's Time to Reaffirm Rehabilitation," *Journal of Criminology and Public Policy* 5 (2006): 665–772, 666; Roberts, "Public Opinion and Youth Justice," 511–514.

40. The questions posed in most polls seldom situate the hypothetical alternatives in a concrete economic context. The endorsement of a particular policy in the abstract does not convey whether the respondent is willing to bear the cost of that policy through increased taxes, a better measure of actual support. As a consequence, conventional polls may indicate more enthusiastic public support for a potentially expensive policy than would likely be the case if the actual cost burden of the policy were revealed. Thus, the WTP methodology likely yields a more accurate estimation of public opinion than does conventional polling.

41. Daniel S. Nagin, Alex Piquero, Elizabeth Scott, & Laurence Steinberg, "Public Preferences for Rehabilitation versus Incarceration of Young Offenders: Evidence from a Contingent Valuation Survey," *Journal of Criminology and Public Policy* 5 (2006): 627–651.

42. Respondents were asked: "Would you be willing to pay the additional $100 in taxes for this change in the law?" The amount was doubled or halved depending on whether the response was positive or negative. Ibid., 634.

43. See also Brandon Applegate, Francis Cullen, & Bonnie Fisher, "Public Support for Correctional Treatment: The Continuing Appeal of the Rehabilitative Ideal," *The Prison Journal* 77 (1997): 237–258.

44. Peter Greenwood, *Changing Lives: Delinquency Prevention as Crime-Control Policy* (Chicago, 2006); Steve Aos, Polly Phipps, Robert Barnoski, & Roxanne Lieb, "The Comparative Costs and Benefits of Programs to Reduce Crime," *Washington State Institute for Public Policy* (Olympia 2001) at www.wsipp.wa.gov.

45. David Olds et al., "Long-Term Effects of Nurse Home Visitation on Children's Criminal and Antisocial Behavior," *Journal of American Medical Association* 280 (1998): 1238–1244.

46. Cullen, Fisher, Applegate, "Public Opinion about Punishment."
47. Steve Aos et al., "The Comparative Costs and Benefits of Programs to Reduce Crime."
48. Ibid. See also Steve Aos, Robert Barnoski, & Roxanne Lieb, "Watching the Bottom Line: Cost-Effective Interventions for Reducing Crime in Washington," *Washington State Institute for Public Policy* (Olympia, 1998) at www.wsipp.wa.gov.

Acknowledgments

This book is a product of a decade-long collaboration between the authors, a legal scholar and a developmental psychologist, that was fostered by our mutual involvement in the John D. and Catherine T. MacArthur Foundation Research Network on Adolescent Development and Juvenile Justice. That Network, composed of social scientists, legal scholars, and legal practitioners, conducted several of the studies we describe, but, more important, it also provided ten years of intellectual stimulation and sustenance that shaped and informed much of what we have written. We are exceedingly grateful to our fellow Network members (listed in alphabetical order), Marie Banich, Elizabeth Cauffman, Jeffrey Fagan, Sandra Graham, Thomas Grisso, Darnell Hawkins, Amy Holmes Hehn, Daniel Keating, Patricia Lee, Orlando Martinez, Paul McGill, Edward Mulvey, Daniel Nagin, Kimberly O'Donnell, Alex Piquero, Robert Schwartz, Jennifer Woolard, and Franklin Zimring for the many ways in which they contributed to our thinking. Our thanks also go to the many colleagues who served as consultants to the Network over the years and, especially, to Richard Bonnie, with whom we had many conversations about the sources of mitigation in the criminal law that contributed to the developmental approach we take; and to Dick Reppucci, who played an important role in two Network studies and has been a valued collaborator and colleague for many years.

Through its generous support of the Network, the MacArthur Foundation funded our work on this book both directly and indirectly, and we are indebted to the Foundation and, especially, Laurie Garduque for this support; indeed, without her commitment and interest, the Network would never have been launched. Jonathan Fanton, the Foundation's president during the bulk of the Network's tenure, and Julia Stasch, the Foundation's vice president during that time, both have been staunch supporters of the Network, and we are grateful to them for their confidence. We are also indebted to Lynn Boyter and Marnia Davis, who administered the Network and organized countless meetings during which many of the ideas that form the basis for this book were discussed and debated. The ideas expressed in the book reflect our own views, of course, and are not an official statement of the Network or of the Foundation.

Several of our Network colleagues deserve special mention. Frank Zimring initially suggested that we write a monograph on this topic for a Network-sponsored series that he has edited, and although we ultimately decided that we had more to say than a monograph's space would permit, we nonetheless are grateful to him for his encouragement. Tom Grisso, who directed the Network's study of competence to stand trial, co-authored articles with each of us on the topic, and our discussion of this issue in Chapter 6 of the book borrows heavily from these previously published pieces. Similarly, Beth Cauffman and Jen Woolard each collaborated with us (along with Dick Reppucci) on early articles on adolescent development and decision-making that substantially influenced the developmental framework in Chapter 2 and the mitigation argument in Chapter 5. Daniel Nagin gave helpful advice that helped shape the Social Welfare Argument in Chapter 7. Finally, Bob Schwartz kindly read the entire manuscript and gave us extraordinarily comprehensive and helpful comments. In our view, Bob is a model for contemporary youth advocates, combining sophistication about the science of adolescence with extraordinary advocacy skills—along with a good humored ability to recognize perspectives different from his own.

We have had various opportunities to present parts of the book as lectures and at colloquia and workshops and have received many useful comments from colleagues on these occasions. These include presentations at Columbia Law School, Drexel University, the Harvard School of Public Health, New York University Law School, the University of Massachusetts Medical School, the University of Pennsylvania Law School, Princeton University, Temple University Law School, Tulane University School of Medicine, and Washington University Law School.

A number of colleagues outside the Network reviewed and critiqued the manuscript, and the final product has benefitted greatly from their careful reading. We are grateful to Elizabeth Emens, Martin Guggenheim, John Monahan, Robert Scott, and William Stunz for their helpful comments on the manuscript and to Elizabeth Knoll, at Harvard University Press, for her encouragement and enthusiasm.

Several law students contributed excellent research assistance that contributed immeasurably to the book. These include Michael Loatman and Abby Perdue, at the University of Virginia Law School, and Anne-Carmene Almonord, Katherine Healey, Nathan Horst, and Jason Novarr, at the Columbia Law School.

We are grateful also to the University of Virginia School of Law, the Columbia Law School, and Temple University, which provided research leave time and generous financial support that contributed to the completion of the book.

Finally, we are very grateful to our spouses, Bob Scott and Wendy Steinberg, for their patience and unflagging support of this project, and to our children, Christy Nielson, Adam Scott, and Ben Steinberg, for their love and support.

Index

Abortion, and adolescents, 68–69, 299n15, 300–301n31

Addington v. Texas, 173

Adolescence: as developmental stage, 298n6; features of development, 29–31; and individual development, 15; as intermediate legal category, 147; key advances during, 288n35; psychology of, 13–16

Adolescent development: and the age-crime curve, 52–55; of the brain, 44–49; and culpability, 130–131; and decision-making, 35–36, 37, 57; and experimentation, 51–52; and future orientation, 39–40; and involved adult, 56–57; and peer influence, 37–39; and personal identity formation, 50–52; in prisons, 206–211; and pro-social peer group, 57; psychological distinctions in, 33–35; and psychosocial maturation, 34–35, 58–60; and risk evaluation, 40–43; science of, 28–31; and self-management, 43–44; social conditions of, 55–60; stages of, 31–33; and trial competency, 158–165; understanding and reasoning in, 36–37

Adolescent-limited offenders: and age of offense, 254; defined, 54; maturation of, 317n38, 348n58; patterns of, 347n49. *See also* Childhood-limited offenders; Life-course persistent offenders; Moffitt, Terrie

Adolescents: differences from adults, 29–31; educational outcomes of, 331n27; immature judgment of, 14–15; impact of adult punishment on, 17–18; legal status of, 68–69; and Life Without Parole, 246–247; mitigation in sentencing of, 129; normative, 14; patterns of criminal behavior of, 15–16; prior criminal records of, 231; in prisons, 245–247; redefined as adults, 10. *See also* Decision-making, by adolescents

"Adult time for adult crime," 9, 99, 205, 350n10

African American youths: assumptions about, 114; gangs of, 113; numbers in justice system, 319–320n52; prejudice against, 12; study on bias toward, 310n81. *See also* Racial bias

359